KT-461-681

Please return on or before the last date stamped below

- 3 NOV 2004

15 MAR 2006

16 MAY 2006

17 APR 2007

12 NOV 2008

18 MAY 2009

- 1 APR 2010

19 JUN 2013

A FINE WILL BE CHARGED FOR OVERDUE ITEMS

190 937

EDUCATION, CULTURE AND CRITICAL THINKING

Education, Culture and Critical Thinking

KEN BROWN

NORWICH CITY COLLEGE LIBRARY			
Stock No.	190937		
Class	370.152		
Cat.		Proc.	

Ashgate

© Ken Brown 1998

All rights reserved. No part of this publication may be reproduced, stored in a retrieval system, or transmitted in any form or by any means, electronic, mechanical, photocopying, recording or otherwise without the prior permission of the publisher.

Published by
Ashgate Publishing Ltd
Gower House
Croft Road
Aldershot
Hants GU11 3HR
England

Ashgate Publishing Company
131 Main Street
Burlington, VT 05401-5600 USA

Ashgate website: http://www.ashgate.com

British Library Cataloguing in Publication Data
Brown, Ken
Education, culture and critical thinking
1. Critical thinking 2. Education - Philosophy 3. Critical thinking - Study and teaching
I. Title
370.1'52

Library of Congress Catalog Card Number: 98-73765

ISBN 1 84014 324 X

Reprinted 2002

Printed in Great Britain by Biddles Limited, Guildford and King's Lynn

Contents

Introduction

A sense of crisis afflicts present-day education. Hardly a week goes by without the official announcement of new measures to raise standards, and it is now widely accepted that the responsibilities of central government encompass both the specification of general educational objectives and the fine detail of the curriculum. Despite its comparatively recent origins, our system of state-maintained schooling has become nearly definitive of both popular and professional concepts of education.

At the same time, concern about the apparent reliance of education systems on rote memorisation and their failure to produce significant numbers of incisive, analytical thinkers has spawned a variety of remedial programmes and a growing literature to support this effort. An international search is on for definitions to underpin strategies for the enhancement of student performance. However, some fundamental disagreements have emerged amongst exponents of teaching 'critical thinking' and there is a danger in the current climate that solutions will be prescribed while the nature of the problem remains obscure and controversial. Popular and official anxieties about educational standards, institutional pressures and inertias, and the demands of mass teaching have cashed themselves in the language of 'skills' and in obsession with predetermined educational targets. All this provides an impetus for the introduction of programmatic methods for remedying passive, rote learning which may well prove self-defeating.

'Critical thinking' has found its way into a proposed school-leaving examination syllabus as one of a number of 'core skills' to promote eventual workplace adaptability. The associated term, 'problem-solving' is already well established as one criterion of educational attainment despite an abundant literature displaying lack of consensus about its meaning. But such measures too neatly absolve educational institutions and governments of responsibilities for the 'thinking skills deficit'. To impose preconceived ideas of what constitutes critical thinking, or indeed knowledge and understanding, through the medium of programmatic curricula is to subvert the traditions of critical thought and to ignore vitally important questions about the purpose of educating people in free, democratic societies.

A conviction widely shared by contributors to the current debate is that critical thinking skills of a general nature not only can be identified but that they can be taught successfully. However, some confusion exists between the 'general', conceived as universal criteria of intelligibility and sound reasoning, and the 'foundational', understood as fundamental and generic processes of mind irrespective of the particular subjects to which they are applied. This latter interpretation seems to be a powerful influence in the present movement and is supported by a legacy of research in psychology, psycholinguistics and, more recently, cognitive science. A notorious problem is that putatively generalizable thinking skills fail the test of transferability between subject-matters; a failure in terms of the very meaning of this idea of generality.

Advocates of an alternative conception of critical thinking emphasise its subject- or domain-dependence. I examine these contrasting theoretical stances and relate them to a wider debate in philosophy and the social sciences about the significance of consciousness and intentionality in the interpretation of culture and behaviour, a perspective which accentuates social, interactional dimensions of thought.

Critical thinking, in any educationally meaningful sense, must be understood in historical and philosophical terms as exfoliations of a universal potential of language in social conditions of heightened dialogue and controversy. Its evolution has depended on institutionalised recognition of an individual right of inquiry and criticism which has clear democratic and libertarian implications. All human societies have displayed impressive problem solving abilities. Indeed, language and thought, even perception, are criteriological. But the very universality of these abilities means that they do not help us to discriminate between different manifestations of human intelligence in a manner consistent with the identification of critical thinking as a significant educational desideratum. In *this* sense, it must be understood as specific to an historically limited range of cultures, none of which have enjoyed automatic guarantees of sustainability. My case is not that 'thinking skills' programmes will necessarily fail to produce results, though the notorious elusiveness of skill-transfer suggests that they may. Even if they succeed, the results will reflect arbitrary decisions about educational purpose which pay scant respect to the historical effort to transcend passive assimilation of traditional myth and dogma.

A theory of critical thinking which takes account of its historical origins and dialectical character provides more than the definition of an objective within the institutional apparatus of education. The critical traditions embody a sovereign principle, a criterion of the effectiveness of educational institutions to represent that legacy and the personal and social liberties in which they are enmeshed. This was the message articulated by John Stuart Mill throughout his lifetime; a comprehensive theory of critical thinking, liberation and personal empowerment, comprehensively overlooked in the present scramble for higher educational standards and, indeed, by the present 'thinking skills movement'.

1 Critical Thinking and its Alternatives

Modern education is all *cram*...The world already knows everything, and has only to tell it to its children, who, on their part, have only to hear, and lay it to rote (not to *heart*). Any purpose, any idea of training the mind itself, has gone out of the world. Nor can I yet perceive many symptoms of amendment. Those who dislike what is taught, mostly...dislike it, not for being *cram,* but for being other people's cram, and not theirs. Were they the teachers, they would teach different doctrines, but they would teach them *as* doctrines, not as subjects for impartial inquiry...Is it any wonder that, thus educated, we should decline in genius? That the ten centuries of England or France cannot produce as many illustrious names as the hundred and fifty years of little Greece? (John Stuart Mill, letter to the Monthly Repository, October 1832, 'On Genius')

Most educational commentators and most of the general public seem to agree on at least one thing: the schools are in deep trouble. Many graduates, at all levels, are characterized as lacking the abilities to read, write and think with a minimum level of clarity, coherence and a critical / analytical exactitude. Most commentators agree as well that a significant part of the problem is a pedagogical diet excessively rich in memorization and superficial rote performance and insufficiently rich in, if not devoid of, autonomous critical thought. (Richard Paul, 1990, p. 102)

The 'Thinking Skills Movement'; a neglected historical dimension

Mill's diagnosis of the malaise affecting the educational methods of his day is significant for many reasons. One of the more obscure but important is his choice of Classical Greece as a standard of intellectual excellence and his implicit assumption that the passage of time had failed to render that example obsolete. Another is the standard set by his own extraordinary educational achievement; the result of a harshly administered but uniquely effective pedagogy devised jointly by his father, James Mill, and Jeremy Bentham to demonstrate the universal potential of methods grounded in a rationalist philosophy. J S Mill's early progress as a critical thinker was a constant focus of interest and debate for an influential group of *philosophical radicals.* It was also intended by his mentors as a paradigm for 'philanthropists, religious or irreligious, who at this time were obsessed with the idea of reforming humanity by pedagogy' (Halévy, 1952, p. 285). Modern educational debate takes place within a different paradigm and Mill is often portrayed as the isolated subject of a unique educational experiment. In fact he is an important representative of an Enlightenment tradition in which the cultivation of reason came to be identified with the political ideals of individual empowerment through more libertarian and representative forms of government. This tradition, substantially modified and developed by Mill, had deep historical roots and was the outcome of interrelated developments; religious dissent with its conception of spiritual equality between individuals, the accessibility of transcendental purposes to human reason, and the rise of experimental science. More fundamentally, it expressed a predisposition to question traditional authority and to justify critical inquiry in contrast with ecclesiastical emphasis on revealed truth and authoritative interpretation. Hooykaas describes the fusion of these trends, maintaining that the defenders of this developing spirit of inquiry were 'perfectly conscious of the analogy between the liberation from ecclesiastical and philosophical tradition by the Reformation and the liberation of science from ancient authority by the new learning' (Hooykaas, 1977, p. 113).

It is ironic that the passages, above, by Mill and Paul convey identical messages despite having been written more than a century and a half apart. That period has seen not only the emergence of systems of comprehensive, state-maintained education but now, some claim, intimations that those systems are in terminal decline. For Mill, writing at the outset of his prodigious career as a philosopher and social analyst, universal education was still a distant prospect. It was for him the necessary, though not sufficient, condition of a civilised democracy which would realise the egalitarian and feminist ideals of the political tradition to which he was heir. Paul, a major contributor to the contemporary debate about critical thinking, endorses similar democratic values. But he castigates a system of public education which has now been rejected for more diverse reasons by many hundreds of thousands of 'home-schooling' parents in the United States. Disillusionment and a sense of crisis afflict British education, too. An eminent Cambridge educationalist has argued for a dismantling of the now-traditional system in favour of 'an infinite variety of multiple forms of teaching and learning' (Hargreaves, 1997).

Enormous social, technological and political changes have occurred since 1832 when Mill wrote the essay known as *'On Genius'*, of course. That was the year of the first, hesitant nineteenth-century concession to a growing movement for electoral reform in which Mill's father, James, Jeremy Bentham and their philosophical radical associates played a significant part. Indeed, the idea of universal access to education was supreme amongst James Mill's democratic ambitions, but partly as the result factionalism amongst the reformers themselves about the role of religion in education, and partly because of hostile competition by the established church, Mill's practical educational initiatives collapsed and the most tangible legacy of his ideals and practical energies is the University of London (Burston, 1969).

John Mill's much-debated reservations about the emerging democracy of his lifetime are largely explicable as alienation from a system of schooling in which the ideal of individual, critical autonomy was not only absent, but sometimes explicitly disavowed. In 1840, less than a decade after the publication of Mill's defence of critical thinking in the essay, *On Genius*, the following instruction was issued to Her Majesty's Inspectors by the Committee of Council on Education. It registers the triumph of an alternative view of educational purpose:

> No plan of education ought to be encouraged in which intellectual instruction is not subordinated to the regulation of the thoughts and habits of the children by the doctrines and precepts of revealed religion. (Morris, 1972, p. 283)

I do not claim that the authoritarianism of that agenda has been typical of the subsequent development of educational policies and practices even though there are contemporary resonances in the centralised, hierarchically organised drive by government for higher educational standards. However, it stands in polar opposition to Mill's conception of educational purpose in which maximisation of the critical autonomy of individual students is paramount. One might loosely describe subsequent educational developments in terms of the gravitational attraction of these polarities; emphases alternating between collective social and ethical values and individual needs - or putatively unproblematic ways of reconciling these objectives. But that would miss a vital point about Mill's conception of the dialectic of critical thought. It does not stand on a continuum of pedagogic objectives; it is not an item on an educational agenda; it is the sovereign principle and self-authenticating end of educational endeavour because open ended commitment to the critical appraisal of all values, all notions of social utility, is the condition of their justifiability for fallible human beings (Mill, 1965, p. 273).

Israel Scheffler and Harvey Siegel articulate similarly radical arguments in support of the educational ideal of critical thinking and their contributions to the contemporary debate are important and unusual in this respect. The perspective offered by Mill, however, encompasses the totality of social life and ethics in fine detail and, as I will argue in my final chapter, provides an unsurpassed account of the internal relationship between individual freedom, democracy and critical thinking - and of the dangers of underestimating the internality of that relationship in the pursuit of other social objectives. Moreover, there is an optimism about human intellectual and moral potentials in Mill's philosophy which is now unfashionable; an Enlightenment faith in the power of educated reason to eliminate the gross differentials between individuals, social classes, genders and races (Mill, 1965, p. 160). I will argue that Mill's contentions have not been effectively refuted; they have never been effectively tested.

The language of 'skills' has now invaded all levels of education and threatens to embrace the definition of critical thinking, conveying a spurious sense of the determinacy of this very complex subject and, consequently, of appropriate ways of teaching it. Mill was implacably opposed to the idea that this could be a question of predefined technique or strategy. Critical thinking, above all, enjoins a Socratic commitment to follow the logic of discourse wherever it leads in pursuit of the truth; a view of education in deep contrast with the idea of nationally prescribed curricula, age-related attainment targets and standardised testing procedures. Contemporary education is not only identified implicitly with national economic performance by large sections of the media and the public; its utilitarian, servile role is now recognised explicitly in the title of the United Kingdom's *Department for Education and Employment*. Such a prioritisation of general social objectives conflicts fundamentally with Mill's conception of the educational ideal of critical thinking and with that of more recent exponents like Scheffler:

> ...the notion that education is an instrument for the realization of social ends, no matter how worthy they are thought to be, harbors the greatest conceivable danger to the ideal of a free and rational society. For if these goals are presumed to be fixed in advance, the instrumental doctrine of schooling exempts them from the critical scrutiny that schooling itself may foster. (Scheffler, 1973, p. 134)

Paul and Siegel urge recognition of the intimate relationships between critical thinking, rational and moral integrity and democratic values. But in the brief course of their development our education systems have acquired an aura of autonomy and of technical complexity which tends to limit public debate to the *means* of achieving predetermined educational ends. And these are often taken for granted or accepted as self-authenticating within the framework of national, or even global, social and economic objectives.

Thus, I have chosen to begin and end my argument with Mill because he provides a much-needed 'Archimedian point' beyond the present 'thinking skills debate' and an education system which is widely perceived to be in crisis. More than any of his successors, including John Dewey who is usually celebrated as the philosophical pioneer of critical thinking (for example, see Fisher, 1989, pp. 37-38), Mill challenges popular, instrumentalist views of education and the authoritative status of collectively determined educational ends. His theory of critical thinking is simultaneously an account of the relationship between mind and society, a sustained critique of the authoritarian mentality and of the pervasive influence of that mentality on our social institutions to the detriment of aspirations for personal freedom, justice, social and gender emancipation.

The disinheritance of Mill's ideal

Some distortions in contemporary accounts of critical thinking need to be corrected by an emphasis on its traditional character; a heritage which has been accumulated laboriously and which remains vulnerable; a product of gradual disentanglement from other ways of life and thought. Critical thinking and its alternatives, which I will try to characterise in the following chapters, cannot be comprehended adequately without reference to cultural and historical environments, unless they are to share the obscurity which now surrounds the anthropological distinction between 'logical' and 'pre-logical' mentalities. In the absence of this attention to context, definitions of *skills of thought* are liable to degenerate into scholastic formalisms. Pedagogic techniques derived from them may amount to little more than routine exercises which are a shallow substitute for genuine critical thought. The indefinitely large, expanding body of intellectual capabilities which it subsumes cannot be pinned down by precise definitions; the attempt to do so seems to rest on the misconception that because reasoning so commonly involves the use of rigorous, clearly defined procedures, it therefore must be explained in terms of them. Critical thinking involves, quite crucially, the predisposition to evaluate *any* accepted rules or procedures. And here it is necessary to make a distinction between an unrealistic (and undesirable) *practice* involving constant re-evaluation and an institutionalisation of open dialogue in which the possibility of critical appraisal is always implicit.

Thomas Kuhn maintains that the history of science must have some bearing on contemporary science, and that an 'unhistorical stereotype' has emerged, drawn from texts which 'seem to imply that content of science is uniquely exemplified by the observations, laws, and theories described in their pages' (Kuhn, 1970). Similar considerations apply in the case of contemporary efforts to define thinking skills and to identify their characteristics with their formalised products. History or social science, taught without regard to philosophical questions about purpose and method become little more than futile, self-perpetuating exercises. In the physical sciences, too, questions about the meaning, epistemic status and ontological implication of concepts are prior to effective critical thought.

Equally, the idea of critical thinking is seriously distorted by efforts to portray it simply as an activity of individual intellects. Social dimensions of dialogue and debate and the organisational means which have evolved for maintaining them are also crucial in its elucidation, as Karl Popper has argued in the case of the sciences in *The Open Society and its Enemies* (Popper, 1969). This socio-historical dimension of critical thought is of much more than marginal, antiquarian interest. Mill stressed the intimate connection between the intellectual triumphs of the Greeks and their cultural environment of pervasive disputatiousness. Matthew Lipman, pioneer of *philosophy for children,* has tendered an explanation, closely resembling those of Mill and Popper, for a 'notorious historical enigma'; Classical Athens and Renaissance Florence were examples of spontaneous *communities of inquiry*, a concept which is the distinctive organisational principle in Lipman's promotion of critical, philosophical inquiry in schools (Lipman, 1991, p. 73). Yet emphasis on education through a discursive, argumentative search for truth does not represent a flight from social and economic imperatives. It was a prominent feature in many of the 'Dissenting Academies' founded in post-Commonwealth England in reaction to the Act of Uniformity of 1662 (Priestley, 1904). These schools promulgated the new empirical, scientific methodologies. In the 18th and 19th Centuries they contributed to the growth of the physical sciences and technology quite disproportionately to their size and number, confirming the intimate connection between religious nonconformity and scientific innovation which Merton and Hagen have described (Merton, 1979, pp. 20-54; Hagen, 1967, pp. 290-309).

There is a disturbing tendency in the contemporary debate about critical thinking to disregard the laborious development of the critical traditions and to take the question of justification for granted. Siegel maintains that critical thinking should be regarded as a 'regulative ideal' in education and has emphasised that a justification of it is long overdue:

> This conception of education, and its role and relationship to the larger society, is a profound one, and indicates the immense depth of the philosophical issues raised by a consideration of critical thinking. (Siegel, 1988, p. 55)

His own 'beginning of a justification' of the educational ideal of critical thinking is couched partly in terms of ethical goals like *respect for students, self-sufficiency, initiation into the rational traditions* and he discerns an intimate connection between *critical thinking and democratic living* (Siegel, 1988, pp. 55-61). In important respects he echoes Mill's prioritisation of individual critical independence as a necessary condition for the justification of all other social, ethical or educational ends. Yet one key aspect of Mill's view of critical thinking strikes a discordant note in the context of modern educational theory and practice and is probably overlooked for that reason. This is his belief in the dynamic potential of an education in critical thinking to eliminate intellectual differentials between 'individuals, races or sexes' which were regarded by most of his contemporaries as innate and therefore 'indelible'. He proposed a 'hand-to-hand fight' with the pervasive doctrine of genetically determined mental inequalities, the principal obstacle to the 'unlimited possibility of improving the moral and intellectual condition of mankind by education' (Mill, 1965, p. 160 and p. 69). The prioritisation of nurture over nature was one of the few of James Mill's philosophical convictions which

John Stuart supported without reservation to the end of his life; but there was nothing, he pointed out, 'more contradictory to the prevailing tendencies of speculation...' Gross educational inequalities still persist despite universal schooling, lending some credence to long-established beliefs in the immutability of intellectual differentials - not only between individuals but entire social classes, articulated forcefully in 1867 in Walter Bagehot's classic work, *The English Constitution:*

> The lower orders, the middle orders, are still, when tried by what is the standard of the educated "ten thousand," narrow minded, unintelligent, incurious...a philosophy which does not ceaselessly remember, which does not continually obtrude, the palpable differences of the various (social orders) will be a theory radically false. (Bagehot, 1963, p. 63)

There are other subtle reasons why Mill's egalitarian educational ideals may be contrary to prevailing beliefs and theories in modern democracies. Not least amongst them is the formidable influence of psychometrics and, more recently, growing popular interest in genetic predisposition. Moreover, the idea that the characterising features of thought are to be found in determinate operations, the *processes* of individual minds, rather than in the social matrices of language, dialogue and cultural tradition enjoys support of another kind. Cognitive science and associated philosophical stances known as 'eliminative materialism' and, rather less respectfully, 'methodological solipsism' invest heavily in the idea that mental operations are, in principle, comprehensible independently of the way in which they 'hook up to the world' through human language and intentional behaviour (Churchland, 1992, p. 301). In other words, there is already considerable momentum at both scholarly and popular levels for the conflation of distinct ideas; criteria of rationality; individual proficiencies in the utilisation of those criteria; and determinate structures, processes and psychological *skills* of thinking.

Although critical thinking might be readily accepted as an educational and democratic ideal by large sections of the educational establishment, important questions remain about its conceptual status and, consequently, its pedagogic and institutional implications. Powerful voices now explicitly subordinate educational objectives to those of economic expediency or tacitly assume an uncontroversial identity between them. The prevalent 'skills conception' of critical thinking is harnessed effortlessly to utilitarian objectives despite the deep controversies about it. Scotland's reformed system of school-leaving qualifications explicitly minimises distinctions between the academic and the vocational in the expectation that students 'may face several career changes during their working life'. In a public information leaflet on these new qualifications, 'critical thinking' has been fitted snugly into a sub category of *core skills,* including 'planning' and 'organising', as one of several means towards the end of vocational adaptability (Scottish CCC, *Higher Still*, 1998).

Mill's letter, *On Genius* was an expression of a beleaguered tradition which upheld a progressive view of human rationality against contrasting views. This letter was also an anticipation of the case for freedom of thought and discussion in Mill's *On Liberty* (1859), 'a statement of liberal principle so radical and at the same time so fundamental that it surely ranks with *The Social Contract* and *The Communist Manifesto* as a source for the political and social theory of the Western world' (Levi, 1969, p. 6). But historical precedent has inclined so heavily against *critical thinking* in the forms of philosophical inquiry, scientific investigation, religious and political dissent that it is remarkable that so many contemporary theorists accept it as a goal of education which will encounter general approval. Indeed, it might be a condition of its political acceptability that the term *critical thinking* is redefined as a determinate repertoire of utilitarian skills to be taught and tested without posing inconvenient questions about established educational curricula or their connections with the wider world.

In fact references to Mill's ideas in the extensive literature of the contemporary 'thinking skills movement' are extremely rare. This neglect is even more poignant because it encompasses Mill's autobiographical account of his early educational achievements, which spectacularly confounded expectations of age-related competence. He wrote explicitly to show '...how much more than is commonly supposed may be taught, and well taught, in those early years which, in the common modes of what is called instruction, are little better than wasted' (Mill, 1965, p. 1). Mill bequeathed a principle of general applicability; that early immersion in rigorous analytical debate could do for others what it had done for him. Despite his renowned modesty, illustrated by his declaration that he was rather below average in natural talent, Mill claimed an educational advantage of 25 years over his contemporaries. Yet his extraordinary education enjoys little more than frequent honourable mention, sometimes qualified by distaste for that remarkable experiment.

That disinheritance might be a consequence of the advent of universal state-maintained education, in many respects a fulfilment of the social and educational ideals of the very movement in which James Mill and Bentham played an important part; and the aspiration which they represented for a form of democratic government founded on an educated, pro-active citizenry. Debate about the educational ideal of critical thinking is now more tightly circumscribed. Definitions acknowledge little of their debt to history. But the long and controversial debate about human cognition cannot simply be discounted by abstracting a portion which seems appropriate to a modern educational agenda; the problems which have characterised the field will be imported with it.

The contemporary thinking skills movement

A many-stranded international 'movement' now exists, which, despite numerous points of contrast in philosophical orientation and method, reflects widespread concern about the perceived failure of educational institutions to teach students to think effectively. Yet few references to it in professional journals are as confident as this opening comment in one article:

> The greatest educational revolution of the millennium may not lie in the computerised classroom. Instead, it is likely to be the simple but subversive concept of teaching children how to think (Times Educational Supplement, 12-2-93, p.14).

Agreement about the undesirable predominance of rote-learning is common. Oddly, there is little analysis of the phenomenon itself or the reasons for its prevalence. Less consensus seems to exist about appropriate remedies, although this may be due partly to the geographical diversity and multi-disciplinary character of initiatives which comprise the 'thinking skills movement.' There are many possible bases of comparison between different methodologies and several valuable reviews are available. In an analysis which concentrates on De Bono's 'CoRT', Feuerstein's 'Instrumental Enrichment' and Lipman's 'Philosophy for Children' programmes, Wolfe Mays makes a point relevant to my preceding discussion of Mill, that:

> One of the main arguments against any attempt to improve intellectual performance is that intelligence is largely inherited...This has led to the belief that attempts to change the structure of intelligence and its course of development can only have a limited success - a few points at the most on the IQ scale. (Mays, 1985)

Other developments have helped to shift the parameters of the concept of critical thinking; where the Enlightenment located them in the moral and social ends of education, they now tend to be more closely associated with the measurable relativities of attainment in the ubiquitous modern *classroom*. Generations of educational research on performance in this uniform setting have helped to invest the concept with an aura of technical significance. It is hard to resist the illusion that criteria of rationality must have a limited range of substantive and specifiable manifestations; 'the activation of particular cognitive mechanisms in the brain' as Frank Smith scornfully remarks (Smith, 1992, p. 8) which can be stimulated by pre-specifiable teaching strategies and appropriately designed resources.

One result has been a vast and growing literature, designed for classroom use, which provides exercises in thinking skills and problem solving. Another has been the publication of tests of thinking skills for use by academic institutions or prospective employers, a prominent feature of which is the closed option exercise to evaluate candidates' abilities to grasp the logical structure and implications of statements. An important American example of this approach is the series of Cornell Critical Thinking Tests, co-authored by Robert Ennis. This use of 'informal logic' can be impressive, and it is tempting to speculate about its potential for enhancing literacy in school curricula and alerting students to subtleties of meaning, modes of implication and valid and fallacious forms of argument. However, there are powerful considerations against adopting such methods as the distinctive contribution of critical thinking to educational practice rather than as one useful innovation. A precursor of this kind of test was the Watson-Glaser Critical Thinking Appraisal which exemplified yet another characteristic of recent trends; the analysis of critical thinking into lists of specific intellectual proficiencies, to which Robert Ennis has made what is perhaps the most detailed and systematic contribution. I will consider the bearing of Ennis' list on the contentious topic of defining critical thinking later, though an indication of the length to which systems of classification may be carried is Ennis' remark about his own system; that the contents are 'perhaps overwhelming' (Siegel, 1988, p. 7).

Theoretical differences about the nature of thinking skills carries over into the design of practical initiatives. One obvious contrast is that between Lipman's 'Philosophy for Children' and various derivative projects, and Feuerstein's programme of 'Instrumental Enrichment'. The latter was developed in Israel, initially as a method of remedying 'cognitive retardation' amongst culturally deprived Jewish children from North Africa and other margins of the Diaspora, but subsequently widely exported and adapted. Here, the salient contrast is between Lipman's emphasis on the uninhibited exploration by children of social, moral and epistemological questions, and Feuerstein's reliance on particularised diagnostic techniques to identify putative cognitive deficits and correspondingly structured remedies, mainly involving the analysis of relationships between abstract symbols. Lipman's method, like Feuerstein's, has been used with apparent success to address the problems of deprived children, although Instrumental Enrichment has been favoured as a means of addressing severe and congenital forms of retardation.

It might be claimed that Lipman and Feuerstein address different problems; that Feuerstein is primarily concerned with *basic* or *elemental* skills of thought rather than the kind of analytic, discursive abilities associated with mature critical thinking; that this accounts for his inclination to specify diagnosis and remedial treatment in terms of the analysis of, and impacts on, cognitive structure. However, I will show that it is far from clear what *kind* of distinction the foregoing could be. It is, in any case, one of deep conceptual complexity; a lesson which emerges clearly from the debate between Chomsky and Piaget concerning the relation between formal structure in language and thought and physiological structure or process, discussed in Chapter 6. Their differences apart, both Lipman and Feuerstein owe much to Vygotsky's thesis concerning the mediated, dialogical character of teaching and learning. For the time being it is sufficient to note Vygotsky's repeated assertion that elementary psychological functions are qualitatively different from higher functions. The latter entail various degrees of 'awareness, abstraction and control,' and the former are unlikely to shed much light on 'subjects and functions that could be expected to be meaningfully related' (for example, Vygotsky, 1989, p. 179 and 186).

Dissemination of the better-known methods of Lipman and Feuerstein has diminished the contrast between them, however. Oxfordshire's 'Skills Programme' evolved out of initial trials of Feuerstein's *I.E.* and while this has been retained for low-attaining students various other approaches including Lipman's philosophical method and Paul's critical thinking strategies have been combined within it (Hanson, 1989, p. 83). This fusion of distinctive approaches seems to have occurred despite Lipman's and Feuerstein's insistence on the need for specifically designed source materials and the training of teachers in their respective methods. Strategies of this kind indicate worrying disjunctions between theory and practice, suggesting that measures endorsed on pragmatic grounds may foist illicitly restrictive notions of critical thinking or cognitive skill on educational practice, as Mays and Chomsky have warned.

The 'thinking skills movement' presents the educational world with a shop window. There is a danger that choice between alternative approaches will be determined arbitrarily, by background training and personal preference, by work pressure or the perception that one programme lends itself more readily to the evaluation of performance by familiar techniques than another. In practice, too, the adoption of a novel method is likely to require the abandonment of familiar ones. Understandably, many people feel the need for clear objectives and seek definitions of critical thinking or thinking skills. But in what terms should such definitions be couched?

Parameters, definitions and the critical tradition

Demand for acceptable definitions of critical thinking has considerable momentum. In his introduction to a volume of essays, *The Generalizability of Critical Thinking*, Stephen Norris highlights the pivotal importance attributed to questions about the meaning, the definition, of critical thinking and the decisive outcome which certain answers might have on its future as an educational ideal (Norris, 1992, p. 4). Symmetrical with philosophical interest in this issue is a practical, pedagogic concern with the identification of parameters 'so that we know what we are talking about when we talk of the desirability of teaching thinking' (Coles and Robinson, 1989, p. 8). We are apt to forget that the debate on critical thinking began precisely because the ideal was cogent enough to register a significant contrast with actual educational attainments. One result of prioritising 'definitions' is the incremental separation of a concept from its anchorage in everyday language to the point where it acquires a baffling autonomy. No doubt with some irony, a principal physics teacher asked a British conference on critical thinking: 'With so much content to get through, how can we ever fit in education in thinking skills as well?' (Dane, *The Times Education Supplement*, 6-5-94, 'Critical Times for Critical Thought'). The question registers a diffuse sense that teaching 'thinking skills' is something distinct not only from contemporary educational practice but from the methods and subject-matters of the academic disciplines; a hotly disputed contention which I examine in the following chapter. On the other hand, one comprehensive review of literature on the related topic of 'problem-solving' reached pessimistic conclusions about the prospects for generally acceptable definitions, despite the continuing entrenchment of the term in educational thinking and curriculum design:

> Problem solving is lamentably ill-defined; it can mean all things to all persons; there is little clarity as to its meaning in curriculum and assessment documents...If problem solving is broadly defined, then practical advice on teaching it is equivalent to advice on teaching people how to live and how to think. This requires hubris. (Holroyd, 1989, section 7.1.3)

Popper condemns preoccupation with definitions, recommending instead the critical discussion of whole theories within which the terms in question are located; a strategy which avoids placing a more specific interpretation on their conventional meanings than, by the nature of language, they are able to bear without ambiguity or contradiction (for example, Popper, 1972, p. 310). In this respect, he echoes Mill's observation in the *System of Logic* that the problem confronting philosophers in the search for definitions is that, in formulating and using particular concepts, people usually did not '...mean to predicate distinctly any attribute at all' (Mill, 1900, Book I, Chapter 7, s. 7). Thus, there may be many who subscribe to Johnson's demand for an account of *the relationship* between critical thinking, problem solving, rationality and metacognition and for 'differentiation between the critical thinker and the creative thinker' (Johnson, 1992, pp. 48-49). But, important though they are, relationships between these things are many and varied, existing at different levels of generality and particularity. Language does not work in a way which permits the detection of systematic relationships of the kind Johnson seems to require.

Of course, definitions vary significantly between mathematics, sociology and literary criticism, as well as between such formal disciplines as these and the numerous ostensive definitions of everyday discourse. As a result, my own assertion that critical thinking needs to be understood in cultural and historical terms might incur the charge that I simply offer a definition of a different kind. However, in anticipation of subsequent arguments, I disclaim such an ambition. The words 'characterisation' or 'elucidation' provide a requisite contrast with the attempt to identify necessary and sufficient conditions for the application of a term; a paradigm which seems to influence some demands for definitions of critical thinking, hypostatising the concept and setting up a corresponding requirement for regressive definitions of the terms into which it is decomposed.

There are cogent reasons for this distinction between 'defining' and 'characterising' critical thought. One is that there is a sense in which an ability to think critically is a universal feature of human language and a condition of social existence. Perception itself is criteriological, involving abilities to discriminate between and classify experiences according to common standards. Vygotsky has remarked how the accidental shapes of 'ink-blot' tests are usually judged to resemble familiar objects; evidence of the active, complex application of criteria in visual perception. We are entitled to ask whether any human society is conceivable in the absence of universal abilities to draw reliable inductive inferences or to invoke criteria of meaningfulness and validity in the course of communication. Yet this comprehensive sense is patently not that in which critical thinking makes its appearance as an educational desideratum. Few would want to deny that the development of the physical sciences offers compelling paradigms of critical thought. But, here, another consideration against the prioritisation of definitions arises; what Kuhn has described as '...the insufficiency of methodological directives, by themselves, to dictate a unique, substantive conclusion to many sorts of scientific questions' (Kuhn, 1970). Neither the form nor the occasion of revolutionising scientific development are predictable from within established conceptual schemata and methodologies, though innovatory thinking nevertheless owes its meaning and intelligibility to those intellectual legacies. Critical thinking can be characterised at certain levels of generality as the application of particular principles of rationality, but there is an open-endedness about the substantive interpretation of those criteria; they change and evolve over time within traditions of thought (Siegel, 1988, p. 134). This will be the basis of my claim that the much-debated *generalizability of critical thinking* consists of philosophical inquiry about the status of the kind of understanding and intelligibility provided by different modes of explanation; not simply *whether* but *how* they instantiate acceptable principles of rational discourse.

Finally in this brief list of qualifications to the idea of definition, yet another significant obstacle to prior legislation concerning the parameters of critical thinking is that it is located on a continuum and should not be too closely associated with the idea of determinate intellectual operations. Any two individuals may perform, say, an identical arithmetical calculation like simple addition without it being true to say that they are 'doing the same thing' in all relevant respects. One distinction between rote and genuinely critical performance might be symbolised by one child's recognition that 3 + 3 + 3 is equivalent to 3 x 3 where her companion correctly completes the identical *addition* without that broader awareness. What individuals bring to any determinate task might vary profoundly according to their personal repertoires of ideas, imagery and strategy. As a result, definitions of critical thinking in terms of task performances are inevitably arbitrary and open to further interpretation. Another consideration is that we all occupy a variety of positions within a cultural *penumbra of critical/rational thought.* That is to say that the rational status of most of our beliefs is a function of established theories which, as individuals, we lack the relevant expertise to evaluate; a condition which might apply as much between the astrophysicist and the palaeontologist as between these representatives of modern science and the layperson. Many of our judgments about the rationality of assertions or beliefs express only our own limited perspectives from within a broad, consensual picture of reason and reality which is a product of the historical traditions of critical thinking. Yet such stances routinely transcend mere prejudice and are necessary features of co-operation between specialists from different backgrounds as well as between specialists and non-specialists. Crucial aspects of individual critical autonomy thus involve a preparedness to entertain authoritative statements with degrees of scepticism; to look for reasons - and possibly to find none, for lack of evidence or expertise; to speculate without entertaining great hope of a solution, and so on. One of the cumulative effects of the critical traditions is that they encourage the formulation of questions and sanction expectations that there are answers to be found. As I will show in later stages of this argument, these expectations are more than the psychological adjuncts of an identifiable core of critical thinking skills. The critical *spirit* or *disposition* is internally related to a tradition of discovery and the awareness it fosters that reality and truth are not simply 'givens' - they yield to disciplined inquiry.

One way of summarising these objections to the enterprise of *defining* critical thinking is to say that, in the sense usually required by an educational agenda, it involves unavoidable arbitrariness. And the problem with stipulative definitions is that they offer no guarantee that instructional programmes based upon them correspond to the matrix of values and principles which have stimulated concern about critical thinking as an educational end. Most of the novel methods of 'teaching thinking' will be related to measurable improvements in one aspect of performance or another. My argument is not that there is a lack of empirical evidence that they meet certain criteria of effectiveness, but that those criteria are likely to be the wrong ones. (I will return to the notorious problem that there is little empirical evidence that skills of thought identified as *generic* actually are generalizable in the sense that they can be shown to transfer between 'cognitive domains'). Another difficulty concerns the uncertain relationship between implementation of a particular skills-programme and improved performance. Psychologists Brown and Ferrara note how enhanced teacher expectations, in the form of a dramatic change in their own 'theory of the child' induced by reciprocal questioning sessions, appear to stimulate performance irrespective of substantive features of the pedagogic method (Brown and Ferrara, 1989, p. 301). This point underlines the ambiguous nature of the link between teaching and learning; it is impossible to determine conclusively whether improvement is due more or less to changes in the pedagogic relationship, the enhancement of 'cognitive functions' in the student, or to the introduction of a new perspective on difficult aspects of a subject. Almost anything, a sketch, a well-selected analogy, a model, a gesture or query *might* be an effective stimulus to thought. The important question is likely to be, not about the particular technique employed, but the way it is integrated with the particularities of dialogue about a subject matter.

Adoption of rigorously specified programmes as a general method in response to a definition of critical thinking might be dangerous. Effectiveness in narrowly circumscribed situations might be due to gross oversimplification of the complex cognitive skills required in more general contexts, particularly if the 'improvement' in question owes itself to familiarity with a limited repertoire of routines, as Chomsky has observed. It is worth recalling that the 'fail-safe' method of the uninspired teacher is to teach by rote because experience has demonstrated that this at least satisfies common, if superficial, standards of achievement. But in case this suggests a clear disjunction between real and rote learning, it is as well to bear in mind that the latter usually involves *some* element of discrimination about the appropriateness of a method or formula to a new problem. The real case against rote is that it satisfies obsessions with *standardised* measures of performance but fails to evoke the more self-referential forms of understanding required to judge the relevance of methods, concepts and formulae in less familiar problem situations.

Some dissenting voices and further implications

A number of commentators stress that concepts of *generic* abilities provide no guarantee of relevance to the objective of enhancing a general capacity for critical thought even though they may meet certain test-criteria. Wolfe Mays points out that people in a closed society can master technical skills without necessarily achieving capacities for mature judgment on 'moral, social and aesthetic questions' (Mays, 1985, pp. 149-163). Authoritarian cultures have maintained high levels of technical sophistication. Many thinking skills exponents should take this objection seriously if only because they do in fact tend to justify their proposals in terms of the empowerment of individuals and the invigoration of democracy. But this is not to direct attention to a contingent, ethical dimension of the subject which applies only in so far as the advocates of a particular programme acknowledge these moral, social or political ends. The ethical problem subsumes a logical one, the exposure of which John Anderson has attributed to Socrates' critique of the training in rhetorical skills provided by the Greek Sophists: '...Socrates...was cutting at the root of the modern psychological theory of abilities. Abilities, taken by themselves, instead of as part of the general activity of the individual, are falsified and misdirected' (Anderson, 1963, p. 208). Chomsky has outlined this kind of logical consideration in different works. In one, he refers to the analytical priority of the criteria internal to systems of knowledge and belief:

> I believe that the study of human psychology has been diverted into side channels by an unwillingness to pose the problem of how experience is related to knowledge and belief, a problem which of course presupposes a logically...prior investigation of the structure of systems of knowledge and belief. (Chomsky, 1972, pp. 43-44)

Elsewhere, Chomsky is concerned with the undesirable consequences of a pedagogy which violates this principle by redesigning curricula in terms defined by new techniques for 'rapid and efficient inculcation of skilled behaviour' in language, mathematics or other domains. The problem is not that it is it difficult to construct objective tests to demonstrate the effectiveness of a given method in achieving specified outcomes:

> ...But success of this sort will not demonstrate that an important educational goal has been achieved...What little we know about human intelligence would at least suggest something quite different: that by diminishing the range and complexity of materials presented to the inquiring mind, by setting behaviour in fixed patterns, these methods may harm and distort the normal development of creative abilities. (Chomsky, 1972, p. 101)

These observations highlight a fundamental requirement in the appraisal of critical thinking; that to delve beneath classifications, definitions and generalisations about the subject entails two distinct but related frames of reference. First is the internal argumentative structure of a particular realm of thought, and one might add, competing structures within that realm at a given time. The propositions of physics may be as close as we could get to understanding the intellectual operations (or 'processes') involved in that mode of scientific reasoning but, in any event, they could not be circumvented by descriptions of a different logical form without constituting a revolutionary development of the science. Likewise for philosophy, for social science, history or 'everyday discourse'. Thought, whether significant or not, is always in some sense, *subject-specific* (though, I will maintain, not necessarily in the sense which has become most typically associated with it in the 'thinking skills debate'). One can affirm the necessity of 'the *general* study of reasons, warrant and justification' which we call epistemology and also the existence of universal principles of rationality (Siegel, 1988, p. 36-38, original emphasis, and p. 134). The latter, exemplified by requirements to *consider evidence which is relevant to a proposition;* to *judge whether conclusions follow from premises;* to *distinguish between necessary and sufficient conditions,* are clearly general in character. Moreover, these epistemological principles have undoubted relevance to pedagogy and genuine importance when interpolated into the substantives of different disciplines. But the propositions of mathematics or the methodologies of historians and social scientists are not closed systems; they are fields which are explored continuously because their implications are indeterminate. And principles of rationality, as Siegel points out, are themselves subject to evolutionary development. Their application at any time to a given field of inquiry, or across different fields, may be contentious, uncertain or laden with unrecognised implications.

A continuing interplay between purportedly universal rational principles and specific subject-matters determines the intelligibility of those subjects; what *counts* in their respective cases as a valid conclusion or relevant evidence - and *why.* Even the most abstruse theories are subject to the ongoing jurisdiction of such universal principles. Indeed, the fact that specialisms can be learned is conditional on the possibility that they can be interpreted at more general levels of understanding. But this is not to say that by virtue of their putative universality these principles are 'immutable or innate' (Scheffler, 1973, p. 80) or, for that matter, that their meaning and relevance will always be obvious and uncontroversial. There is an ongoing requirement for philosophical clarification of their contextualised significance.

The second frame of reference indicated by Chomsky is the matrix of values in which a realm of thought is located. This, too, is complex and controversial and sometimes a source of outright conflict. Conclusions embodied in science, religion, history or social science are intimately, and reciprocally, related to social valuations because they contribute to, or challenge, our understanding of the human situation. Siegel and others emphasise the fundamental importance of critical thinking to democratic ways of life. These two things are historically and logically interrelated because both challenge monolithic values and notions of absolute authority. Putnam maintains that Dewey offered an *epistemological justification of democracy* and civil liberty (Putman, 1995, pp. 180-200) though I will argue later that Mill did just this, but with greater consistency and insight into perverse forms of democracy likely to follow neglect of that justification. Historical impulses towards democracy have been coeval with transformations of human consciousness effected by the development of traditions of critical thought. But the demarcation between these traditions and alternative conventions cannot be established satisfactorily by reference to the characteristics of modes of thought alone, nor in terms of universal principles of rationality, important though they are. There are crucial social dimensions which constrain or enhance the evolution of both and are which are implicated, constitutively, in notions of intellectual authority and in the interpretation of rational principle. Striking intellectual ingenuity can manifest itself in scholastic interpretations of the world in terms of the propositions and prescriptions of a few revered texts; in the elaboration of conceptual schemata without due regard for empirical evidence, or the classification of empirical 'data' in the absence of a coherent conceptual framework. Controversy continues in all disciplines on issues of this kind and should serve as a warning that there may be no commonly acceptable, overarching principles for resolving which form of critical thinking is appropriate in particular cases. Disputes amongst some of the most exceptional thinkers involve the mutual charge, not of deficiency in critical thinking, but that particular lines of reasoning are *wrong*.

Frank Smith is sceptical about attempts to establish classifications of intellectual operations, warning that 'Psychological or educational tests based on such arbitrary and ill-founded conceptualizations can only be misleading and dangerous.' He insists that we are already familiar with critical thinking because we do it well in everyday life (Smith, 1992, p. 11). But while that is true at a quite fundamental level, as I have already pointed out, the absence of a unique demarcation between critical thinking and other mental processes fails to address very real concerns about kind of educational deficits identified in the quotations at the beginning of this chapter which have motivated the 'thinking skills debate'. Any departure from the familiar connotations of terms like 'critical thinking' in order to achieve a more illuminating explanation must encompass evidence of an historical and cross-cultural type. Anthropology has entertained - and abandoned - the distinction between *logical* and *pre-logical* or *primitive* mentalities, but the conceptual issues which discouraged its use are symmetrical with those raised by the implicit distinction between *critical thought* and its alternatives, and they may still shed some light on the complexities of the critical thinking traditions and the conditions for sustaining and developing them through education.

Darwin's lost supper: some features of a 'critical tradition'

In his celebrated book, *The Voyage of the Beagle*, Charles Darwin gave a brief account of the different explanations which he and his native guides advanced for the failure of boiling water to cook potatoes in the high Andes. His anecdote illuminates some of the obstacles facing attempts to distinguish neatly between more and less critical ways of thinking. The distance between the two explanations cannot be measured against a yardstick of individual cognitive performance, nor are concepts of general or domain-specific critical thinking skills adequate to characterise the differences in question. There is a need for reference back to features of the contrasting cultural and linguistic environments of Darwin and his guides in order to identify the conceptual resources available to them. The moral in the tale of the raw potatoes underlines the significance of immersion in traditions of critical inquiry:

> At the place where we slept water necessarily boiled, from the diminished pressure of the atmosphere, at a lower temperature than it does in a less lofty country; the case being the converse of that of a Papin's digester. Hence the potatoes, after remaining for some hours in the boiling water, were nearly as hard as ever. The pot was left on the fire all night, and next morning it was boiled again, but yet the potatoes were not cooked. I found out this, by overhearing my two companions discussing the cause; they had come to the simple conclusion, "that the cursed pot (which was a new one) did not choose to boil potatoes". (Darwin, The Voyage of the Beagle, Chapter XV)

Darwin's work provides abundant examples of disciplined conjecture but the solution to the problem of the uncooked potatoes was not one of them. For *that*, he simply relied on a well-established scientific theory, directing attention instead to his native guides' ostensibly animistic explanation, now reminiscent of the distinction popularised by Lucien Lévy-Bruhl between the *logical* mentality of modern cultures and the *pre-logical* or *primitive* mentality of traditional cultures. Descriptions of this kind have fallen into disrepute partly because of the difficulty of sustaining a distinction between viable societies on that basis. The persistence of cultures governed by ostensibly irrational beliefs establishes a presumption in favour of the view that a context must exist for interpretations which 'make sense' of those beliefs (Gellner, 1972, pp. 115-149). One way to make better sense of the guides' conclusion is to accord it status as an episode of sound reasoning within a culture of the kind which preceded the traditions of critical scientific inquiry.

An important criterion of rational thinking must surely be the ability to distinguish what Siegel describes as *relevant reasons and rules of evidence* (Siegel, 1988, p. 43). The elimination of irrelevancies, such as the position of the planets at one's time of birth as a guide to personality, or the malign disposition of one's neighbour as a potential cause of disease in one's pigs, may be regarded as a hallmark of the rational thinker. Nevertheless, the phases of the moon are relevant to the state of tides. To paraphrase Kuhn, there are no unique principles for determining the fields from which evidence might be drawn and, as Popper insists, a crucial feature of scientific rationality is a willingness to *test* even those conjectures which seem most improbable by the standards of existing paradigms (Popper, 1963, p. 102). Darwin's guides did not invoke remote or magical possibilities; they were confronted with a fire, a potful of boiling water and the enigma of potatoes which remained uncooked. There was nothing in their intellectual environment to suggest that the sky above, the air around or the mass of the earth beneath them were at all relevant to the solution of the problem. Indeed, the choice of the pot's disposition as the relevant variable is understandable. It was, as Darwin observed, a new pot. In the experience of the two Chilenos all other pots cooked potatoes where this one failed. What, they might have asked, could be the relevance of their location? Potatoes cooked in Valparaiso and Copiapo, didn't they?

Darwin did not appeal directly to laws of physics to explain the obstinately raw potatoes, but to the converse effects of a pressure vessel, the 'digester' designed in an earlier century by Robert Boyle's assistant, Papin. He plainly did not believe this move beyond his own pioneering knowledge of natural history required a justification. He tacitly accepted that the educated, middle class readership for whom *The Voyage of the Beagle* was written would be aware of the kind of physical principles responsible for this phenomenon, though few would have observed it directly in the 1830's. It is also unlikely that many could have related the account to a system of discrete law-like propositions or could have devised experimental methods for demonstrating them. Darwin appealed to what I have described as the *cultural penumbra* of rational, scientific thought; a diffuse, holistic understanding of what science has 'demonstrated to be the case', an instantly accessible though extremely fallible measure of the credibility of physical explanations.

A simple experiment will confirm that most primary-age schoolchildren dismiss as absurd the animistic explanation of Darwin's guides; 'the cursed pot ...did not choose to boil potatoes'. Pots and other inanimate objects simply do not have volition; to suppose that they do is to be somehow at odds with the rational ethos of modern society. This, of course, is not an example of the critical rejection of an explanation but of that consensual picture of reality which has emerged as a result of scientific traditions to embrace even young children. Despite survey-findings which suggested that two-thirds of the British public do not know that the earth orbits the sun in about one year, (Durant et al, 1989, pp. 11-14), one might conjecture that very few adults indeed would find the animistic explanation of Darwin's guides remotely convincing; it simply does not 'fit-in' with prevailing conceptions of how the world works. And even in cases of less gross ignorance, these conceptions are often only tenuously related to empirically demonstrable scientific principles or to an understanding of the formal characteristics of a discipline like physics. And, of course, the distal relationship of the inexpert to specialised forms of understanding has a bearing on the important concept of *individual critical autonomy* and the institutional conditions in which it can be exercised effectively in a technically diverse, pluralistic society. For most of the time, most critical thinking is a matter of negotiation and arbitration between *interrelated* forms and levels of understanding. Lay people can have a critical, rational attitude concerning the safety of nuclear power generation or beef consumption without a deep understanding of nuclear physics or microbiology. One connection between critical thinking and democracy concerns the absence of a consistent and radical distinction between ways of thinking and ways of living. I will argue that institutions do not simply foster or inhibit critical thinking but are constitutive of it, or of its alternatives, and therefore must be part of its 'definition'.

A point about Darwin's anecdote should be emphasised. The guides' conclusion, 'that the pot did not choose to boil potatoes' *was a conclusion* which had been preceded by a discussion of probable causes. It differed from examples of deliberate, voluntary restrictions on the search for rational explanations which Darwin provides elsewhere in the same chapter. One such was the simple lack of curiosity evinced by native guides who answered his queries about the origins of archaeological features in the Chilean desert with an indifferent, 'who knows?' Another, of significance for later stages of my argument, was a response he recorded to his questions about the Andean environment: 'some, however (like a few in England who are a century behindhand), thought that all such inquiries were useless and impious; and that it was quite sufficient that God had thus made the mountains'. Like medieval peasants who lacked a sense that past and future might differ from the present and who spoke predominantly in the present indicative tense (Le Roy Ladurie, 1980, p. 282) those with little or no access to traditions of argumentative inquiry have little conception of the possibility of alternative explanations; and few bases of comparison to engage their critical potential. There is a continuum between critical and uncritical thinking. Where any given episode is located on it may require a complex understanding of its relationship to traditional ideas and theories and conceptions of epistemic authority which limit consensual views of reality. One crucial point is that historically accumulated knowledge is prolific source of new 'contexts of discovery' and new 'modes of justification'.

The guides' ascription of intentionality to their cooking pot nevertheless merits consideration as a genuine conclusion and the important question concerns the adequacy of the supporting evidence. Accustomed though they were to trans-Andean expeditions, they plainly had not tried to boil potatoes at such an altitude on previous occasions. If they had been used to cooking at various altitudes, it is reasonable to expect that they might have formulated a conclusion to the effect that: 'potatoes (and other foods) cook with diminishing efficiency as altitude increases, although water boils regardless of altitude.' For people lacking the apparatus for measuring temperatures and barometric pressures, this would be a useful 'common-sense' inductive generalisation of the kind which large areas of human activity have always depended upon, in agriculture, seafaring and so on. Examples include folkloristic but fairly reliable weather forecasting and observations about the effects of rain or deliberate irrigation on plant growth. Nor is it unreasonable to suppose that, as a result of experience, Andean cuisine would have gradually eliminated irrelevant factors like the shape, size, age and composition of different pots from the basic generalisation about the effects of altitude.

Darwin's revolutionising thought is typified by a willingness to plunder the theoretical resources of geology, palaeontology, meteorology and natural history for illumination. But as he made clear in earlier pages, his survival depended on his guides' experience of the mountains and their ability to predict localised weather conditions - a matter of dependable generalisation from the relevant, accumulated experience of Andean travellers. Elsewhere, in his discussion of the relationship between seismic events and unseasonable rainfall, Darwin supported the common native view that the two were connected, but failed to reach a conclusion *beyond* a sense of 'some more intimate connexion between the atmospheric and subterranean regions'. Significantly, he *did* discuss explanations tendered by von Humbold and a Mr P. Scope in terms of the atmospheric effects of volcanic vapour and the effects of reduced atmospheric pressure on accumulating seismic forces, respectively. His inconclusive discussion, like so many other conjectures addressed to the reader, illustrates the reliance of even such a prolific thinker as Darwin on the ideas of others, working within many-stranded traditions of inquiry, in order to determine the kind of field from which relevant evidence might be selected to test an hypothesis.

Another point about the guides' ostensibly animistic inference concerns Darwin's translation of the term 'did not choose to...'. Of course, there is no way of assessing the particular case, but it is worth pointing out that various shades of meaning attach to this kind of volitional analogy. Consider, for example, our own use of the verb *will* as possible etymological evidence of a former period when distinctions were not clearly drawn between the potentials of inanimate objects and the aspirations and capabilities of people; 'the pot *will not* boil the potatoes...' The point, here, is that the meeting of minds which endorses particular word meanings is the result of a longstanding dialogic process, although generally of a tacit character. Singular meanings are not guaranteed by the use of individual words and word-function is not adequately conveyed by 'atomic' metaphors; the context and the historical background of usage is also vitally important in conveying precise intentions enshrined in the choice of vocabulary. Words are not indissolubly tied to particular referents, and metaphor plays an essential role in extending meanings, though the pre-history of ideas may be preserved in contemporary usages. That common metaphor about the *rising* sun might, after all, limit many people's grasp of relative Earth-sun movements in the way which so shocked Durant and his colleagues.

Language is self-referential and reconstructive; its terms are elucidated by reference to conventional usage; novel and refined uses are perfectly possible and, of course, are how richness and variety of expression develop; but only where extensions of meaning can be negotiated on the basis of prior agreements. And there are conditions which may favour or constrain such development. A crucially important one, I will argue, is the state of literacy in a culture and its effectiveness in recording linguistic usages and promoting debate across cultures and historical eras.

Whatever terminology Darwin's guides used in their own language, the semantic possibilities were constrained by their cultural and linguistic milieu, and did not necessarily translate readily into a corresponding English usage. I will discuss this acknowledged anthropological problem in subsequent chapters for the light it can throw on the origins evolution and character of critical thinking. The linguistic-conceptual repertoire accessible to individuals in a literate culture massively outstrips that of the non-literate culture, revealing semantic incommensurabilities which defy neat classification. Language emerges as the irreducible medium of thought because each attempt at a clarification of the context of an utterance invokes further judgments of equivalence between terms; a process involving dialogue and continuous reciprocity which we describe as *learning a language*. And it is one which involves various degrees of mutual assimilation (as it does in the case of the anthropologist or in the historically typical meeting of two alien cultures, but often *does not* in the more circumscribed case of the classroom where closely related languages may be taught as though meanings are transparent).

Modes of thought are embedded in cultural and linguistic milieux. Literacy, particularly the readily accessible alphabetical script, unleashes potentials for the accumulation, review and critical appraisal of information, for the growth of a sense of historical change and, thus, sceptical appraisal (Goody and Watt, 1962-3, pp. 304-345). Literacy also provides for the development of language in increasingly abstract and specialised forms, consequences of the accelerated exchange of ideas over time and distance and of the ability to record different usages and shades of meaning. These are features of widespread literacy which have not received due attention as the necessary conditions of the sustained modes of creative, analytical thinking which comprise the critical traditions. And these traditions consist of a rich texture of disciplines, modes of thought and the penumbra of dispositions to view the world in many faceted and often competing ways. Measures of individual critical thinking ability, if they are to be of significance in the field of education, should be measures of the degree to which an individual is integrated within these critical traditions and consequently able to make creative use of a range of the powerful modes of thought and repertoires of imagery which they embody. I do not believe these are abilities which can be subsumed reliably within an inventory of 'general critical thinking skills' but neither are they subsumed by determinate disciplinary logics or methodologies. Darwin evidently did not try to correct his guides' conclusion about their cooking pot; to have done so might have involved a long and regressive debate about the nature of physical reality and the many ways of testing our conjectures about it.

I have used the preceding 'case-study' from Darwin as an initial outline of my subsequent argument. That will be that the polar opposition between exponents of *general skills of critical thinking* and upholders of the *domain specificity of critical thinking* is an exaggerated antithesis, neither extreme of which promises a satisfying account of critical thinking, or more than partial relevance for educational theory. I will examine some philosophical antecedents to these opposed positions and consider some of their wider philosophical and practical ramifications. Only by doing this, I believe, is it possible to gain a vantage point which will place the concept of critical thought in its true perspective as the characterising tradition of democratic, liberal cultures and to begin to form clear ideas about ways of ensuring their sustainability.

2 The 'General Thinking Skills' Controversy

> I wish to redirect attention away from generic *processes of reasoning*, be these logical skills or general strategies, and have you consider the proposition that the content of various subjects and/or problems determines (i.e. creates) the appropriate *process* of reasoning, and not vice versa. (John McPeck, 1990, pp. 68-69, original emphasis)

General or generalizable?

A basic controversy in the 'thinking skills debate' revolves around claims that critical thinking consists of generic skills. Is the idea of *general skills of thought* intelligible, and if so, can it generate unambiguous pedagogic strategies? Some approaches are indeed predicated on a positive answer to this question, although there are different interpretations of the notion of *generality*, with correspondingly different educational implications.

Amongst 'generalists', Robert Ennis is particularly noted for contributing a very extensive list of 'aspects' of critical thinking under a dozen original headings which include: *grasping the meaning of statements; judging ambiguities, assumptions or contradictions in reasoning; identifying necessary conclusions; assessing the adequacy of definitions and the acceptability of alleged authorities* (Ennis, 1962, pp. 82-83). Frank Smith bluntly dismisses this list with the remark: 'None of the above "skills" is generalizable in any sense. Their application on any particular occasion depends on the specific subject matter that is involved' (Smith, 1992, p. 97). This might be chemistry, sociology, geophysics or animal husbandry and Smith identifies a core objection to the 'generalist' case, at least in broad terms. Specific subject-matters determine the meanings and applications of items on Ennis' list and the complex task of interpolating them into those specifics far transcends the importance of preliminary generic descriptions.

But the issue is not so straightforward. Smith is surely wrong to say that none of Ennis' 'aspects' of critical thinking is generalizable *in any sense*. He echoes a common failure to distinguish between universal descriptive categories of thought, like the requirement for sufficient reasons for assertions, and procedures for determining their particular applications. Ennis is certainly not guilty of simple confusion; he recognises that there are many different levels in the way the components of critical thinking on his frequently elaborated lists may be applied to different subjects; that his definitions have a provisional and summary character (Paul, 1990, p. 107).

From this perspective, Ennis' view is compatible with a variety of pedagogic approaches, including one which prioritises open ended, philosophical inquiry about the subjects of the traditional, liberal curriculum. However, he is committed to the standardisation of critical thinking tests and believes that, questions of definition apparently having been satisfied, 'the issue is now an empirical one and should be dealt with empirically' (McPeck, 1990, p. 58 and note). It is against this conception of the possibility of standardised, objective measures of critical thinking that the history and philosophy of modes of understanding come into play. Arguably, the evolution of philosophy, science and social science has been one of competition between different conceptions of the criteria of rational thinking and the educational task is to promote understanding of that competition. A seminal historical example of a universalising principle of rationality is that known as *Ockham's Razor*; the requirement for parsimonious scientific explanation as it was articulated by the medieval scholar and cleric, William of Ockham; *'it is vain to do with more what can be done with fewer'*. But how, if at all, this fits into the conceptual frameworks of modern cosmology, particle physics, behavioural psychology or eliminative materialism remains a controversial, many-sides issue. Yet if such controversies typify something fundamental about the development of human understanding, what non-arbitrary, overarching principles could replace them for the purpose of teaching critical thinking? Perhaps the problem of generalizability needs to be redefined.

Siegel, for instance, identifies an ambiguity which 'plagues' the debate about generalizability; inadequate acknowledgement of a distinction between the general, theoretical applicability of principles of reasoning across varied subjects or domains and practical transferability across the curriculum of the skills involved in utilising such principles: '...it is important to realise that even if principles of critical thinking are general in the sense that they are, theoretically, broadly applicable, it does not follow that they enjoy a high degree of transfer or are, pedagogically, usefully generalizable' (Siegel, 1991, p. 19). The distinction is profound because it could mean the difference between a pedagogy based on philosophical inquiry about the status of different forms of understanding and an arbitrary pre-specification of 'thinking skills' which violates what I will maintain are very basic principles of language, thought and learning. Although Siegel agrees broadly with Ennis on generalizability he maintains that critical thinking theorists and the Informal Logic Movement, with which Ennis is closely identified, must grapple with philosophical questions about the nature and aims of education and the justification of critical thinking as a central educational ideal (Siegel, 1988, pp. 2-3). The fact that Ennis identifies his list of items as criteria of 'statement assessment' seems to underline the need for this wider perspective.

Another point about the kind of criteria on Ennis' list is that, rather than describing general features of critical thinking, they are over-general in the sense that they comprise universal conditions of intelligible discourse. Communication would be impossible if we could not routinely grasp meanings, identify ambiguities or contradictions and so on. And, as Smith points out, *grasping the meaning of statements* is a prior condition of the other items on the list. Indeed, it can be simply another way of saying that we do not find statements ambiguous or contradictory.

The attack on 'general thinking skills'

Opposed to the generalist view is John McPeck's notoriously subversive thesis that *there are no such things as general thinking skills.* Phrases like *ability to define a problem* or *ability to recognise underlying assumptions* 'semantically masquerade as descriptions of general abilities' (ibid., p. 97). Skills of thought are subsumed by the range of individual subjects in which they have been developed as part of a distinctive logic, methodology or philosophical orientation. McPeck claims no advantage from the scarcity of empirical evidence that training in putative general thinking skills facilitates transfer across cognitive domains. It is only 'what commonsense would predict' because the decisive issue is conceptual and cannot be resolved by scientific investigation (ibid. , p. 92). He does, however, cite several authors, including Thorndike, Gagne and Ausubel concerning preponderantly negative results of numerous tests of psychological skill-transfer (ibid., pp. 55-56). These findings are noteworthy because they have a direct bearing on the previously-discussed question of *defining* critical thinking. After all, there is massive evidence of transfer at a fundamental level in the child's ability to utilise grammatical form in endlessly novel ways; an important strand of Chomsky's thesis of linguistic creativity. Manifestations of the transfer of mental skills are ubiquitous and necessary features of social life; from the rambler's ability to relate map data to real landscapes to that of the lawyer to identify precedents relevant to his brief. Experimental failures to detect the generalizability of *skills* across different *domains* suggest that experimenters might be operating inadvertently with arbitrary, stipulative definitions of one, or both, of these terms.

I criticise McPeck's argument in some detail in following chapters because, although not entirely original, it is acknowledged (by Siegel and others) to have raised new and fundamental considerations about the nature of critical thinking and ways of teaching it. McPeck's real contribution, I maintain, has been to introduce the subject of human intentionality into the thinking skills debate under the rubric of *the subject-specificity of thought*. By relating this idea to the precedents for effective, critical thinking enshrined in the traditional academic disciplines, McPeck has opened up a prospect of the historical dimension necessary for any truly significant distinction between critical thinking and its alternatives; the repertoire of gradually accumulated but often conflicting theories, concepts and images which determine what kind of thing counts as the application of rational principle in any given situation. One of the shortcomings of McPeck's argument is a failure to acknowledge the internal diversity of modes of thought and the extent to which they are themselves products of argument concerning the interpretation of principles of rationality in various fields of inquiry. Another is his narrow interpretation of subject- or domain-specificity and his consequent underestimation of a form of *general understanding* to which he, himself, subscribes. That is, philosophical appraisal of the mainstream disciplines which, he says, are all too often taught as if 'chiselled out of epistemic bedrock' (ibid., p. 17). McPeck's solution is an infusion of philosophy into these disciplines to enhance awareness of the problematic nature of their contents. This is, of course, more than a criticism of the way they are taught; it is an assertion, from a universalising perspective, of their *questionable epistemic status.* Critical thinking is generalizable in the sense that criteria of meaningfulness and sound reasoning within specialised modes of understanding fall ultimately under the jurisdiction of common standards of intelligibility and rationality. And that is why specialisms can be taught and learned.

McPeck's thesis is more radical than some of his critics, like Paul, have taken it to be. He does not simply stress the technical specialisation of critical thought, a move which Paul counters by emphasising the everyday and the interdisciplinary, but insists that formal characteristics of thinking are always specialised in terms of their content. A rule like *consider all relevant evidence* means such different things in physics or psychology that it actually begs the question of relevance because those disciplines are, in effect, ways of deciding what kinds of evidence are appropriate to different problems. The characteristic methods and contents of the familiar disciplines, or domains of knowledge, constitute the skills to which we refer when talking about critical, or creative thinking.

Despite appearances, McPeck's argument does not rest on a categorisation of 'forms of knowledge'. It expresses, he says in response to Paul, 'a Wittgensteinian view about the nature of logic, language and thought' which contrasts fundamentally with the prevalent North American emphasis on formal, syntactic features of thinking and reasoning. In the latter case, logic is seen as '...an exogenous system of rules and principles into which language can be plugged as a variable' (ibid., pp. 113-4). McPeck insists that, according to the Wittgensteinian view, the relationship between the form of a particular mode of discourse and its content is an internal one; but the insistent question then becomes: 'what *is* a mode of discourse?' I will show that McPeck does not really provide an answer. He equivocates between Wittgenstein's metaphor of diffusely overlapping, self-authenticating *language games* comprising the minutiae of linguistic transactions, and a portrayal of the broad divisions of the academic disciplines as discrete modes of experience more reminiscent of Oakeshottian idealism.

One task will be to evaluate this kind of domain-theory and to demonstrate the relevance of the conclusions to a wider debate about the concept of *human intentionality* and its implications for methodology in the social sciences. Essentially similar divergences of view exist between those who seek general frameworks of social analysis and others who maintain that social life is intelligible only in terms of criteria internal to it. This broader perspective will help to substantiate my own argument, that critical thinking is fundamentally dialogic and philosophical; that it has evolved by way of traditions and that these cannot be adequately comprehended simply as the internal logical or methodological profiles of disciplines or domains in their contemporary form. There are social, technological and cultural factors which are crucial to a satisfactory account of critical thinking and its alternatives, although neither can be explained simply by reduction to those factors.

Some pedagogic implications

For a domain-theorist like Michael Oakeshott, induction into the 'languages' of the principal academic disciplines actually *is* teaching critical thinking. McPeck's self-contradictory demand for philosophical appraisal of disciplinary understanding is compounded by his belief that this approach is not appropriate to earlier stages of education; a dogmatic, empirical assertion which begs important questions. Is the learning of particular disciplinary 'languages' appropriate because they reflect something fundamental about human cognitive organisation, as he proposes on *a priori* grounds? If so, why do these categories of understanding need to be supplemented by the conceptual, analytical methods of philosophy? But if understanding, by its nature, requires philosophical investigation of the foundations of disciplinary knowledge why should that approach be denied to people in the formative periods of cognitive development?

McPeck does not answer these questions directly by giving an account of particular *modes, domains,* or *forms* of knowledge in terms of their internal logical characteristics and boundary criteria. Nor, despite his heavy reliance on Wittgenstein's metaphor of *language games,* does he follow that philosopher's procedure of demonstrating how logic inheres in particular types of utterance *without commitment* to the idea that boundary criteria could be identified, even in principle. Instead, he persistently refers to subjects like 'math, literature, science, morality', sometimes prefaced by an 'e.g.' and sometimes enclosed in parentheses. This tactic maintains him an elliptical orbit around the two distinct bodies of thought represented by Wittgenstein and Oakeshott. The implication of the latter is that boundary criteria do exist; that they segregate the different 'languages' and 'unique logics' of foundational academic disciplines: 'Each of these manners of thinking is a genuine mode of explanation; each operates with clear criteria of relevance; each is capable of reaching conclusions appropriate to itself...' (Oakeshott, 1967, p. 329). The difference is that Oakeshott's major work, *Experience and its Modes* was an attempt to elucidate those criteria. And he regarded familiarity with distinctive, explanatory 'languages' as a precondition for effective, interdisciplinary or multidisciplinary discourse. As a result, he characterised school-education as 'learning to speak before one has anything significant to say' and the content of the school curriculum as having the quality 'of being able to be learned without necessarily being understood....' (ibid., p. 306). Likewise, McPeck says of young students: 'To passively absorb information is the natural and appropriate way to learn...Possessing basic knowledge and information is a prerequisite for critical thinking, not a deterrent to it' (ibid., p. 44). Yet in the light of his reservations about the epistemological foundations of disciplinary knowledge, it would appear more consistent for McPeck to maintain that the dialectical 'give-and-take' of philosophy, exploration of the meaning of concepts and grounds for belief in them, most faithfully expresses fundamental attributes of cognition from the earliest stages and encourages mature, critical thinking. I will argue that the latter is indeed the case. McPeck smuggles in an unjustified assumption about cognitive stages or 'readiness' for critical thought. Mill's largely unacknowledged contribution to the pedagogy of critical thinking, which I will examine in my final chapter, is to make critical epistemological inquiry the ultimate ideal and method of education from the earliest stages because that method most faithfully reflects the nature of human knowledge. For that reason, it is the means of transcending intellectual differentials which have been consistently but incorrectly ascribed to innate potentialities and consolidated by teaching methods which express prejudices about normal individual development and epistemic authority.

In stark contrast are implicit and explicit theories of cognition purporting to identify general skills of thought which may be presented as programmatic exercises in critical thinking. Experimental failures to confirm 'transfer' in such cases has sometimes been claimed as evidence that thinking is 'domain-specific' although it should be noted that *this* concept of 'domains' is ambiguous. Is the existence of particular *cognitive domains* to be inferred from the simple absence of empirical evidence of generalizability? And is it not a more straightforward conclusion that the putative skills concerned are inconsequential and have no educational relevance? The readiness with which controversial theory can acquire authoritative status in the practice of hierarchical institutions should not be underestimated and the stakes are consequently high in the debate about critical thinking. The theory of cognitive-stage development developed by Piaget and the Genevan School is the result of years of research. Many scholars now question the internal coherence of that system and Piaget himself has warned against premature application of psychological theories developed in the context of pure research. Nevertheless, this is a body of concepts and data which has long been recognised as a major influence in educational practice, and, as I mentioned (above), with intelligence-quotient theory it appears to have been a constraint on many teachers' perceptions of what may be achieved by children at any given age. One crucial but neglected consideration, I believe, is the negative effect on creative and speculative thought exercised by the 'institutional logic' of education systems which bear the impossible burden of transmitting virtually the whole cultural repertoire of the critical traditions. The relative uniformity of pedagogic relationships and the constraints they impose on the presentation and acquisition of knowledge deserve more analysis than they receive in the 'thinking skills debate'. The critical traditions emerged as dramatic transformations of human life and thought, but not necessarily in a classroom.

In subsequent chapters I will consider Vygotsky's thesis that *word-meaning* is the appropriate psychological 'unit of analysis'; his recognition of the deep complexity of human consciousness and the consequent dangers of excessive formalism in depicting modes of thought and mental competences. Yet the notion of elemental cognitive structures and functions, which Vygotsky qualifies with this emphasis on a cultural repertoire of semantic meaning, has been a seminal influence in research on thinking and learning. I will suggest this prejudice has systematically distorted the discussion of critical thinking by misrepresenting thought as the processes of individual minds which could be rendered intelligible - in principle, if not in practice - by identifying their structural elements in abstract, formal terms. And this, in turn, must bolster a 'skills conception' of critical thinking which attributes to it a dangerously misleading sense of determinacy.

The internality of 'logics' and the problem of relativism

The idea that different modes of thought have a *logic* internal to them and *sui generis* is problematical. In later chapters I will consider examples from the fields of social anthropology, psychology and comparative linguistics which illustrate how Wittgenstein's principle of 'internal relations' may be invoked to characterise human thought in general and to dispute the possibility of general explanations of social behaviour of the kind sought by many pioneering social scientists. McPeck recognises that this principle militates against attempts to subsume descriptions of thought and thinking skills within a general and systematic conceptual framework. However, his overall stance justly incurs accusations that it involves an ultimately self-defeating relativism:

> a. ...there are almost as many distinguishable logics, or kinds of reasoning, as there are distinguishable kinds of subjects. And there is no way to learn these different logics apart from learning the language (or meanings) of those subjects.
>
> b. ...just as different 'rules of predication' constitute different language-games, so different modes of reasoning constitute what we call "subject areas." Each is a different "category of understanding" (in a Wittgensteinian sense), and each has its own "rules," as it were, of reasoning. This is what renders a general thinking skills approach *implausible* from a theoretical point of view, and *ineffective* from a practical point of view... (McPeck, 1990, pp. 36-37, original emphasis)

As already noted, McPeck's interpretations display both (a), Wittgensteinian and (b), Oakeshottian credentials; the former in emphasis upon 'internality' as a general feature of thought, but the latter in the identification of 'logics' with particular subject areas, also ambiguously categorised as *subjects* in the sense of academic disciplines. My own argument is less with his conclusion that thought is always *subject-specific* than with his equivocal account of what a subject is. For this conceals precisely what is so important about critical thinking. It is a product of modes of inquiry which are both distinctive and rule-governed but also subject to internal controversy, revolutionary development, and to cross-disciplinary boundary disputes which invoke external, general principles. These principles, however, are also subject to evolutionary change, as Scheffler and Siegel point out; something I will consider at later stages of my argument.

The main question turns on disciplined creativity and open-endedness in human thought, the quality which Chomsky has articulated as 'the character of free creation within a system of rule' (Chomsky, ii, 1972, p. 45). I will elaborate this theme as it is central to the concept of critical traditions which I develop in contrast to that of Oakeshottian 'domains' characterised by internally seamless but mutually incommensurable logics. Critical thinking and the values currently placed upon it are heavily indebted to rare traditions of inquiry which sprang from growing realisation of the relativities in human beliefs and practices and, crucially, from various attempts to transcend them. But first it is necessary to consider a powerful elenchus encountered by attempts to describe these relativities.

As his critics have been quick to point out, McPeck's claim that *there are almost as many kinds of rules of reasoning as there are subjects* looks very like a declaration of the self-authenticating character of any system of belief and its immunity to rational criticism. Arguments for the internality of the criteria of intelligibility and rationality of domains of thought, disciplines or ways of life themselves appeal to principles of reasoning which purport to be universally valid; a point made repeatedly by Siegel and by Putnam, who observes that the relativist case is self-refuting as soon as it is stated (for example, Siegel, 1988, p. 73; Putnam, 1995, pp. 176-7). To articulate a case against universal principles of rationality is necessarily to try to invoke them and, indeed, McPeck appears to do just that through his general argumentative strategy and in his appeal for the infusion of philosophical criticism into subjects in the school curriculum. However, arguments at this high level of generality do not engage satisfactorily with a range of defensible intermediate positions, nor do they take account of a further contention of McPeck's, in the form of another paraphrase of Wittgenstein, that intelligibility 'is determined at the *semantic* level of discourse' and 'the *syntax* of a system cannot yield semantic *meaning*' (ibid., pp. 36-37, original emphasis). This is a recognition of the inadequacy of formal, logical descriptions to account for the multiplicity of ways in which ideas are contained in particular developments of language and thought as the result of a process of semantic accretion.

Although he attacks McPeck's claims concerning the self-authenticating nature of language games, Paul questions the idea that critical thinking can be taught as a series of discrete, generally applicable skills. He proposes a 'dialectical/dialogical' approach to the broader context of the beliefs, prejudices and attitudes which are typically a source of controversy or conflict in the real world. The kind of 'pure skills' conception promulgated by Ennis, techniques of argument analysis, fail to engage with these wider beliefs and commitments; holistic features of thought described by Paul as 'argument networks' and 'world views'. In practice moral or ideological disagreements are rarely capable of being resolved by strictly defined procedures. Although the possibility exists (as McPeck also acknowledges), it is untypical. Disagreements are more commonly about the meanings and connotations of ideas than about the process of inference. 'World views', as Paul describes them, suggest some affinity with Wittgenstein's 'language games', with which McPeck identifies his concept of domains of knowledge, and the related but less frequently mentioned 'forms of life'. Paul's formulation allows for eventual rational reconciliation of conflicting world views. Siegel maintains, nevertheless, that there are only two tenable positions on the question of relativism; acceptance, in which case 'critical thinking collapses as a coherent notion distinct from 'uncritical' thinking and as an educational desideratum' or, alternatively, the admission of general, 'atomistic' criteria of rationality exemplified by phrases like: *considers all relevant evidence; deals adequately with objections* (Siegel, 1988, p. 14).

Siegel criticises McPeck for failing to recognise that such atomistic criteria do not 'refer to any specific subject matter' (Siegel, 1990, p. 77). McPeck could agree with this without detriment to his argument simply by adding that the *meaning* of the criteria and the skills involved in their application are rooted firmly in their differing contexts and that Siegel's general formulations amount to little more than useful mnemonics. On the other hand, Siegel's argument encompasses the idea that such 'skills' really summarise the application of criteria which are employed in the *philosophical* task of trying to render explicit the intelligibility of particular kinds of explanation which McPeck actually advocates. It would be a mistake to confuse a classification of general criteria of rationality for the operational principles of a general thinking skills *strategy* which could be equally efficacious when applied to different subject-matters or disciplines. What Siegel describes as 'atomistic criteria of appraisal' may, and often do, involve a regressive debate about relevance and the nature of evidential relationships. The point which Paul seems to be making is that there are questions *beyond* any enumerable sets of rational criteria *which are not inconsistent with them*. What *counts* as 'considering all relevant evidence' or 'dealing adequately with objections' will surely depend on the complex conceptual network which constitutes a particular world view. We might ask what would count as evidence that the earth orbits the sun for a sceptical member of an isolated, traditional society, or for the allegation that the United States pursued imperialistic foreign policies in the Far East in the 1960's? 'Relevant evidence' is not of one kind. The adequacy of particular conceptual schemata or data-selections will rarely be a neatly circumscribed question but one requiring insight into its significance for those with historically differentiated intellectual and cultural perspectives. Siegel's insistence on the two clear-cut alternatives, acceptance of relativism or rejection in favour of 'atomistic criteria of rationality', is symptomatic of a problem about levels of generality in the critical thinking debate; that what at first sight might appear to be an outright contradiction between views arises because they are broadcast on different wavelengths.

This becomes apparent when authors address the problems posed by the historical evolution of critical traditions. McPeck mitigates the impression of Heracletean flux created by his vision of proliferating language games and logics with the comparison of Kant's categories of understanding. Unlike Kant's categories, however, 'language games are not fixed and immutable' but evolve 'to accommodate changes in different forms of life.' But, he says, so long as these categories of understanding 'are in place at any given time, they constitute coherent thought' (McPeck, 1990, p. 37). This implicit admission of what is an otherwise unelaborated *universal criterion* of the appropriateness of reasons to times and places is not congenial to the case for domain specificity, an issue I explore in the next chapter. It reflects a major tension between the normative commitment to putatively universal principles of rationality and the inescapable fact that such principles have been articulated differently according to time and place. Scheffler also denies that these principles are 'immutable or innate' and he explicitly acknowledges that the educationalist's task is to help rising generations to improve them by 'passing on...the multiple, live traditions in which a sense of their history, spirit and direction may be discerned' (Scheffler, 1973, p. 80). And Siegel follows Scheffler in acknowledging the changeability of criteria of rationality 'crystallized at a time in a rational tradition' (Siegel, 1988, p. 135). But this idea requires cautious interpretation. A vital feature of the critical traditions is that they never are 'crystallised' in the sense that there are overarching principles which determine the historical and cultural appropriateness of forms of rationality. The evolution of the critical traditions has been intimately connected with recognition of the problems posed by the apparent relativities of understanding, and institutional recognition that the progress of reason is a function of the conflict of ideas. Putative resolutions of the tension inherent in this dualism between the historically particular and the universal, the view 'that change is ruled by an unchanging law', are seen by Popper as the source of a perennial conflict between totalitarian ideologies and the idea of an 'open society' (Popper, 1969, Chapters 1-3, for example). He directs attention towards *procedures* rather than solutions; the crucial open-ended principle which unites critical thinking with free, pluralistic and democratic social institutions.

A rational appraisal of statements often requires one to enter labyrinthine conceptual schemata encompassing very particular experiences, information and values. One of Paul's contributions to the current educational debate has been to point out that few real controversies are amenable to direct analysis; one has to enter this labyrinth. There is rarely a straightforward choice between atomistic analysis and a relativism in which all points of view are held to be equally valid according to their own criteria. Examples are best drawn from the anthropologist's experience of the incomprehensibility of alien customs or from methodological and epistemological differences within the most highly articulated areas of the critical thinking traditions. For, I will argue, these are paradigms which instantiate something fundamental about thought in general. Participants in controversies may be committed, not only to the idea of universal criteria of rationality, but to most or all of the specific features which have been identified by Ennis and others; grasping the meanings of statements; assessing definitions; evaluating the authoritative status of sources; identifying ambiguities and so forth. As I have already argued, the important questions are nearly all about the application and meaning of such criteria in particular contexts. Galileo's dispute with the church was not about the cogency of the heliocentric model of the solar system but his insistence that its ontological import was justified by a reappraisal of scriptural authority. He did not even *oppose* empirical evidence to the idea of divine revelation but, in a letter to the Grand Duchess Christina, redefined revealed truth *in terms of* this kind of evidence:

> ...we ought to begin not from the authority of scriptural passages, but from sense-experiences and necessary demonstrations; for the holy Bible and the phenomena of nature proceed alike from the divine Word, the former as the dictate of the Holy

> Ghost and the latter as the observant executrix of God's commands. (Goodman, 1973, p. 32)

This statement marks a truly significant development in critical thought. Yet it shifts the field of *relevant evidence* from scripture to experience by means of a reinterpretation, rather than a rejection, of supernatural authority. Elsewhere, as Popper points out, Galileo paid homage to Aristarchus and Copernicus for their 'greatness of mind' in entertaining theories which were, 'in violent opposition to the evidence of their own senses (Popper, 1963, p. 102). This observation highlights another feature of genuine critical thought; the formulation of novel ways of explaining familiar things, as well as a commitment to consider *what kind of things might count as evidence* for a purely conjectural model. And this element of creativity tends to be seriously underemphasised by the generalist conception of enumerable skills or criteria of thought and, alternatively, the domain-specifist's concern with the binding authority of the contents and methods of academic disciplines. I wish to argue for a view of the critical thinking traditions which emphasises their deep, historical complexity, internal controversiality and open-endedness. I also wish to stress the *cumulative* nature of this tradition as the source of justification for teaching critical thinking in the context of established disciplines by virtue of the sheer weight of precedent which they represent. As I hope to make clear, this is not to claim that precedent alone is justification-conferring, but that its contribution to critical thinking has been in the accumulation of a rich semantic repertoire without which the idea of principles of rationality is general to the point of vacuity. Clarification will be achieved through an understanding of the history of the critical traditions, for general principles of critical thinking have been themselves defined in the course of a history of argumentation and need to be understood against that background. Consequently, pedagogic solutions are not the definitive, programmatic ones which are so enticing to some hard-pressed educationalists. They will be found, instead, in institutional realisation of a Socratic commitment to follow the logic of inquiry wherever it might lead.

The 'problem' of transfer; syntax and semantics

Despite McPeck's indifference, the largely negative results of empirical research contribute significantly to a clarification of the generalizability issue. 'Why,' ask Singley and Anderson in one review, 'has general transfer in problem solving been so hard to detect?' (Singley and Anderson, 1989). I have already noted the peculiar contradiction between such inconclusive findings and 'everyday' manifestations of the transfer of skilled behaviour, suggesting that researchers might be operating with arbitrary and misleadingly abstract conceptions of cognitive skill. At least part of the answer, I believe, is to be ascribed to the indefinitely complex relationship between language and thought; specifically, to the kind of thing McPeck identifies in his Wittgensteinian prioritisation of *semantic meaning* over *syntactic structure* (ibid., pp. 36-37). Systematic attempts to study thinking and reasoning are unavoidably interpersonal, involving communication in language or language-dependant symbols as I will try to demonstrate, below.

Empirical investigation of cognition is constrained by differentially shared meanings, conventions and cultural-historical values. While this does not diminish the value of empirical research, it does suggest that huge obstacles face any search for 'foundational' skills of thought which could be represented in formal, abstract terms. Yet even where the explicit aim is not necessarily to identify such elements, the idea of cognitive structure exercises a widespread fascination and has been the conceptual basis of much research into the subject of thinking. I believe this idea has provided a metaphorical infrastructure for the notion of *general* critical thinking skills which are transferable between varying subject-matters and that this idea has been a potent but misleading influence in education. There is always the possibility of discerning *analogies* between different intellectual tasks, but the point about analogy is that it denotes resemblance only in certain respects. If an abstract problem-solving strategy involves the same skills as (say) an aspect of scientific investigation, that judgment of identity must depend in the last analysis on an understanding of the nature of the scientific investigation. The only valid conclusion might well be that an illuminating parallel has been drawn by the teacher; the scientific method has been elucidated - though not necessarily that there is an identity or *isomorphism* between the symbolic representation of the problem, the cognitive operations of the student and the scientific problem itself. This last point is central to the issue of critical thinking. It is, after all, fairly common for schools to produce students whose understanding of academic subjects bears a resemblance to features of that subject; they may be able to name chemical elements without knowing what an element is; they may be able to multiply but not divide, or have too inadequate a grasp of the relationship between these algorithmic operations to know which to employ for the solution of a given mathematical problem.

If there is one distinction which unites opposed factions in the 'thinking skills debate' it is this one between rote and real learning addressed by quotations from Mill and Paul at the beginning of Chapter 1. Yet it must be clear that the prevalence of this kind of learning is evidence of the effectiveness of certain pedagogical techniques for communicating information and skills *of a sort*. Inadequate though they may be, these methods work according to certain empirical assessments of effectiveness; as examples of successful *transfer*. And it seems fair to assume that few in the 'thinking skills debate' would endorse such assessments because they are not those which determine effective use of criteria in the fields of knowledge to which they are applied. Yet some authors draw a distinction between the pedagogic effectiveness of method and the epistemological characteristics of the forms of knowledge to which it is applied. John Andrews argues that a rejection of general skills of thought, justified on the philosophical grounds that they are specific to cognitive domains, does not necessarily imply the rejection of a psychological conception of heuristic strategies which 'may or may not be contingently helpful depending on circumstances'. He stresses that there is no accepted theory of *domains* and is consequently speaking hypothetically (Andrews, 1990, pp. 71-79). In the next chapter I will consider fundamental flaws in the concept of domain specific understanding which militate against the successful formulation of such a theory. But it should be noted that there is an equivocation in Andrews' hypothesis.

If the character of episodes of thinking depends on their relation to the epistemological characteristics of a domain or subject-matter, this must preclude an independent, *general* system of appraisal. Any admission of 'contingent helpfulness' is just that; the fortuitous discovery of a way of enabling a student to grasp an idea or principle, the meaning of which is sanctioned only by the epistemology of the domain concerned, however that is defined. There might be such contingent relationships, but they would lack the coherence or systematicity which could qualify them as independent objects of research or as pedagogic strategies. Such time-honoured methods as beatings and inducements of honour have been contingently helpful in promoting the transfer of skilful thinking, although they are patently of a different order to any mental skills in question. But whether or not a strict argument for domain-specific logics is granted, there is still only one basic criterion for deciding whether a skill involved in thinking about substantive issues in any field is *the same skill* as that promoted by a contingent thinking skills strategy. And that, despite the admitted empirical features of the situation, is an epistemological, *not* an empirical criterion. After all, two people can perform what in outwardly observable respects are the *same* tasks; completing a calculation or reading a complex piece of prose, for example. But the *sameness* in question is ambiguous because they can bring different degrees of understanding to these tasks which are not features of the observable situation. Rote-regimes meet empirical criteria of effectiveness; that is why they exist. Their inadequacy is due to their failure to meet the requisite epistemological standards. Performances sanctioned by such regimes are parodies of those intended because an essential understanding has not been achieved.

Belief in something identifiable by empirical methods, independently of the semantically meaningful and substantive content of thought, has been a longstanding source of confusion. Because it is possible to represent this content in abstract formal terms, it is too readily assumed that abstract symbolisms present a close analogy to elemental features of a cognitive architecture which makes possible the organisation and manipulation of an indefinitely variable semantic content. The problem, I suggest, is that this has encouraged premature investigation of what are presumed to be general characteristics of thinking and reasoning in unduly abstract terms which disregard what Chomsky has described as the logically prior investigation of systems of knowledge and belief in their own right (Chomsky, 1972 b, pp. 43-44). It is this prejudice which often seems to encourage the reification of general *principles* as psychological *skills*. This, however, is to overlook the role of conventions which always govern the interpretation of symbolic relationships, the defining sense of which is dialogic and *semantic*.

The prejudice in question reveals itself in the problem addressed by Singley and Anderson, that *general transfer in problem solving has been very hard to detect*. This common observation is reiterated, for example, by Holroyd, (1989) in his extensive review of strategies for teaching problem-solving and by Hunt, from a different perspective:

> ...research workers in Artificial Intelligence...have found from bitter experience that there are no domain-independent inferential rules which could be used to construct a general intelligence. This should not be interpreted as a narrow technical failure, but as an important general truth about the nature of human thought and the disciplines to which it is applied. (Hunt, 1989 pp. 23-29)

However, the implications for the organisation of thought in alleged failures of transfer do not constitute evidence for any particular theory of cognitive domains. Nor, as I have already suggested, do they refute a perfectly respectable sense in which skill-transfer is universal; a norm of social existence. The 'problem of transfer' is the result of a misconception about the organisation of mind. In particular, that thinking and reasoning boil down to discrete formal and elemental operations in individual minds which can be represented veridically as abstract and formal relationships, an idea perhaps bolstered by the analogy of computer machine-code.

Thorndike's prolonged research on the subject of skill-transfer led him to conclude that the mind is segregated into independent capacities and that training has a much narrower influence than is generally supposed. His thesis is disputed by Vygotsky who remarked that 'The ability to gauge the length of lines may not affect the ability to distinguish between angles, but the study of the native language - with its attendant sharpening of concepts - may still have some bearing on the study of arithmetic' (Vygotsky, 1989, p. 178-9). Thorndike's pioneering work, however, illustrates a research genre reflecting common preconceptions about the nature of mind and cognition, which I will consider further in Chapter 6.

Burden and Florek refer to Feuerstein's hostility to the term 'thinking skill' because the purpose of his theory and methods is to have, 'a profound effect upon the underlying cognitive structures of all thinking and learning' (Burden and Florek, 1989, p. 71). Feuerstein's is an unusually explicit commitment, but as Smith points out, contemporary educational thought is heavily influenced by the language of *structure* and *process* which 'takes a meaningful word out of the world and makes it another mystery in the head' or 'the activation of particular cognitive mechanisms in the brain' (Smith 1992, p. 8). Moreover, as Siegel points out, there is confusion between the general, theoretical applicability of *principles* of critical thinking and the practical transferability of the *skills* involved in utilising those principles. Ennis supplements his classification of *aspects* of critical thinking with the idea of *proficiencies* in their utilisation and there is a widespread tendency in 'thinking skills' literature to do what McPeck describes as 'reifying the existence of a pervasive 'ability' from its description' (McPeck, 1990. p. 56).

Despite my intentions, it might appear that these observations have been directed against the empirical investigation of language and thought. There are two different but related issues here. One concerns legitimate multidisciplinary inquiry into the biological basis of perception, cognition and language development, the subjects of rigorous and explicit investigation by psychologists, linguists, philosophers and biologists of the interfaces between their disciplines. Chomsky, for instance, accepts in principle that language acquisition and other features of learning are ultimately reducible to physiology, but questions whether they will ever be understood fully in those terms. He warns against premature inferences about the nature of these processes and deplores a tendency in psychology to opt for, 'the approach to human intelligence that begins by postulating, on a priori grounds, certain specific mechanisms that, it is claimed, *must* be those underlying the acquisition of all knowledge and belief' (Chomsky, 1972, p. 7).

The other issue, which I address, concerns a pervasive but largely *inarticulate* model of physiological determinism which seems to exercise a kind of magnetic attraction for many who attempt to remove ambiguities in the description of intellectual abilities. It is a model which encourages the view that *particular skills* should be isolated from their enshrouding everyday contexts as though in preparation for an investigation of the elusive physiological correlates of mind. This is not to deny the heuristic value of explicit model-building; but models are methodological devices and not objects of research. I have already argued that it is very difficult to think of any act of cognition which lacks criteriological elements in an absolute sense. Rigorous investigators could have no justification for pre-empting the results of their research by designating some of these elements as more foundational or functionally relevant than others.

The aspirations of the broad 'thinking skills movement' are radical rather than conservative. Proponents seek to break through the diffuseness of everyday descriptions by discovering features of cognitive operations which will make it possible for individuals to acquire the recognised skills more rapidly; by enhancing existing skills through correct identification and appropriate stimulation; or perhaps by extending skills to sections of the population previously considered unlikely to be able to acquire them. Ironically, for the reasons I have stated, programmes of this kind may be little more than edifices based on conjectured analogies between commonly acknowledged thinking skills and the schemata which purport to represent them; concepts of critical thinking which are, in effect, arbitrary and stipulative or parasitic on established precedents. And that is to petrify critical thinking abilities and render them unresponsive to novel kinds of problem by implicitly excluding the creative reformulation of concepts, principles and methods which, I argue, are cardinal features of the traditions of critical thinking. The problem with such courses of action is that there are no bench-marks against which to validate an identification of unitary, atomistic skills. Failures of transfer in experiments are really evidence that the appearance of clarity thus achieved is spurious.

Vygotsky's criticism of the early experiments by Thorndike is cast in that form. It might appear that judgments of length and judgments of angle are closely related. This was no doubt the reason for Thorndike's selection of the exercise for one of his experiments. According to Singley and Anderson, his conclusion, after thirty years of empirical research, was that 'the mind was composed not of general faculties but rather of specific habits and associations, which provided a person with a variety of narrow responses to very specific stimuli'. This is similar to the suggestion put forward by Singley and Anderson, themselves, that *'we can conclude that the units of knowledge in the mind are functionally separate with respect to their potential for improvement'* (ibid., p. 29, my emphasis). The latter authors' choice of terminology, 'units' which are 'functionally separate,' is significant. It establishes a momentum towards a certain view of mind without postulating it; an infrastructure of discrete constants, each with its intrinsic system of variables. And formal extrapolations from meaningful intellectual operations become self-fulfilling predictions. They are indeed unitary because they fail the test of generalizability as we recognise it in less artificially systematised intellectual pursuits.

Hanging over the entire enterprise of laying bare 'core skills' is that objection that we have, ready to hand, massive evidence of transfer at a very fundamental level; in a young child's rapid acquisition of the skills necessary to recognise, name and manipulate the multifarious objects of perception. In other words, although we often use 'skills' and 'problem-solving' language without difficulty in everyday situations, the suspicion must arise that we are no longer dealing with the same thing when the effort is made to translate them into a notation which will serve the different purpose of specifying *processes* rather than investigating *intentional* socio-linguistic activities. In Vygotsky's terminology, we are confusing 'elementary' and 'higher' mental functions which are qualitatively different because of the mediation of language in thought (ibid., page 83):

> Psychology winds up in the same kind of dead end when it analyses verbal thought into its components, thought and word, and studies them in isolation from each other. In the course of analysis, the original properties of verbal thought have disappeared. Nothing is left to the investigator but to search out the mechanical interaction of the two elements in the hope of reconstructing, in a purely speculative way, the vanished properties of the whole. (Vygotsky, 1989, page 4)

A foundational skill, shorn of its context of meaning, is an arbitrary construct. This is not quite as sceptical a view as it might appear. It makes sense to identify thinking skills and their potential for transfer as long as this is done within a convention which provides a system of reference; a basis for agreement about what a problem is and what kind of conclusion would constitute a solution to it. That might be an abstract problem of logic, of course, but as I argue in the following section, logical operations are carried out within a system of semantic conventions and without that prior semantic agreement, logical form is not self-evident. I hope the following example will begin to elucidate this claim.

An example; the Wason Card Test

Singley and Anderson cite the example of the 'classic Wason Card Test' as a well known instance of the failure of transfer in what is, ostensibly, a logical problem of the form, *if p, then q* (Singley and Anderson, 1989, pp. 23-29). The test consists of 4 cards bearing, on the uppermost side, the symbols E, K, 4 and 7. Subjects are told that each of the four cards bears a letter on one side and a number on the other and are required to judge the truth of the following rule, which applies only to these four cards: *'If a card has a vowel on one side, then it has an even number on the other side.'* Subjects are asked *to turn over only those cards necessary for the truth or falsity of the rule to be judged.*

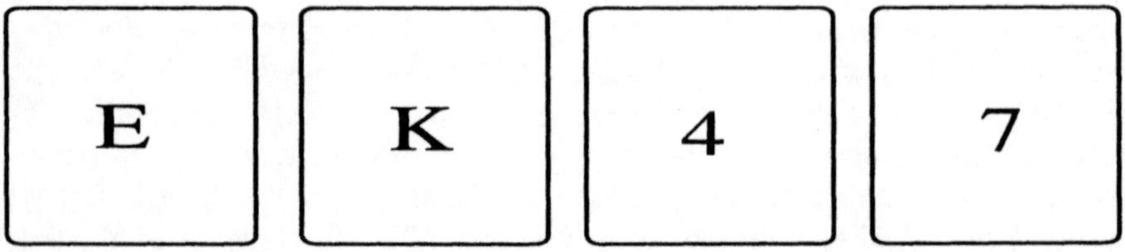

E	K	4	7

Card E should be turned because it must have an even number on the reverse if the rule is true (this is a necessary but not sufficient condition of 'proving' the truth of the rule).

Card 7 should be turned because it must *not* have a vowel on the reverse. If it does, the rule is disproved.

Card K is irrelevant to the rule because it is a consonant and need not be turned.

Card 4 is also irrelevant because the proposition does not require that cards bearing even numbers must have vowels on the reverse.

Although subjects in some cases were trained in logic and should have been familiar with this form of proposition, very tiny percentages (e.g. 4%) were reported to have turned over the correct cards. These are cards E and 7, because 'an odd number behind the E or a vowel behind the 7 would have falsified the rule.' The card bearing a K could, of course have either an even or an odd number on the reverse side, because the rule does not encompass consonants, and the card bearing the number 4 would not determine the truth or falsity of the proposition, which does not exclude the possibility that a card might have an even number on one side and a consonant on the other.

It is worth noting, however, that *if* card 4 is turned, and proves to have a vowel on the reverse, that this tends to *confirm* the rule. This inductive procedure of accumulating data to reach a conclusion is so much more familiar than reaching one by imposing artificial constraints on how much data we collect. Perhaps, for this reason, the highest proportion of error involved turning this card in addition to the most obvious card, E. But there may be explanations which have less to do with habit or psychological predisposition and more to do with the ambiguity of the rule, itself, I suggest.

It was reported that the 'same' test, an 'isomorphic' or 'logically equivalent' version, couched in more familiar terms, produced very high success rates: 'If a person is drinking alcohol, then he must be over 21.' The authors of one of these versions argued for the existence of a 'permission schema' which allows people to transfer the *identical reasoning process* successfully to more familiar and thus more readily *recognisable contexts*, but not to the more abstract one of cards bearing symbols (ibid., p. 124).

But surely the notion of a 'permission schema' (perhaps best pictured as the equivalent of a 'goto' command in the cerebral programme) leads up a blind alley? This additional 'process' in the individual subject is introduced as an explanation for differential performances on apparently identical tasks, but the more cogent explanation is that *they are not identical tasks* because to supply a recognisable context is to import criteriological features which were absent in the initial test.

Of course, the task is remote from familiar, everyday ones because it has been designed as an exercise in *formal* reasoning which, ostensibly, involves the removal of vague or ambiguous instructions which might obscure either its structure or what a subject believed she was being asked to do. But note the ambiguities which are built into the task specification as a result of this attempt at economical explanation:

> 'If *a* card has a vowel on one side, then it has an even number on the other side.'

Here, the very indefiniteness of the indefinite article intrudes on the presentation of the task because *a* card might reasonably be interpreted as *one* card - as in 'a cow in the field' or 'a boat on the lake'. Use of the same word for the indefinite article and the number one, after all, is a common feature of many languages and our own carries vestiges of this identity. In fact, large minorities of subjects were reported to have turned over card E only, and this might reflect just such an interpretation of the indefinite article or the researchers' intentions in using it. Moreover, the very informality, and thus ambiguity, of the way in which the rule is expressed might have encouraged misinterpretation according to precedent: i.e. as an abbreviated version of 'cards with vowels have even numbers on the other side, cards with consonants have odd numbers on the other side.'

Of course, such ambiguities might have been removed by a more precise task-specification. Subjects could have been told that:

> 'For each and any of these four cards (but only these four cards) which have a vowel on the side displayed, or on the side concealed, there will be an even number on the other side.'

And, instead of being asked to turn 'only those cards' necessary to test the rule, they might have been asked to turn 'only the card, or cards, necessary to demonstrate the truth of the rule. Though note the heightened emphasis on the meaning of the words - *a new convention* is being proposed in order to differentiate between conceivable alternative interpretations of the original formulation; a proposal which refers implicitly to the ambiguities in the original rendering of the rule. But if that were to be done, I suggest, the logical form of the task could also fairly be said to have been altered by the more explicit introduction of the idea of *necessary* and *sufficient* conditions of proof. The point is that the words expressing the rule are intrinsically ambiguous without a context of meaning: they offer no good basis for distinguishing between the 'logical' and the 'psychological' aspects of the operation; the situation is that of a novel, and incompletely specified, language-game.

It might be argued that these objections ignore the preamble to the experiment, but then it should be noted that the preamble (in whatever varying forms it might occur) becomes a constituent of both semantic and syntactic aspects of the task, strictly defined. And strict definition seems to be the intention in cognitive research which is designed to isolate and study performance in such precisely specified fields. In terms of the methodological premises of this experiment, to vary contextual cues is arguably to change the problem - a point also relevant to my later discussion of Piagetian 'conservation' tests (Voneche and Bovet, 1982, pp. 89-91).

The high failure rate of subjects trained in logic might have the simple explanation that while the researchers understood the test to be a logical proposition of the form, *if p, then q,* their attempts to divest the task of such technical connotations for the sake of generalizability invited common modes of reasoning rather than the artificial disciplines of formal logical reasoning.

None of the foregoing implies scepticism about the possibility of achieving precise, logical form in the use of words and symbols; that would be nonsensical and would disregard the precision achieved routinely by logicians and mathematicians. On the other hand, this example does illustrate the reliance of logical procedures on the establishment of linguistic conventions One can isolate a logical task. But that, and the ability to perform it satisfactorily, presuppose fairly protracted induction into the use of words in particular contexts. The moral is that a unitary sample of logical form, in isolation from the very specific linguistic conventions which identify it as such is syntactically and semantically ambiguous. As the object of an experiment to investigate particularities in cognition, it is intrinsically unreliable because the subject's perception of that form (and thus her 'cognitive processes') will vary according to her familiarity with those conventions.

Margaret Donaldson has used the Wason Card Test to argue the importance of 'human sense' in problem solving. She attributes the very much higher success rates on a version of the Wason Card Test (modified in such a way as to present the task in familiar, concrete terms) to this factor:

> There can be little doubt, then, that when we set such store by disembedded modes of thought we make the pursuit of education in our society a difficult enterprise for the human mind - one which many minds refuse at an early stage...children who relied on human sense and did not reason tightly from the premises got them wrong. (Donaldson, 1990, page 81)

The weakness of Donaldson's reference to 'disembedded modes of thought' is that it overlooks the dependence of logical form on the context of meaningful language. She accepts, as do Singley and Anderson, that a modified, 'human-sense' Wason test is a *logically isomorphic* version of the first task: '...it is the *same* task as regards logical structure.' My point is that even though a perfectly legitimate distinction is to be made between (a) the logical structure of the problem, and (b) subjects' perceptions of the problem, it does not follow that this distinction is sustainable in operational terms. Subjective perceptions of the task are not strictly distinguishable from the ambiguities inherent in the linguistic specification of that task; a vagueness about what would constitute what Donaldson describes as 'tight reasoning from the premises'. And that failure occurred because, in its original form, the task *itself* lacked a clear, logical structure for subjects who were unfamiliar with the conventions governing the *specialised* language needed to interpret the problem as its authors intended. And in cases where failure occurred despite familiarity with formal logic, it was probably because subjects had not been alerted to the relevance of a very specific set of conventions. In other words, logical form is an extrapolation from more common modes of reasoning which is the result of highly sophisticated developments in language-use; it is no more a skeletal framework within 'human sense' than that proverbial angel is contained within the block of marble. Human sense is not a single kind of thing, either. It reaches out into all those varied situations in which a mode of reasoning is sufficient for immediate purposes. Symbols comprising mathematical equations or logical propositions have no intrinsic significance They represent complex developments of language, and failure amongst educationalists to appreciate this might account for the special difficulty which many experience in dealing with such abstractions.

Donaldson's introduction of the concept of a supportive 'human-sense' context, like a reassuring cocoon around the stringent requirements of logical form, directs attention away from an important fact: the search for elemental intellectual skills which can be expressed in some formal notation (like traditional logic) is suspect because it is impossible to define either skills, functions or tasks in isolation from their socio-linguistic contexts - certainly in the absolute sense which could ensure that all subjects are engaged on precisely the same, elemental cognitive operation. An ineradicable ambiguity separates the definition of a problem from perceptions of it; each successive clarification is tantamount to a modification of the form the problem assumes from the subject's point of view, and this will vary according to idiosyncrasies in personal experiences of language-use. This is not to deny the possibility of eventual agreement about the form of a problem. But by virtue of the mutuality between language, social context and logic, the terminology of 'cognitive structures' and 'units of knowledge' is deeply misleading if it relies on a postulate of *isomophism* between the specification of a given task and the form of reasoning involved in its successful completion. The precise and elemental forms of logical relationship are extrapolations from modes of reasoning, not their dynamic principles.

Singley and Anderson do indeed acknowledge that there is a problem about the *identity* of any two or more stimuli (that is, different versions of the same experimental task). But they write the difficulty off in the case of Thorndike to his vagueness 'about the exact nature of his elements' and, in general, because of 'the absence of an explicit representation language for cognitive skill' (ibid., p. 5). My argument in this section has been that there can be no precise determinations of these things in the intended sense. They are logically embedded in the language which describes them, and the test of linguistic meaning is discourse; it is *between* people rather than *within* them. Singley and Anderson suggest a rationale for sustained interest in the transfer of cognitive skills, despite difficulties of the kind just discussed:

> One reason why the notion of general transfer keeps rising from the grave is that it is such an attractive proposition for psychologists and educators alike. It is the one effect that, if discovered and engineered, could liberate students and teachers from the shackles of narrow, disciplinary education. Sustaining these longings is the fact that it is very difficult to prove something does not exist. There is always another manipulation in the psychologist's toolbox to try. (Singley and Anderson, 1989, pp. 23-29)

What kind of faculty are we talking about, though, which could liberate students from, say, physics, history, logic or mathematics? A discipline embodies its own characteristic forms of reasoning even if, as I maintain, it could not be logically autonomous as McPeck claims.

3 Epistemic Bedrock or Logical Quicksand?

> ...confusion, *ignoratio elenchi,* is itself the most fatal of all errors, and...it occurs whenever argument or inference passes from one world of experience to another...the importance of a criterion for determining this confusion is extreme. (Oakeshott, 1933, p. 5)

Domain theory and some of its limitations

In the previous chapter I discussed some difficulties confronting theories about the generalizability of critical thinking. Now I wish to consider some objections to the commonly opposed notion, that critical thinking is predominantly or exclusively domain-specific. I hope, as a result, to develop an alternative interpretation of the terms *generality* and *specificity* which have assumed misleading roles as polarities in the 'thinking skills debate'.

McPeck champions the idea that significant thought is domain-specific. He reaches conservative pedagogic conclusions because his emphasis on the mutual exclusivity of cognitive domains implies lengthy periods of induction to them. However, there are significant lacunae in his own thesis and I will argue that his reliance on Wittgenstein's metaphor of *language games* is an insecure foundation for his particular thesis. But before making that case I will examine domain-theory in the more architectonic, universalising form articulated by Michael Oakeshott in decades preceding the contemporary 'thinking skills debate'. My reason is that he makes clear something that is insufficiently explicit in this debate; that it is really about the characterisation of human thought in general, a question which extends beyond the aims and methods of formal education and subsumes them. Oakeshott seeks 'a point of view from which the relative validity of any world of experience can be determined...' (ibid., p. 2). And issues of this generality need to be addressed because they encompass the origins and justification of critical thinking as a social and educational ideal.

McPeck echoes an equivocation in Oakeshott's theory of discrete disciplinary languages; an emphasis alternating between the internal, logical cohesion of the disciplines on the one hand, and the historical process of disciplinary specialisation, on the other. The quotation at the beginning of this section illustrates Oakeshott's characteristic preoccupation with criteria of demarcation and mutual incompatibility. Elsewhere, there is his acknowledgement that the complex evolution of intellectual traditions precludes exact definition of them. But this acknowledgement marks more than *just* a difference of emphasis. It is a shift from insistence on an internal criterion of identity to general criteria; the tacit acknowledgement of a fatal flaw in the theory of domains; that they must be characterised, ultimately, in terms of their evolution within cultures. This is not a once-for-all procedure. Its implications for the teaching of critical thinking are not the same as the more conservative and authoritarian educational implications of the concept of logically discrete and mutually exclusive realms of knowledge. But McPeck and Oakeshott argue similar cases and draw similar pedagogic conclusions from their analyses which, I believe, are at least as inimical to genuine critical thinking as some of the approaches they oppose.

Emphasis on the specificity of disciplinary thought may preclude certain cherished methods. For example, Oakeshott and McPeck hold views which are inconsistent with the idea of child-centred education and reciprocal, egalitarian teacher-pupil relationships. As I have already noted, their conceptions of specialised disciplinary 'languages' implies a need for authoritative interpretation and long periods of initiation before the novice can communicate effectively within them. Oakeshott's view is that 'School education...is learning to speak before one has anything significant to say; and what is taught must have the qualities of being able to be learned without necessarily being understood' (Oakeshott, 1967, p. 306). McPeck follows with the claim that passive memorisation, receptive learning are appropriate to earlier school grades because '...first students must learn the basic information about their culture so that they will have something to be critical about' (McPeck, 1990, p. 44).

Despite McPeck's support for a cross-curricular infusion of philosophy, his view of educational priorities clashes with Matthew Lipman's idea of *democratic communities of inquiry* as vehicles for philosophical dialogue amongst young children, and between them and their teachers. Oakeshott's view is wholly inconsistent with such ideas; the 'language' of philosophy is, for him, one of the distinctive features of a *university* education *(Oakeshott, 1967, pp. 301-333)*. There is, in addition, an obvious incompatibility between such an emphasis on specialisation and Jerome Bruner's 'provocative', Millian hypothesis '...that any subject may be taught effectively in some intellectually honest form to any child at any stage of development' (Bruner, 1974, p. 413).

McPeck and Oakeshott stress the disjunctive attributes of disciplines, selecting examples like science and history in which the differences appear most self-evident. Neither says much about the variety of disciplinary subdivisions, their history of gradual differentiation, or the many spheres of common interest and contested fiefdoms; the sociologist's concern with history; notions of mind which are shared and disputed between philosophers and psychologists. This kind of omission is more understandable in McPeck's case because his interest is mainly with the school curriculum. Oakeshott, on the other hand, surveys the broad spectrum of human experience and in university education, for example, he detects a few foundational disciplines. For him, the study of politics is interdisciplinary but the disciplines concerned are philosophy and history - and these, he claims, are discrete languages (Oakeshott, 1967, pp. 301-333).

But this key metaphor is double-edged. *Languages* are not only mutually intelligible in principle, they can be learned, even several at a time, by young children and the illiterate as well as by the educationally sophisticated. In other words, there are common, general, criteria of intelligibility, however complex and elusive they may be. The more the case for the *internal, logical coherence* of different modes of thought is pressed, the more apparent it becomes that this is to invoke *general* criteria of discrimination within the plethora of languages and idioms. As I will show, Oakeshott is forced to abandon the idea of exclusive, domain-specific 'logics' and instead, to adopt historical, philosophical and sociological characterisations - a reluctant acknowledgement that it is from the common ground within the diversity of human thought that we obtain descriptions of its more specialised developments and establish their validity and truth. The fact that we *learn* can be accounted for only in terms of reciprocities between specialised understanding and more general forms of comprehension.

These preliminary points do not register an intention to refute domain theory in all respects, for I believe it has a core of validity. Thought is, as McPeck maintains, definitively *subject-specific*, a pedagogically significant consideration which will be elaborated in my subsequent discussions of human intentionality and semantic meaning, and one which should prompt serious reservations about current enthusiasms for the pre-emptive modelling of general thinking skills. However, McPeck over-identifies subject-specificity with broad intellectual traditions or academic disciplines (subjects) like history, science or philosophy. But philosophy, I maintain, is thought at its most highly articulated level of generality. It includes the investigation of specialised forms of understanding, their reciprocal implications and (in contrast to Oakeshott's conception of philosophy as a general form of inquiry) their connections with 'everyday' and 'common-sense' understandings. Domain theory leads to a self-defeating relativism of the kind Siegel has identified; the conclusion that no effective criticisms of modes of thought can be mounted from standpoints other than those internally sanctioned by particular methodologies and subject-matters. This is uncongenial to the idea of critical thinking; it sacrifices a sense of the richness, diversity and controversiality of the critical traditions for the illusion of monolithic 'forms of knowledge'. Stress on internal homogeneity diverts attention away from competing conceptions of reality and reason which foster critical thought, substituting for argument and debate a fictional unanimity as its cardinal feature. In an extreme form, domain theory imposes false limitations on the potential of young minds by stressing the esoteric at the expense of the generic; it sanctions a view of early education as *learning without understanding* and replaces critical thinking by self-authenticating dogma.

The 'languages' of the formal disciplines

Oakeshott is insistent about the domain-specificity of thought. Three decades after the publication of *Experience and its Modes* (1933) in which he presented the thesis in its most elaborate form his only specific retraction in a later collection of essays concerns an unspecified 'single foolish sentence' in that earlier work. In all other respects he continues to maintain that:

> ...the 'languages' of history, of philosophy, of science and of mathematics - are all of them *explanatory* languages; each of them represents a specific mode of explanation...each operates with clear criteria of relevance; each is capable of reaching conclusions appropriate to itself; in each it may be said that this or that is in error, but also (and more significantly) that this or that is out of character... (Oakeshott, 1967, pp. 327-8, original emphasis)

Oakeshott opposes the concept of internally coherent modes of thought to the rationalist's alleged faith in 'a "reason" common to all mankind, a common power of rational consideration, which is the ground and inspiration of argument...'. He even characterises the rationalist as one who misguidedly follows Parmenides' precept, *judge by rational argument* and, moreover, one whose preoccupation with technical knowledge leads to exaggerated faith in the efficacy of rules, principles, directions and maxims which can be taught and learned by heart - 'in the simplest meanings of these words' - and applied mechanically, like the logic of the syllogism. This is, in fact, a convincing attack on some problem-solving and thinking skills programmes which enjoy contemporary popularity (despite the notorious rarity of empirically confirmed skill-transfer). Oakeshott is consequently the intellectual foe of those who seek, or claim to find and teach general thinking skills which could be remotely applicable to the subject-matters of the formal disciplines; highly specialised inheritances which, according to his caricature, the rationalist implicitly disavows. Had these arguments been made a quarter of a century later, in the context of the thinking skills debate they would place Oakeshott decisively in opposition to the Informal Logical Movement. A token of the seriousness of Oakeshott's attack on rationalism is the remark by Karl Popper that '...there was not much in the rationalist literature which could be considered an adequate answer to his arguments' (Popper, 1963, p. 121).

McPeck invokes Oakeshott's example in his argument for the introduction of philosophical analysis into the teaching of the mainstream academic disciplines; specifically in relation to the teaching of history (McPeck, 1990, p. 17). There is some irony in this choice because Oakeshott describes history and philosophy as different explanatory languages, each with its intrinsic criteria of relevance and error. What, we are entitled to ask, could *philosophy* contribute to a *history* which is so seamlessly self-consistent, or vice-versa? Both authors ground their arguments on evidence other than observations about the way historians or philosophers happen to go about their work. Indeed, McPeck emphasises the *a priori* nature of his assertion of domain-specificity. The autonomy of domains of knowledge represents a categorical organisation of thought itself, a principle of epistemology which, he maintains, is fundamental.

Both authors equivocate in their accounts of this principle. Despite occasional renunciations of 'settled doctrine', Oakeshott's proclivity for differentiating modes of thought in terms of absolute disjunctions and defining these, in turn, as matters of logic is borne out repeatedly in later essays. It is evident in the insistent vocabulary of 'discrete universes of discourse', of 'unique utterances, not to be assimilated to any other' and of 'logically distinct universes of discourse'. On the other hand, both authors do entertain conceptions of the flux within which forms of knowledge have taken shape historically and of the potentially limitless variety of forms which they might assume. Oakeshott envisages 'no limit to the possible modifications in experience' although he considers them to be internally homogenous and mutually exclusive (Oakeshott, 1933, pp. 320-331). McPeck expresses this same view in his references to 'language games' and 'forms of life' - distorting the metaphor by insisting simultaneously on two incompatible points of view. There are, he says, 'almost as many distinguishable logics, or kinds of reasoning, as there are distinguishable kinds of subjects' but follows this proposition with the claim that '...categories of understanding are not static...but so long as they are *in place at any given time*, they constitute coherent thought' (McPeck 1990, pp. 36-37). With this move, McPeck inconsistently shifts the burden of his argument to an unspecified *external criterion* of suitability to time and place, as already noted.

It is as though McPeck withdraws at the last moment from the epistemological relativism inherent in his idea of self-authenticating language games. However, the solution cannot be a straight choice between domain theory and the generalist thesis. Mutually contradictory though they are in one sense, each thesis sustains itself by locating its 'Archimedian point' in features of the other. The domain-theorist resorts to an artificial criterion of general applicability in an effort to establish the rational justifiability of any given mode of thought. In order to avoid abstraction to the point vacuity, the generalist is bound to acknowledge a point of Scheffler's concerning the historical particularities of universal principles of reasoning, that:

> ...the way in which (their) demands are concretely interpreted, elaborated and supplemented in any field of inquiry...varies with the field, the state of knowledge, and the advance of relevant methodological sophistication. (Scheffler, 1973, p. 78).

Indeed, Scheffler adopts an almost Oakeshottian vocabulary: 'To teach rationality in history is, in effect...to introduce the student to a live tradition of historical scholarship' (ibid, p. 79). The idea of universal principles faces the difficulty, recognised by Scheffler in the same passage, and also by Siegel; they change and evolve with the traditions which embody them. However, both authors maintain that these principles will be 'crystallised' for a time within a rational tradition (Siegel, 1988, p. 135) - a phrase which might seem reminiscent of McPeck's own conception of categorical forms of understanding 'in place at a given time'. While I do not wish to conflate what are the very distinct positions of McPeck, Scheffler and Siegel, I suggest that the *specifist* and the *generalist* arguments represent horns of a single dilemma which cannot be tackled effectively 'head-on' because neither case can be coherently formulated in such a way as to obviate the qualifications just mentioned. In fact, Siegel argues that generalists and specifists are both correct and that the conflict is misconceived. In other words, as Siegel points out and McPeck himself asserts (though inconsistently), an indispensable component of critical, rational thought concerns the conscious appeal to purportedly universal epistemological principles to determine the intelligibility and justifiability of theories within ostensibly different domains.

The significance of this latter move is that it shifts emphasis from the logical and epistemological characteristics of thought to human activity and institutional behaviour; the historical arena of debate concerning the nature and applicability of principles within various traditions of inquiry. One of the vital signs of a critical tradition is that criteria of rationality are never 'fixed' in the way implied by McPeck's reference to time and place. Taken in conjunction with his argument against superordinate, universal principles of reason this could only mean that judgments concerning relevance to time and place are contingent upon historically-specific notions of human status and authority and are consequently arbitrary. But even those things which appear to be most enduring and unchallengeable in our repertoire of constants may be subverted by alternative paradigms, as the independent categories of time and space were by Einsteinian relativity. Competing notions about the nature of sound principles of argumentation have been the philosophical dynamic which has driven the critical traditions from the time of the pagan Greeks, through the Galilean revolution to the present. Galileo underscored this point; that in the struggle to reconcile authoritative, universal principles with newly discovered and contradictory evidence the central issue is redefined as one of social conventions of discourse:

> ...God delivered up the world to disputations...In my opinion no one, in contradiction to that dictum, should close the road to free philosophizing about mundane and physical things, as if everything had already been discovered and revealed with certainty. (Goodman, 1973, p. 35)

The dialectic between contrasting theories of knowledge reveals the interpersonal character of semantic meaning and reason, and appreciation of the institutional conditions which promote dialogue and controversiality, themes I will explore in more detail in the following chapters.

The demarcation between cognitive domains

Oakeshott is correct to draw attention to the possibility of confusion between different categories of description and explanation. His mistake is in believing that the categories are capable of being distinguished comprehensively; that a 'criterion' could be found in order to determine 'the relative validity of any world of experience', and to distinguish it from others, obviating the error and confusion which 'follow from a failure to determine the exact character and significance of (for example) scientific or historical experience' (Oakeshott, 1933, pp. 2-5). He insistently stresses the mutual exclusivity of these two domains and the dire consequences of any conjunction between them, making no allowance for the provisional nature of our solutions and the ongoing need to reassess our procedures and methodologies in the light of newly-discovered paradoxes or inconsistencies. But he can sustain this argument only, for example, by stipulating that science, unlike history, is an attempt to explain reality in quantitative terms (ibid., p. 172). This arbitrary definition, which neglects the use of quantitative method as a mere instrument for achieving more precise insights into reality in other terms, also seems to rule out archaeology, geology or anthropology as *scientific* sources of historical illumination. But of course they often *are* extremely valuable sources of historical understanding which may expand, amend or contradict the written record (for example, about the scale of ancient communities, diet, life-expectancy, typical illnesses, patterns of trade or conflict, to supplement or amend the written record). The application of scientific procedures to the subject-matter of other disciplines does not import, bag and baggage, all the philosophical presuppositions and implications of scientific method. It is probably from within moments of co-operation and conflict that a more reliable characterisation of disciplines will emerge than from the attempt to identify their necessary and immutable characteristics, thereby dismissing challenging contradictions in our views of the world as *category errors*. Conflict between modes of understanding is not evidence of systematic irreconcileability and mutual unintelligiblity as Oakeshott believes (Oakeshott, 1933, p. 349). For instance, the 'solution' of dismissing the free-will/determinism issue as a category error fails to engage with common real life issues in which we contrast voluntary, reasoned behaviour with behaviour which is the causal consequence of hormone levels, brain trauma or the use of psychotropic drugs. Yet concrete situations like this determine what we mean by 'free-will' and 'causal determinism' and the varying patterns of contrast we detect between them.

What, then, is Oakeshott's criterion of demarcation between the modes of experience? His philosophical stance is explicitly that of Hegelian Idealism and the following quotation illustrates the point succinctly with its presupposition of an ultimately coherent realm of experience-as-a-whole, free of all contradictions and inconsistencies:

> What is achieved in experience is an absolutely coherent world of ideas, *not in the sense that it is ever actually achieved,* but in the more important sense that it is the criterion of whatever satisfaction is achieved. (ibid., p. 35, my emphasis)

But there is something odd in the notion that something never actually achieved can be a *criterion* of thought. I will discuss later the idea of *truth* as a normative feature of social life; a universal, regulative ideal. The contrast I want to draw, here, is not between truth and coherence. It is between truth as something accessible in many situations, our familiarity with which makes the concept meaningful as a more generally achievable *end*, and the frustrating paradigm of absolute metaphysical certainty which encourages sceptical renunciations of the idea of universal principle. We are specifically not committed to a transcendental view of truth which operates as a criterion of, or constraint on, the forms which the dialectic of inquiry can be permitted to take.

Paradoxically, Oakeshott refers to the Platonic concept of the *dialectic* as the source of his notion of 'coherence'. The true form of experience, he says, is argument. And argument is invariably based on a belief in a system which is (ultimately) coherent, in which 'there is no permanent place for what is incoherent or irrational' (ibid, p. 37). My own contention is similar; knowledge is dialogic and interpersonal; argument, *in a crucial sense*, presupposes the possibility of eventual agreement on the basis of common principles of rationality; the *elenchus* which defeats scepticism and relativism. However, this is not the same as Oakeshott's belief that this ultimate ideal of *coherence* can be articulated prospectively in order to assign particular episodes of thought to one of a number of segregated modes of experience. Unresolved inconsistencies within the modes of experience to which he ascribes a unique self-consistency, like those arising from relativity theory in physics, or the conflict between Oakeshott's own historical idealism and dialectical materialism, have driven critical inquiry. To legislate in advance about the boundaries between the coherent and the incoherent is to establish an arbitrary standard which would obviate genuine critical, dialectical argument. But, it seems, Oakeshott's conception of the dialectic is just such an arbitrary standard, a criticism overwhelmingly justified by his peculiarly inconclusive metaphor of 'conversation' to describe the limited opportunities for meaningful exchange between different disciplines.

The possibility of a 'conversation' implies that there are at least some common criteria of intelligibility and sound reasoning. But in *these* conversations, Oakeshott claims, participants 'are not engaged in an inquiry or a debate; there is no 'truth' to be discovered, no proposition to be proved, no conclusion sought. They are not concerned to inform, to persuade, or to refute one another...' (Oakeshott, 1967, p. 198). The image of disciplinary specialists talking past one another, conjured by these words, is reminiscent of Oakeshott's own metaphor of the 'Tower of Babel' in an essay expressing his view of a crisis in post-war European morality. There is an evasiveness about this statement; an inclination to reassert domain specificity strongly and invest it with the strict necessity associated with 'logic', having qualified it in anticipation of the problems which this poses from philosophical and historical points of view. In order to account for the comparatively recent proliferation of disciplines, Oakeshott retreats from assertions of domain-specific logics, necessary and sufficient conditions, to the imagery of a 'miscellany of utterances' which only gradually acquire a *specific character* (ibid., pp. 151-2).

I do not believe that this represents a genuine revision, if only because Oakeshott returned to a much stronger emphasis on the distinctiveness of the disciplines on subsequent occasions, as I have indicated. Yet there are clear historical and sociological implications in what he says about the emergence of recognisable disciplines from that miscellany. His characterisation of domains of thought cries out for an account of the historical transition from standards of intelligibility and rationality governing more general modes of discourse to the *specific* and putatively *unique* logics of foundational disciplines. *That* requires an understanding of the cultural environments which have fostered and influenced such developments as well as a rigorous account of the point at which the *general* becomes the *domain-specific*.

This is a most significant equivocation in the position of the radical domain-theorist which raises the prospect of a more intellectually satisfying conception of *traditions of critical thought*. Indeed Oakeshott adopts precisely this term, 'tradition', in his attack on rationalism. McPeck also uses 'tradition' in contrast to the programmatic approach of the Informal Logic Movement. However, both authors appear to be motivated by a sense of the inadequacy of such a loose formulation to justify the pre-eminence of mainstream academic disciplines in education; the absence of an incontrovertible inner cohesion in the idea of tradition. Their desire for this leads to that gross underestimation of the diversity and controversiality of intellectual history which marks a retreat from the commitment to critical inquiry. Oakeshott's retreat, in the form of a largely unhistorical and arbitrary account of the internal cohesiveness of three modes of experience, is clearly illustrated by his treatment of one of them; *history.*

The character of history

The preceding commentary has focused on aspects of the general case for domain-theory mainly as Oakeshott articulates it, rather than on the internal character of a domain, which is equally necessary to the credibility of such a theory. I believe Oakeshott's account of history displays some of the contradictions and lacunae which must inevitably afflict that endeavour. In *Experience and its Modes* the subject is depicted as 'the attempt to explain the historical *past* by means of the historical *past* and for the sake of the historical *past*' and as 'a world of abstractions...a *homogenous, self-contained* mode of experience which falls short of self-completeness' (ibid., p. 145, and p. 156, my emphasis). This world of experience has three cardinal features. It is distinct from the practical concerns of everyday life, and there can be 'no relation or commerce' between history and practice; whenever this occurs 'the result can be only the destruction of both' (ibid., p. 157-8). There are no 'plots' or 'themes' in history, and the historian's concern is exclusively with detail. History is part of the world of present experience; it is nothing more than present evidence and 'what is beyond the evidence is actually unknowable' (ibid., p. 108).

These formulations hardly assist Oakeshott's portrayal of history as an internally seamless activity. Despite his tendentious portrayal of exclusive concern with *the past* for its own sake, his denial of the possibility of knowledge about anything beyond 'present evidence' invites the question whether *evidence* can refer only to itself. And, if so, does this mean that we are never justified in believing that an historical document actually had an author, a context or a point? This simultaneous assertion and denial of a *past* marks a chaotic departure from the common meanings of words; a flux within which Oakeshott evidently feels at liberty to establish his own, arbitrary definitions of a domain of thought. History is whatever he wants it to be; and he seems to want it to be the activity of politically and ethically neutral academic 'historians' who establish imaginary connections between the words contained in books and documents, for according to his account they have no justification for believing in the reality of anything or anyone beyond words on pages. Indeed, it is not too extreme an interpretation of Oakeshott's scepticism to point out that his theory of 'present evidence' removes all justification for believing that two items could refer to the same thing; they seem to be discrete by virtue of their lack of connection with anything beyond themselves.

This self-authenticating domain seems to be immune from the personal testimony of living individuals whose experience of past events influences their practical concerns and whose interpretations are influenced by those events, because these are not the abstract and dispassionate ones of the historian. Oakeshott's rejection of the past, construed strictly, has bizarre consequences. It removes any basis for discrimination, on grounds of reliability, between competing bits of evidence. For unless made in purely quantitative terms, judgments of this kind entail plausible reconstructions of past events; narratives which reach beyond available evidence. There has to be, for example, a presumption that human motivations at least approximated to those of the present; that linguistic usages were at least sufficiently similar to present ones for us to reconstruct the significant differences and their semantic and historical import.

Convention has it that authors of the past, whose works constitute source materials for contemporary research, were rarely prompted by dispassionate interest and historians have always conducted their inquiries in a world which contains individuals whose living testimony eventually comprises the corpus of historical understanding. Cumulative, anecdotal evidence provides the checks and balances to the historian's interpretation of scholarly sources - or the demagogue's revision of accepted interpretations of the past and its significance. A recent example is Claude Lanzman's documentary film, *Shoa* (BBC2, 7th & 8th Jan. 1995), made explicitly to refute neo-Nazi denials of the reality of the holocaust by recording and correlating the direct testimony of its victims and administrators. Lanzman's disturbing evidence of an historical reality was made precisely because of its bearing on present-day political developments. Does that mean that this investigation does *not* constitute historical evidence of past events? Oakeshott appears to exclude such material by *fiat* and, with it, almost everything which we usually understand by 'history'.

The continuity of past and present through the testimony of successive generations of living people is not only our warrant for asserting the *reality* of past events; it is an essential constituent of the meaning we attach to a term like 'the past' in everyday language, and it thereby establishes the parameters of what anyone - including historians and philosophers - can say about it without becoming unintelligible. Oakeshott's sceptical argument that history is nothing *but* the investigation of present evidence is parasitic upon his conception of the past as a reality, and derives whatever meaning it has from that contrast. Moreover, an understanding of the past entails the exploration of *themes* and the employment of *generalisations* as much for the historian as for others. Our sense of the historical past is united with present experience; we are committed to the recognition and critical examination of broad and competing patterns, trends and institutions, because they make intelligible what would otherwise be an incomprehensible variety of individual motives and actions. And, as I will later argue, these 'generalisations' are also constitutive elements of our motives and actions. Historical understanding is a necessary component of contemporary ideas and beliefs. We clarify our grasp of them by tracing their evolution in the intellectual and practical lives of human beings - a significant consideration in elucidating the traditional character of *critical thinking.*

The contradiction inherent in domain theory

A paradox is implicit in domain-theory. On the one hand, there is the denial of superordinate and general criteria of rationality. This seems to imply that there must be logical structures internal to the different modes, at least if there is to be any possibility of rational justification. On the other hand, the inherent relativism of this position - the justification of propositions and methods by internal criteria alone - prohibits meaningful statements *about* different modes of thought when taken to its conclusion, because boundary criteria and standards of relevance are not even *specifiable* from an uncommitted point of view. Indeed, it is only by arbitrary, stipulative definitions that some appearance of order can be imposed on the vicious regress into an infinity of *languages, modes of thought and forms of life*, each of which is held to possess its own criteria of meaning, relevance and validity. Ernest Gellner satirised the position in his assault on Wittgensteinian idealism:

> So, by looking at language *games*, we hunt with the empirical-naturalistic hounds; but by accepting their *contents*, we run with the transcendental hares, or any others we care to run with...And moreover: by suitably determining the limits of 'games' (language itself does not do it), and by choosing the terms with which to describe them, we can have our universe just as we wish, unchallengeable and beyond doubt. (Gellner, 1968, p. 167)

Gellner's parody of language games is questionable in so far as he treats them *as though they are to be regarded as phenomena* rather than as heuristics for comparing diverse forms of expression; 'the morphology of the use of an expression,' as Wittgenstein once described it (Malcolm, 1968, p. 50). Nevertheless, the parody makes a telling point about the dilemma in which Oakeshott and McPeck find themselves. This is revealed particularly in the latter's contention that '...there are almost as many distinguishable logics, or kinds of reasoning, as there are distinguishable kinds of subjects'. If the features which distinguish a subject, and its 'logic', are wholly contained within it, McPeck's only recourse is either to impose a definition or to admit that there are criteria of a *general* or interdisciplinary nature, as Siegel has pointed out. These general criteria are implicated in the possibilities of (a) distinguishing disciplines and 'modes of thought' by identifying their salient characteristics and the epistemic status of their contents, (b) the possibility of learning this content and thus achieving eventual understanding, as well as (c) providing a rationale for selecting from a potentially unlimited number of subjects those few appropriate to an educational menu. In fact McPeck imposes his definition by selecting those subjects which he holds to be of special value in a liberal education, namely, mathematics, history, science, art and so forth.

A prioritisation of subjects comprising a liberal education may be broadly justifiable on the ground that they represent the cumulative results of substantial traditions of inquiry rather than products of a categorical organisation of human thought. Paul Hirst, another authority cited by McPeck, and one of the originators of this latter sanction for liberal education, revised his early concept of the 'forms of knowledge'. In a later essay he acknowledged that: 'The logical interrelations between the different forms of knowledge are manifestly many and complex. How far a general map of these can be outlined, I am far from clear'. Moreover, the concept of liberal education which he had developed on that basis had been 'explicitly stipulative' (Hirst, 1974, pp. 30-53 and 90-91). Nor could the radical epistemological perspective of an Oakeshott or a McPeck be other than stipulative and ultimately arbitrary. In some respects their views of educational method accord with those of Thomas Kuhn on the teaching of science; the difference being that Kuhn acknowledges that his prescriptions are for the arbitrary imposition of order on an essentially disorderly subject-matter (Kuhn, 1970). McPeck's recommendation for an infusion of philosophical debate about the epistemic status of curricular subjects seems to be a partial acknowledgement of this indeterminacy and it is compatible with my own thesis, but he appears not to recognise that this admission of the insufficiency of internal disciplinary 'logics' destroys the cohesion of his main argument. He concedes that there are non-trivial skills of thought which, if not *general* in the contemporary sense, are extrinsic to the form and content of particular subject-matters (ibid., p. 17). This is to say that *general, non-specific criteria of rationality* are necessary to the appraisal of the very foundations of disciplines.

Domains and language games

Apart from the important proposition that *intelligibility is determined at the semantic rather than the syntactic level,* which I will examine in subsequent chapters, McPeck's rejection of general thinking skills rests on his contention:

> Just as there are different kinds of "language games," which stem from what Wittgenstein called different "forms of life" (e.g. mathematics, morality, religion, art, etc.) so there are different rules of predication, or "reasoning," if you will, which govern the different kinds of thought. (ibid. p. 36)

The suggestion, and it is never more than this, is that *forms of life* or *language games* are to be identified with the academic subjects, listed in parentheses, which comprise the elements of a liberal education. I have already referred to the fundamental difficulties posed for the domain theorist by defining coherent thought as appropriateness to time and place. But an equally serious objection to McPeck concerns the above quotation. 'Language games' are not only not static; they are never 'in place' because they are not phenomena of any kind. The concept, which evolved gradually over a long period in Wittgenstein's later philosophy, is a metaphorical device for drawing attention to features of language and logic which, by their very nature, cannot be subsumed within a formal system of description. Like all metaphors, language games relate to the things they represent in partial, fleeting ways. There is no sense in which they are structural components of thought or language; they are, perhaps, examples of what Wittgenstein meant by saying that certain things can be *shown*, but not *said*. It is exactly this diffuseness, further emphasised by Wittgenstein's simile of 'family resemblances' between linguistic usages, which led Ernest Gellner to protest:

> Empirically, there is no non-arbitrary way of isolating such self-contained games within the flux of our thought and language...because, logically, it is impossible...There are no inherently isolated language games in the world, any more than there is an absolute, all-embracing one. (Gellner, 1968, p. 175)

But this was precisely the kind of point that the language-game metaphor illustrates. It is amplified in Wittgenstein's own words in various contexts, and especially in his *Philosophical Investigations:*

> We remain unconscious of the prodigious diversity of all the everyday language games because the clothing of our language makes everything alike. Something new, (spontaneous, specific) is always a language game (PI, IIxi, p. 224). ... How should we explain to someone what a game is? I imagine that we should describe *games* to him, and we might add: "This *and similar things* are called 'games'". And do we know any more about it ourselves? Is it only other people whom we cannot tell exactly what a game is? - But this is not ignorance. We do not know the boundaries because none have been drawn... (PI, I, 69)

Language games are not appropriate building blocks for McPeck's concept of internally coherent, logically bounded domains of thought. Indeed, Wittgenstein emphasised this point by asking whether our concept of a game, or games-in-general, which we can use effectively but cannot articulate, is equivalent to an 'unformulated definition'. His answer was: 'If someone were to draw a sharp boundary I could not acknowledge it as the one that I too always wanted to draw, or had drawn in my mind. For I did not want to draw one at all...' (Wittgenstein, 1968, PI, 76). And again:

> Our clear and simple language games are not preparatory studies for a future regularisation of language - as it were first approximations, ignoring friction and air resistance. The language games are rather set up as *objects of comparison* which are meant to throw light on the facts of our language by way not only of similarities but also of dissimilarities.
>
> For we can avoid ineptness or emptiness in our assertions only by presenting the model as what it is, as an object of comparison - as, so to speak, a measuring rod; not as a preconceived idea to which reality *must* correspond [the dogmatism into which we fall so easily in doing philosophy.] (ibid., PI, 130 ;131, original emphasis)

These few examples should be sufficient to demonstrate that McPeck has recruited Wittgenstein's metaphor to his own thesis in a very different spirit to that intended by its originator. There are other justifications for the formal disciplines, but the idea of language games is amongst them in a quite different sense. This, I will argue, is that the disciplines are a continuation of the historical effort to explore the diversity of meanings and modes of implication in language and thought. Although I do not wish to labour this point here, I will refer to language games in subsequent discussions of the relationships between language, thought and 'forms of life' and their implications for pedagogic method. For this reason, and because McPeck *is* at least partly correct in his attack on the idea of superordinate systems of rules of effective argumentation, I offer the following considerations:

The 'game' metaphor does not specify the kind of subject which occupies identifiable categories of discourse. Nor does it deny the powerful explanatory force of disciplined inquiry by introducing an anarchic principle. It reflects the fact that problems may, and do, arise in the course of generalising from particular uses of language and that there is no final, epistemological court-of-appeal because there is no definitive way of categorising the various linguistic usages. The analytical value of these 'games' is exhausted, so to speak, when we appreciate the creativity of language and its potential for ambiguity - illustrated for example, when we assume we are dealing with one set of linguistically meaningful relationships but are actually dealing with another. Like Wittgenstein's earlier metaphor at the conclusion of his *Tractatus* (T, 1969, p. 151), the metaphor of language games is like a ladder, to be discarded when it has been climbed; having fulfilled its function as a warning against the assumption that ostensibly similar linguistic conventions have an underlying identity of semantic and rational import. Its relevance is to the minutiae of everyday speech as well as to the large and small questions which arise within and between the disciplines. Perhaps the major significance of the *Philosophical Investigations* is the bearing it has on the unsuccessful search for elementary propositions; there is no way of escaping from the different linguistic usages in which 'elementary' and 'proposition' have their range of meanings, and thus no sense in an attempt to construct an account of the relationship between language and reality on the basis of fundamental, 'atomic' propositions. Wittgenstein admitted that he had 'nowhere said what the essence of a language game, and hence language, is; what is common to all these activities and, and what makes them into language or parts of language' (PI, I, 65). Instead of attempting to investigate the *general form of propositions* and of language, Wittgenstein was drawing attention to the multiplicity of linguistic relationships within which the inquirer has to navigate.

Even on the face of things, there is a paradox in any assertion of fundamental logical distinctions between modes of thought *which may nevertheless be taught to and learned by novices.* The problem turns out to be one of emphasis, after all, because no matter how mysterious the actual process of learning may be, its possibility implies the existence of some kinds of general (non-specific) criteria of intelligibility in a quite crucial way. Specialised concepts owe their intelligibility to the fact that they *can* be portrayed in non-specialised language. This formal consideration, by itself, reveals little or nothing about the kind of things which count as general criteria, but this is precisely the point I have already made against the position of Ennis. Language is enmeshed in textures of human thought and social practices. But, despite his misplaced emphasis on the exclusivity of languages and language-games, McPeck is correct in his contention that intelligibility is determined at the *semantic* and not the *syntactic* level, a consideration of crucial significance for the nature of critical thinking, as I hope to make clearer in subsequent stages of my argument.

4 Language and Consciousness

> I do not think I truly remember emotions which I experienced before I was taught. I knew I had them because I have a tactual memory of shedding tears, screaming, kicking, and other acts which indicate feeling. Yet in no case can I recall the emotions as such...I am astonished that there should be such distinct images of different acts in my mind side by side with such a vacuum of emotional memory. (Helen Keller to William James, quoted in Lash, 1980, p. 363-4)

> ...as the cool stream gushed over one hand (Annie Sullivan) spelled into the other the word *water*, first slowly, then rapidly. I stood still, my whole attention fixed upon the motion of her fingers. Suddenly I felt a misty consciousness as of something forgotten - a thrill of returning thought; and somehow the mystery of language was revealed to me. I knew then that W-A-T-E-R meant the wonderful cool something that was flowing over my hand...I left the well-house eager to learn. Everything had a name, and each name gave birth to a new thought. As we returned to the house every object which I touched seemed to quiver with life. (Keller, ibid. p. 57)

> The word is a thing in our consciousness...that is absolutely impossible for one person, but that becomes a reality for two. The word is a direct expression of the historical nature of human consciousness. (Vygotsky, 1989, p. 256)

Syntax, semantics and human intentionality

Helen Keller's discovery of *word-meaning* plausibly depicts the sudden emergence of a human consciousness. Her partial release from the isolation of life without sight, sound or significance illustrates Vygotsky's thesis that human development changes from the biological to the sociohistorical with the advent of language; that the task of psychology is not the investigation of general, structural components of thought, but the analysis of word-meaning and its varied cultural expressions in intentional behaviour. Thought is interpersonal, and it is only by grasping the *internality* of the relationships between the cultural 'specificity of human vocalisation' and particular qualities of consciousness that the study of thought can rise above the production of mere generalities (Vygotsky, 1989, pp. 4-5).

Helen's recollections of overt manifestations of emotion in a vacuum of emotional experience cast in high profile the way each new name she learned brought objects to life in her mind. This anecdote *proves* nothing, of course. On the other hand, I believe it helps to illuminate a theme concerning the impact of language on consciousness which I will develop. We imbue experience with affective, epistemic and ontological significances which vary according to qualities of language use and social interaction. Language makes it possible for us to represent experience abstractly, to ourselves and others; to benefit from vicarious experience and to dissect and recombine it in an infinity of ways so that we can entertain images of people, things, situations and places of which we can have no direct experience. The critical traditions have been exponential developments of this imaginative faculty sustained by language; a legacy of cumulative social experience and its burden of conflicting intimations. Critical traditions foster the experience of reality as complex and problematic rather than 'given' and they extend the scope of meanings.

In this chapter I explore some wider ramifications of the claim that *semantic meaning* is logically prior to syntactic structure in thought, the valid core of McPeck's otherwise exaggerated case for domain-specificity which I have already criticised. Here, however, I will examine the prioritisation of semantics over syntax as it has been articulated in other contexts in order to demonstrate the universal significance of that thesis in the characterisation of thought. This strategy involves examination of the role of language in social relationships, of consciousness and intentionality, and of the connection between the notions of 'language-games' and 'forms of life'. For the Wittgensteinian concept of the internality of criteria of reason and intelligibility, recruited by McPeck against the idea of general thinking skills, bears close affinities to Vygotsky's conception of 'the internal aspects of speech', communicated and learned in culturally specific contexts, and their contribution to particular forms of consciousness. Wittgenstein's emphasis on 'internal relations' has also been deployed by Peter Winch against the possibility of identifying general features of thought and behaviour to achieve scientific understanding of social phenomena:

> ...the relation between idea and context is an *internal* one. The idea gets its sense from the role it plays in the system. It is nonsensical to take several systems of ideas, find an element which can be expressed in the same verbal form, and then claim to have discovered an idea which is common to all the systems. (Winch, 1958, p. 107)

Winch's thesis embraces human thought and behaviour as a whole. An error to which he draws attention is that of indicating overt similarities between ideas or activities and then identifying them as *intrinsic* to those phenomena; of reifying a general classification and incorrectly investing it with substantive significance. For example, observations by uncommitted observers about the apparent universality of social practices like 'ritual purification' may conceal how very differently they 'fit' into the textures of ways of life and signify important contrasts in the conscious lives of members of different societies. And the lack of such understanding could vitiate both the explanatory and predictive values of the outside observer's description of two practices or modes of reasoning as the *same* kinds of thing. As I have already suggested, similar considerations apply to judgments about whether criteria of sound reasoning, like *consider relevant evidence*, have been met in different cultural contexts. In reality, there is no unique, *general* criterion of the 'sameness' of institutional practices, modes of thought or methods of inquiry. Generalisations may be articulated with varying degrees of explicitness and awareness of their heuristic status, but understanding comes with incremental amendments to these provisional judgments as their conceptual status is negotiated through dialogue.

Winch compares the task of the social scientist in coming to terms with this *internality* of meaning in thought and social relations to the 'exchange of ideas in a conversation' (ibid., p. 128). I want to suggest that this is more than an extremely appropriate analogy for social processes. The exchange, conflict and reconciliation of semantic sense is the basic dynamic in the evolution of thought in the earliest and most intimate learning situations as well as at the most sophisticated levels of social interaction. Winch argues that where the physical scientist deals with one set of rules, those governing her particular investigation, the sociologist has to deal with the rules of sociological investigation *and* engage directly (effectively as a participant) with the rules governing activities or systems of beliefs:

> ...And it is these rules, rather than those which govern the sociologist's investigation, which specify what is to count as 'doing the same kind of thing' in relation to that kind of activity. (ibid., p. 87)

An examination of some key arguments for this notion of human intentionality should clarify some ambiguities and contradictions afflicting the two broadly distinct conceptions of critical thinking I have considered. This will involve an excursion beyond the field of education and pedagogic method - into social anthropology, for example. I will try to justify the move in later chapters which are an elaboration of the following propositions:

a. *Education is the ubiquitous process of enculturation.* This is the matrix from which our conceptions of critical thinking have emerged in the historical transmission of diverse, often competing traditions of thought. Yet much educational research fails to acknowledge the significance of cultural and historical context, and a tendency has developed to look to comparatively recent (and thus partial) measures of competence in the formal educational context for the characteristics of critical thinking; a procedure involving dangerous oversimplifications. Only by continuing to review the historical interplay of ideas and cultures can we develop an adequate conception of the nature of critical thought. A corollary of this is that an education with the ideal of enhancing rationality must promote awareness of its history and thus of the kind of problems which have stimulated critical inquiry. This is the general philosophical task of determining the contributions of specialised areas of knowledge to the intelligibility of experience and reality.

b. *Learning language is a dialogical process.* Obvious though this might be, it was less widely accepted as a principle with educational implications before Vygotsky drew attention to the matter with his concept of a *zone of proximal development;* the notion that learning is the product of interpersonal relationships utilising various *psychological tools.* There can be no satisfactory measure of learning-potential or competence in an individual which is not, at the same time, a measure of the quality of interpersonal exchange and of the efficacy of the linguistic or other 'tools' employed in any pedagogical relationship. This means that critical thinking is as deeply implicated in the social organisation and ethos of education as it is in the psychology of individuals - and the latter is not an independently specifiable variable.

Vygotsky directed attention to the cognitive implications for individuals of their involvement in a heritage of particular linguistic meanings. Words do not have an atomic or stand-alone significance in speech; they embody specific cultural perspectives established through cumulative usages; a process of semantic accretion. Helen Keller's celebrated experience at the water-pump was much more than a new-found ability to name things. With the transformation of the *sign* for water into the *word,* 'water', came metalinguistic recognition of a system for classifying previously uncomprehended experiences. She discovered the internal relationships between words and referents, thought and subject-matter, behaviour, purpose and affect. Helen's transformation into a language-using human being is a vivid illustration, from the inside as it were, of the gulf between human actions conceived as overt responses to stimuli, susceptible to objective description, and alternatively, as intrinsically meaningful, intentional behaviour. It is also a reminder of the impossibility of imagining our world in the absence of the structure which language confers on experience.

Helen discovered language in the highly articulated form of the western, literate tradition which she was later to exploit as an author. Her first word was one item in a vocabulary which vastly exceeds the learning capacity of any single individual. It has been estimated that the average English speaker knows about 50,000 of the half million words contained in the most comprehensive dictionaries. Even this is a poor measure of the subtleties of everyday expressions and the specialised linguistic conventions which govern them, a diversity which is the product of historical evolution:

> Tracing a word's development back in time shows that in many cases what are now separate lexical items were formerly one and the same word. The deep prehistory of our language has nurtured little word-seeds that over the millennia have proliferated into widely differentiated families of vocabulary. (Ayto, 1990, Introduction)

With the realisation that 'everything had a name' Helen began to inherit something like Popper's 'World 3' - a vast interpersonal legacy consisting, for example, of the contents of books and libraries, and their potential for the re-combination and development of ideas, implicated in what Popper describes as a 'full consciousness of self':

> ...*full consciousness of self* depends upon all these (world 3) theories...animals, although capable of feelings, sensations, memory, and thus of consciousness, do not possess the full consciousness of self which is one of the results of human language and the development of the specifically human world 3. (Popper, 1972, p. 74)

The qualities of Helen's emerging consciousness would have been quite different in a small, non-literate society lacking the capacities for linguistic accumulation, metaphor and abstraction which an accessible script affords. This is not to suggest that the language of such a simple society would be structurally simple. Indeed, the converse is often the case and extreme syntactical complexity is frequently an obstacle to the linguist who wishes to learn the language of a very simple and isolated hunter-gatherer community (Black, 1968, p. 4) - a caution against assumptions that the overt complexity of a syntax implies a corresponding sophistication of ideas or, indeed, that the properties of syntactical systems are reliable guides to their potential for semantic meaning, an issue I will return to briefly in this chapter. The sophistication required if grammar is to be simplified (ibid., p. 4) is indicative of the wide scope of tacitly accreted meanings embodied in words and of the hidden complexity of traditions of language-use and thought.

In simple, traditional societies with relatively small vocabularies, words must be more closely bound to concrete referents in the physical environment, and to a more limited range of social relationships. In such a society, concepts of time and space may be constrained by the absence of written records or methods of communication which transcend the limitations of face-to-face contact. And such limitations obviate consistent reflection and comparison, the sense of historical change and cross-cultural difference which unsettles minds and stimulates sceptical, critical appraisal of traditional understandings and cultural meanings (Goody and Watt, 1963, pp. 304-355). Thus there are intimate reciprocities between *forms of language* and *forms of life* which pose serious problems of mutual intelligibility between the representatives of different cultures and these can rarely be transcended by appealing directly to common criteria of meaning or rationality - and never in an absolute sense. I will try to justify these claims with specific examples in following chapters.

It must be obvious, however, that by the simple device of early adoption, an infant from one of the few remaining 'stone-age' societies could inherit, in one generation, those modern intellectual and cosmological perspectives which have been accumulated over centuries or millennia; a possibility which hints at the indefinite scope of human mental potentials. I suggest this modest 'thought-experiment' is a reminder that profoundly different conceptual universes are intelligible as products of culture rather than as identifiable-*in-principle* structures and functions of individual minds, or as discrete, specifiable generic mental skills. Those who are persuaded by 'twin-studies' of the overweening influence of genetics in the formation of personality and intellect might reflect on these huge cultural differentials and what they imply about the content and potentials of individual minds; even those of the most closely related human beings. The impact of culture on a genetic infrastructure is simply not expressible in the popular terms of arithmetical ratios; the relationship is dynamic and exponential; a function of very particular kinds of human interaction.

Different consciousnesses signified by the term, 'human intentionality' are mutually commensurable only in the course of negotiation and this may become very protracted where cultural differences are large. A massive enhancement of these argumentative, dialogical relationships was a necessary condition for the development of the critical traditions and I also maintain that it is a necessary condition of their sustainability.

Conceptual gridlock; subjective idealism or reductionist behaviourism?

Helen Keller's experience of language-acquisition also symbolises the radical distinction Vygotsky drew between elementary and higher mental functions. His emphasis on the decisive importance of *consciousness* in the explanation of human behaviour identified him with the 'idealist and intuitionist tendencies' in 'the irreconcilable split between subjective idealism and reductionist behaviourism' (Bruner, 1989, p. 4), a controversy which runs like a geological fault through the arguments of philosophers and social scientists and which is reflected in the diverging views of protagonists in the present 'thinking skills debate'.

Vygotsky attempts a solution to this longstanding gridlock. He criticises both the search for elemental mental skills and idealist assertions of the unassailably *a priori* nature of concepts. His dissatisfaction with the latter view is expressed in remarks about Stern's account of the origins of language-use in child development:

> ...the "intentional tendency" appears out of nowhere; it has no history and no derivation. According to Stern, it is basic, primordial; it springs up spontaneously "once and for all"; it is the propensity enabling the child to discover the function of speech by way of purely logical operation. (Vygotsky, 1989, p. 62)

Here, Vygotsky pinpoints a tension which is also notable in the *domain-theorist* stance. Assertions of the internal, logical coherence and autonomy of domains of thought cry out for explanation in evolutionary terms, as I observed in Chapter 3. *How* is such exclusive inner consistency achieved? Vygotsky attempted to solve this problem by describing human consciousness and meaningful behaviour as products of culturally specific, 'psychological, tool-mediated' learning. And the psychological tool of greatest significance is the *word*, and *word-meaning* in the languages of different cultures (Davydov and Radzikhovski, 1989, pp. 35-63).

True languages, unlike systems of animal communication, provide innumerable ways of confirming interpretations of the meaning of a particular utterance at some level of dialogue. This is quite different from making unilateral judgments of equivalence between action and utterance, as an observer of animal behaviour might. It involves exploitation of the recursivity of words; the meaning of one can be progressively 'homed-in-upon' by reference to others with which it is linked in particular conceptual repertoires. Learning languages is a circumlocutionary, reciprocal and cumulative process. The meanings of individual words and concepts may be strictly untranslatable from one tongue to another, or even within a common tongue, as Quine maintains, but they can be negotiated by reference to phrases and situations about which there are other levels of approximate agreement between parties. Languages exhibit contrasts and affinities as the result of historical differentiation and assimilation. Vernacular and idiomatic forms of speech inhibit mutual comprehension between generations and social groups within what are broadly the same geographical communities. Languages, dialects and idioms evolve rapidly, assimilate one another and become extinct; patterns reflecting Wittgenstein's use of the 'game' metaphor in the *Philosophical Investigations* (1968) and notes published under the title *On Certainty* (1969):

> ...new language games come into existence, and others become obsolete and get forgotten' (PI 23)...when language-games change, then there is a change in concepts, and with the concepts the meanings of words change. (OC 65)

Language also registers the multiple forms which human thought has assumed and of the precipitation of some as relatively stable modes of description and explanation:

> ... grammar is created and stored in the memory of the linguistic community. It is

also possible to conceive of a plurality of linguistic systems or language-games which represent different linguistic worlds and cultures. (Gier, 1981, p. 173)

Linguistic meaning represents an exfoliation of images and concepts within the broad constraints of traditional usage rather than a system of word-referent relationships articulated within syntactic structures. In the tortuous but rather inconclusive debate which Wittgenstein initiated about the conceivability or otherwise of a 'private language' one consideration seems to stand out; 'any use of language at all presupposes a community in which there is agreement in the application of words and signs' (Malcolm, 1989, pp. 150-153 and 156-157). Language, like money, is essentially transactional both in its uses and its origins. The ubiquitous role of metaphor is evidence of a constant appeal to tacit, arbitrary agreements about identities and resemblances; there are no unique criteria to justify such judgments. Metaphor either works, or it doesn't work; the criteria are lost in an infinity of prior usages. Now, of the numerous affinities between the ideas of Vygotsky and Wittgenstein, perhaps the most intriguing is their shared sense of an inscrutable, prelinguistic and instinctual basis of what the latter describes as *agreement in forms of life*. That 'agreement' is manifested when, for example, people communicate using simple words with a certainty and confidence which cannot be predicated on the possibility of demonstrating that they are all being used consistently from one context to another:

> Now I would like to regard this certainty, not as something akin to hastiness or superficiality, but as a form of life...But that means that I want to conceive it as something that lies beyond being justified or unjustified; as it were, as something animal. (Wittgenstein, On Certainty, quoted by Malcolm, 1989, p. 153)

Consistent use of words is a *condition* of intelligible discourse. Discussion about particular meanings is possible only because others are treated as transparent. And another illuminating comparison, detected by Malcolm (ibid, p. 72) is the conclusion which Wittgenstein appears to share with Chomsky, that for there to be a possibility of language, there must be a natural linguistic potential. The difference, of course, is that Wittgenstein's references to naturalistic origins are extremely circumspect, conveying a sense of profound inscrutability and the impossibility of reaching beyond language to explain language. Chomsky's interest in this biological infrastructure is famous and he has attempted to make its inherent syntactical structures explicit, though his frequent references to the probable limits to our understanding of the linguistic basis of thought should be noted (for example, Chomsky, 1972 a, p. 101). Pinker, by contrast, invests this idea of a universal human language instinct with a substantiveness which fails to grapple with manifest cultural differences and the evolution of ideas. Concepts of 'freedom' and 'equality', he maintains (with apparent indifference to the controversy and strife accompanying attempts to articulate these ideas) are innate universals. But innate potentialities notwithstanding, the meanings of the most commonplace expressions have their origins in histories of dialogue which long precede those who utter them. In the most highly articulated uses of language there will be dissonances necessitating reciprocal clarification; appeals to meanings accumulated by tacit adaptations of usage. And attempts to resolve incommensurabilities of this kind constitute some of the most important sources of critical and creative thinking.

Different views of the relationship between language and thought

Pinker takes issue with the idea that substantial linguistic differences register differences in forms of consciousness. He upholds the idea of a 'universal mentalese' - a mental life which is independent of the specificities of particular languages, whether English or Apache. Indeed he says that 'People without a language would still have mentalese', and so, '..concepts of freedom and equality will be thinkable even if they are nameless' (Pinker, 1995, p. 82). But at what level of generality could the medieval peasant's concepts of freedom and equality categorised with those of, say, an Amazonian hunter-gatherer or a Locke? It is easy to sympathise with Pinker's claim that regardless of differences in culture, gender roles and history, to 'imagine seeing through the rhythms to the structures underneath' is to 'sense that we all have the same minds' (ibid, p. 430). This is essentially the principle of human mental equality espoused by Mill, but an important difference is Mill's recognition that universal potentials are mediated by cultural pressures which convert the properties of elements into the qualitatively different properties of compounds.

I will return in the next chapter to Pinker's argument when I consider some examples from social anthropology, including evidence purporting to demonstrate fundamental differences (which he disputes) between the mental lives of native American tribespeople and European Americans. Meanwhile, I suggest that Pinker conflates two distinct things. First, what may be called a genetically-based, universal linguistic capability and, second, culturally specific systems of semantic meaning which are the socially-mediated, cumulative developments of the language capabilities of all individuals. In other words, Pinker confuses the idea of universal syntax with that of universal semantic meaning. His assertion of the independence of thought from language is surely correct to the extent that people do not necessarily *think in words,* though only to that extent. There are, after all, huge differences in interpretations of 'freedom' and 'equality' between cultures and historical epochs. But even if Pinker rejects Winch's injunction, above, against arbitrary judgments of 'sameness' between superficially similar beliefs and practices in different societies, he surely cannot wish to maintain that all humans have (and always have had?) essentially the same concepts of *god* or *gravity*, the *shape, size and age of the Earth*, the *origins of life and human society* or the *nature of the cosmos* or the *divine right of kings?* These are paradigmatic examples of conceptual and epistemic differences relating to times and places, as well as of the evolution of ideas through debate and criticism. Pinker's notion of 'universal mentalese' could encompass a variety of ideas like this only in a system of classification which was so general as to be quite vacuous.

Another portrayal of relationships between language and thought should be distinguished from the one which I wish to develop in these pages. This is the thesis that an empirical study of different linguistic usages by dispassionate or uncommitted observers can provide reliable indications of differences in their conceptual of epistemic content. I referred earlier to the absence of any necessary correspondence between syntactic and semantic complexity, a point illustrated by Black's reference to the complex syntactical organisation of relatively simple tongues.

This observation has wider significance. In one study Becher has compared history, sociology and physics to test the hypothesis that, 'differences in fields of knowledge' might be expected 'to be reflected in differences of linguistic form' (Becher, 1987, pp. 261-274). Although his use of the word 'reflected' is ambiguous, the hypothesis seems to be tautological because it is hard to see what evidence, other than *some* kind of difference in linguistic expression, could indicate different 'fields of knowledge'. And surely differences in linguistic form, in any context, entail some differences in what might be described as their cognitive correlates? Becher evades the central issue of salience. For example, he concludes, from a study of contemporary disciplinary inquiry, that the historian's preoccupation with detail means her subject is largely 'atheoretical' whereas sociology is 'taken up with the status of knowledge' (ibid, p. 263).

This aspiring epistemological enterprise ignores Winch's claim that the rules governing *sameness* and *difference* are internally related to the fields in question according to their characteristic, historically-determined criteria and methods. The sociologist's use of *models* might be described either as a definitive contrast with the historian's preference for detail, or as a more explicit attempt to clarify the kind of generalisations to which historians are unavoidably committed; *renaissance, reformation, revolution, nation, war, modernisation, industrialisation,* and so on. Moreover, Becher's analysis of discipline-specific terminology and modes of publication offers no insight into the substantial overlaps between history and sociology. And these, for example, include controversies about the epistemic status of structural and/or functional models of social institutions which may exclude reference to their historical origins and development. Questions about relevant similarities and differences, between disciplines and between social practices, are philosophical. And that is neither discipline-specific nor general; in a crucial sense, it is *both.* Methodological differences are not necessarily reflections of relevant differences in the epistemic status of disciplinary inquiry. A classification of them is, at best, the beginning of a search for eventual insight into the respective standards of intelligibility they comprise; and this is a continuing philosophical undertaking.

There is *no ultimate procedure* for defining modes of thought. A characterisation of critical thinking which ignores its complex root system in the dialogues of history can be nothing more than a parody of many varied intellectual traditions. I maintain, for example, that the 'skills' conception of critical thinking bears a similar relation to the intentional content of modes of critical thinking as Becher's formal characterisation of physics, sociology and history do to the subject-matters of those disciplines; as a preparatory classification for epistemological investigation. Another consideration, which I will elaborate further, is that differences in linguistic form are tantamount to differences in human consciousness but the resolution of these differences is not a *once-and-for-all* procedure but a protracted negotiation between those concerned, in which some will be more successful in asserting their linguistic-conceptual perspectives than others. Helen Keller's sudden grasp of the significance of words was an awakening of a consciousness with an indeterminate history. As Vygotsky observed, 'the word is a direct expression of the historical nature of human consciousness' (Vygotsky, 1989, p. 256).

The centrality of consciousness and intentionality

John Searle has condemned the indifference of philosophers and psychologists to the subject of consciousness as 'something of a scandal' because it is 'the central fact of human existence' (Searle, 1984, p. 16). He argues, in harmony with McPeck and many others, that 'no computer program can ever be a mind' because computer programmes are syntactical and minds 'are semantical, in the sense that they have more than a formal structure, they have a content' (ibid., p. 31). Searle also echoes Winch's proposition that because social institutions and practices are the embodiment of ideas and concepts in human minds:

> ...What we want from the social sciences and what we get from (them) at their best are theories of pure and applied intentionality. (ibid, p. 85)

The question is, what difference does Searle's thesis make if it is correct? In what sense, if at all, are consciousness and intentionality central to an understanding of the way people think and behave? I believe Winch and

Searle *are* correct and that Winch's comparison of explanation in the social sciences with 'the exchange of ideas in a conversation' - a matter of tracing the implications of concepts - is particularly illuminating (Winch, 1958, p. 128). Intentionalistic interpretation is not simply important because it offers insight into the way people think and behave. It is the essential condition of understanding thought because it concerns the engagement by individual minds with a differentially shared, language-mediated imagery. I will try to clarify this claim in ensuing pages after considering some misleading interpretations of intentionality in social relations.

There is, of course, widespread acceptance amongst social scientists of the need for *empathetic* interpretation of social phenomena, notably in the anthropologist's stress on the importance of induction into the language and customs of an alien society. Such periods of familiarisation nevertheless frustrate any aspirations for strict objectivity because they 'contaminate' the study in at least two significant ways. Limited equivalencies between the language of the observer and that of her subjects may flaw her understanding. For instance, Kluckhohn and Leighton caution administrators and interpreters of American Indian affairs that 'The Navajo language represents an importantly different mode of thinking and must be regarded as such' (Kluckhohn and Leighton, 1960, p. 194). No matter how meticulous the anthropologist's investigation, periods of enculturation involve *reciprocities* which alter the significance of social practices for the participants themselves, if only by undermining their confidence in the manifest significance of their beliefs and behaviour. Paradoxically, the more protracted the observer's dialogue with her subjects (in the interests of full understanding), the greater the effects of this microcosm of mutual cultural assimilation. Both these factors are important because they are implicit not only in social scientific research but in all cases of cross-cultural contact and assimilation. I also maintain that identical problems affect the reliability of experimental conclusions about cognitive development in children for essentially the same reasons.

Winch's philosophical sociology draws on Wittgenstein's portrayal of *forms of life*. The criteria of logic '...arise out of, and are only intelligible in the context of, ways of living or modes of social life' (ibid, p. 100). This argument must encourage regressive sceptical conclusions if interpreted as an invitation to draw concrete sociological inferences from language game analysis. Questions about the intelligibility and justification of particular beliefs and practices, it might be concluded, cannot be resolved from any other standpoint than that sanctioned by their role in specific social contexts; an objection symmetrical with Siegel's previously cited criticisms of McPeck's thesis. I believe a mistake of this kind is facilitated by plausible identification of particular social institutions with Wittgenstein's 'forms of life' regardless of his own disclaimer, which I emphasised in Chapter 3, that he had not tried to describe the 'essence' of a language game and did not seek to identify boundaries distinguishing one from another. Nor, he pointed out, did these concepts reflect aspirations for a future regularisation of language. Gier endorses Winch's view that Wittgenstein's conception of 'forms of life' created a genuine revolution in philosophy with seminal significance for epistemology and sociology (Gier, 1981, p. 19). Winch also exposes the disguised relationship between Wittgenstein and continental phenomenology in which, by contrast with Wittgenstein's philosophy, there was *a clear systematising intent* (ibid., p. 223). Gellner, however, attacks Winch's 'strong functionalism' on precisely such an assumption, condemning the vicious regress involved in postulating an indefinitely large number of internally significant social practices and institutions:

> ...Wittgenstein is also the author of the insistence on seeing the meaning of utterances as their use, and on seeing language as a "form of life"; in anthropological terms, on interpreting them in the light of their function in the culture of which they are a part. (Gellner, 1972, p. 122)

But this is the result of reading a *systematising* intent into the concepts of *forms of life* and *language games;* to view them as the real objects of a phenomenology rather than as heuristic tools which might reveal something important about relationships between language, culture and the way people think. These metaphors illuminate both the continuities and incommensurabilities of language and thought. There is an absence of categorical boundaries between different ways of living and thinking, but many points of contrast, similarity and eventual accommodation. John Searle helps to clarify this point.

Any generalisation about observed behaviour which fails to take account of its intrinsic semantic significance cannot be regarded either as a proper description or as an explanation. Institutions like *money, marriage and war* are intelligible only in terms of the rules which participants understand as defining those phenomena. 'Money' refers to whatever people use as and think of as money; there is no physical (or behavioural) correlate of the concept which is distinct from and independent of the range of practices in which it is employed (Searle, 1984, pp. 79-82). The implications of the example of money for understanding unfamiliar cultural practices are illustrated by the Melanesian custom of exchanging cowry shells for other objects during perpetual circular voyages between South-Sea islands. Such traditions may be religious or social with the accent on fulfilment of ritual or social contact - or they may be forms of economic exchange in which the shells occupy the status of 'money.' The *true* explanation, one might say, spirals ever more closely inwards towards the initially obscure motivations of the voyagers. Eventually a point is reached where the western concept of money becomes irrelevant to the anthropologist's grasp of the significance of the practice; except to whatever extent western concepts of monetary exchange have contaminated those of the Melanesian voyagers. This dialectic does not lead to a finitely specifiable understanding, but one in which concepts change as they accommodate to each other.

In opposition to Winch, Rudner has raised the question of how we check the *accuracy* of our *verstehen*, our grasp of the 'inscape' of others' beliefs and actions (Rudner, 1966 pp. 68-83). This question suggests that he regards the meaningfulness of human beliefs and actions as a psychological variable accompanying independently identifiable cognitive states and actions. Winch and Searle, by contrast, describe this internal meaningfulness as constitutive of, and logically inseparable from, the very nature of beliefs, thought and action. Rudner, however, maintains that empathetic understanding can only be validated against a prior characterisation of the phenomenon under investigation.

The point is significant, because it exposes a central problem about intentionalistic interpretation. Naturally, a social scientist will wish to test the accuracy of her hypotheses. Yet Winch's argument appears to deprive observers of any perspective other than that of the participants themselves. Gellner argues against the 'functionalism' which he detects in the Wittgenstein-Winch formulation of intentionalistic behaviour on the grounds that people are often deliberately or accidentally misled by propaganda and the manipulation of information. Dominant ideologies may, for example, cast exploitative behaviour in a favourable light which becomes that in which the exploited see their predicament. How, he asks, could we account for the kind of social and ideological change which arises as a result of the recognition by some members of a culture that their dominant beliefs are internally inconsistent, absurd or ambiguous? (Gellner, 1972, p. 141). This objection is substantial because that seems to be precisely how both conceptual and social changes often occur. However, Gellner does not insist on a categorical distinction between what he calls 'contextual interpretation' (learning the internal significance of cultural beliefs and practices) and the kind of independently established hypotheses which Rudner considers necessary features of social-scientific interpretation. He recognises that the problem cannot be resolved by appealing either to independently specifiable criteria determining the meaning of concepts and social practices, nor to criteria which are comprehensively internal to those concepts and practices. Instead, he recommends empathetic interpretation seasoned with awareness that the ideas and beliefs interpreted may contain absurdities (ibid., p. 147).

Rudner's objection conveys the widely held but misleading feeling that somewhere there must be a *paradigm explanation* of any given social phenomenon. But agreement with Winch does not imply the essentialist conclusion that the paradigms are to be located exclusively in the beliefs of particular social collectives. That would, of course, create the regressive problem of how the social scientist should identify those features which distinguish one social grouping from another (and within another); a problem, perhaps, for the functionalist but not necessarily for Winch. There *are* no absolute paradigms of demarcation between social collectives. This is the burden of the claim that the investigation of social phenomena is more like entering a conversation, and tracing the implications of the concepts employed within it, than studying the phenomena of the physical sciences. Social change is accounted for in terms of the inter-penetration of ideas within, and between, societies, including the forcible inculcation of some beliefs and the denigration and extinction of others. The social scientist, knowingly or otherwise, is a party to this interaction, and scientific objectivity must not be defined as an ability to stand back and examine a subject-matter dispassionately. Thus, as Gellner rightly points out, explanation in the social sciences has a normative function - it can become an integral feature of the purposive behaviour of the people under investigation.

The *language game/form of life* metaphor captures the dynamic of dialogic accommodation between alien ideas; there can be no ultimate, veridical descriptions of modes of thought or social institutions. The relativism which Gellner perceives in Wittgenstein and Winch owes itself partly to a false construction he places on the indeterminacies of language and thought. There are meeting places between the external, general and the internal, particular perspectives, but they are not in the kind of uncontaminated, objective realms where social scientists have often tried to locate them. It is impossible, as Gellner is inclined to admit, to draw up general rules with any finality. Hilary Putnam describes how he relinquished his original hope that Wittgenstein's portrayal of linguistic usages 'could be completely surveyed and analyzed in a functionalist way' - in recognition that it is not possible to identify the necessary and sufficient conditions for the use of words. He recounts his dismay on reading how Wittgenstein substituted the idea of 'persuasion' for that of the attempt to refute alien beliefs according to rational criteria. Yet Putnam exonerates Wittgenstein of the relativism many have read into this kind of proposition. The illusion, he maintains, is to believe that there is a secure metalanguage according to which we can justify our own language games. But, in the last analysis, we have to take something on *trust* if we are to make any meaningful assertions (Putnam, 1955, pp. 166-179). And this is not to deny that there can be general criteria of rationality and intelligibility, but to identify them as regulative principles rather than final destinations; one can navigate without knowing where the land is. Such, I think, is the force of Winch's prioritisation of philosophical discourse. His analogy between the study of human (social) phenomena and exchanges of ideas in conversation (ibid., p. 133) becomes more than mere analogy. It is a description of the evolution of thought and of the way we learn.

Successive dialogical approximations

There is a missing link between intentionalistic interpretation and the methodology, recommended by Rudner, of constructing hypotheses necessary to validate those interpretations. It might be called the process of *successive dialogical approximations;* the protracted manner in which initial prejudices, hypotheses or heuristic models of behaviour and beliefs are refined through discourse. There is a parallel here with Vygotsky's recommendation that psychometrics should be regarded as only a starting point for the creative interpretation of individual cognition against the broader background of relevant social and behavioural norms (Vygotsky, 1993, p. 285). In this dialectical procedure neither researcher nor subject has an absolute veto on the other's interpretation; and neither is immune from the influence of the other's interpretations, though one party will probably be more influential and dominant than another. This principle of *successive dialogical approximation of linguistic meanings* applies indiscriminately to formal and informal conversations, including those between anthropologists and their subjects, parents and children, teachers and pupils. It also applies to the study of cognition in individuals. There are no paradigm explanations of what a person accomplishes in a given task; answers lie in the indeterminate logical territory between the intentions of the psychological researcher, the form in which a task is presented and the form in which it is grasped by the subject. In later chapters I will review some powerful evidence for such a conclusion which comes, rather ironically, from Piaget's empirical studies of the ways in which children think and reason.

The intentionalist case does not diminish the importance of rigorous empirical research though it underlines the fact that the empirical and the conceptual are inextricably intertwined at every level of inquiry and the latter are not reducible to the former. Neither, on the other hand, does it lend credence to the Oakeshottian idea, which I referred to in Chapter 3, of a 'conversation' between those representing different modes of experience, leading neither to truth nor genuine clarification. The principle of human intentionality does, however, invalidate certain conceptions of social scientific method, particularly where the temptation is to postulate models, on *a priori* grounds, as templates for assessing the meaning of people's own understanding of their beliefs and activities.

Where the social scientist investigates institutions in her own culture much of the explanatory power of her account will take for granted the intelligibility of her organising concepts. There is a real sense in which her models and the relatively unexamined, traditional concepts of her countryfolk merge; in the description of political institutions and familiar categories of social relationship, for example. Indeed, the models of the social analyst often enter constitutively into our understanding of everyday events; become part of the ill-defined penumbra of everyday thought. This is also true of investigations of learning and cognition within the culture of the school. The familiar curriculum is a convenient source of hypotheses about cognitive operations. But the availability of well defined tasks can encourage the development, by analogy, of stipulative definitions of these cognitive operations as particular skills of thought. The mistake, here, would be to believe that the rules governing the specified tasks are entirely at the disposal, and fully within the comprehension, of the researcher or the teacher. Winch's reservations about judgments of similarity between ideas or activities in social-scientific analysis apply with equal logical force to the study of thinking skills, and to another contribution to the 'thinking skills debate' in the form of Stephen Norris' claim that:

> The question of whether or not people can apply the *same* critical thinking ability to a number of fields is a question of whether or not the same mental power operates in different contexts. This is *not* a conceptual question, but a scientific one... (Norris, 1990, p. 71 , original emphasis)

People may apply the *same* ability in different fields according to overlapping and internally differentiated conventions. As in the case of Becher's empirical analysis of disciplinary discourse, overt similarities in forms of expression do not necessarily hold good at a conceptual level. As I have already remarked, rote persists in education because it yields - in some sense - the *same* results as more critical or creative performances; and the uninspired, field-dependant scientist works within the *same* 'Kuhnian paradigm' of scientific method as its brilliantly creative originator. Formal identities between the rules which we extrapolate from modes of thought belie the varieties of conscious awareness which they represent. The key to enhancing critical thinking is neither the adoption of preconceived models nor submission to *particular* conventions and strategies. It is the insight that thought constantly transforms itself through rigorous appraisal of its former modalities; and there are important educational implications in this.

In my first chapter I mentioned Chomsky's warning that '...new knowledge and techniques will define the nature of what is taught and how it is taught'. These novel methods could even be confirmed, spuriously, by objective tests which nevertheless 'will not demonstrate that an important educational goal has been achieved' for they are 'set on *other* grounds and in *other* terms' (Chomsky, 1972 a, p. 101, my emphasis). The real danger is that understanding will be defined in these terms; that the student's task becomes a *unilateral* accommodation to alien concepts and formularies which make no concessions to her unique perspectives on the world.

5 Side by Side Through Different Landscapes

It seems odd, if not absurd, to a European when he is told that a twin is a bird as though it were an obvious fact, for Nuer are not saying that a twin is like a bird but that he is a bird. There seems to be a complete contradiction in the statement: and it was precisely on statements of this kind recorded by observers of primitive peoples that Lévy-Bruhl based his theory of the pre-logical mentality of these peoples, its chief characteristic being, in his view, that it permits such evident contradictions - that a thing can be what it is and at the same time something altogether different. (Evans Pritchard, quoted by Gellner, 1972, p. 131)

So the people of Montaillou lived in a kind of 'island in time', even more cut off from the past than the future. *There is no other age than ours,* said Raymond de l'Aire of Tignac...This absence of a historical dimension went with a general use, in speech, of the present indicative tense, without logical connections with past and future. (Le Roy Ladurie, 1980, p. 282)

...one human being can be a complete enigma to another. We learn this when we come into a strange country with entirely strange traditions; and, what is more, even given a mastery of the country's language. We do not *understand* the people. (And not because of not knowing what they are saying to themselves.) We cannot find our feet with them. (Wittgenstein, 1968, PI, p. 223)

Intentionality and 'forms of life'

This chapter is concerned with ways in which possibilities of thought are constrained or expedited by particular forms of culture and language use. Ultimately, I want to relate the following argument to the requirements for an appreciation of mature critical thinking; to the traditions which comprise it, and to the social and educational conditions necessary for its development. For I believe such an approach will help to substantiate two related propositions. One is that the traditions of critical thinking constitute explosive transformations of human consciousness, and the other; that these transformations are evidence of what Mill described as the unlimited possibilities of intellectual and social improvement implicit in the educational ideal of critical thinking. Mill's optimism, I suggest, is an urgently-needed antidote to a prevalent, limiting conception of 'skills' of critical thinking as requirements for successful adaptation to existing social and economic imperatives. First, however, I examine the problem of incommensurabilities between alien ways of life and thought which resist description in terms of anything we could identify confidently as universal characteristics of human nature.

My first quotation (above) reflects that anthropological dilemma; different language-uses may express ways of thinking which apparently cannot be reconciled in terms of common criteria of rationality or intelligibility. Yet a characterisation of these asymmetries by means of that distinction between *logical* and *pre-logical* cultural mentalities raises the previously discussed problem that the latter may be integral to perfectly viable ways of life. Indeed, certain totemic systems seem to embody quite fundamental principles of classification and social organisation. Wittgenstein's account of internal relations militates explicitly against a general framework of explanation which could subsume the diversity of cultural expressions and validate Sir James Frazer's thesis that, '...the movement of higher thought...has on the whole been from magic through religion to science' (Frazer, 1993, p. 711). It is equally incompatible with Lévi-Strauss' search for '...elementary principles common to all thinking' - his incentive for trying to establish 'the rudiments of a semantic algebra' (Leach, 1972, pp. 183-203). But a generalising strategy of this kind is strenuously endorsed by Pinker, in his development of Chomsky's theory of innate linguistic potential. To a psycholinguist, he says, 'not speaking the same language' is a superficial difference. There is a 'single mental design' beneath the variety of cultures and languages and preoccupation with their apparent incommensurabilities must not be allowed to obscure the reality 'that we all have the same minds' (Pinker, 1994, p. 430).

In the next chapter I consider some problems facing the seductive, even compelling, idea of an innate and universal mental design. Not least among these seems to be the tautology that this design must be, in some sense, coextensive with the totality of past, present and possible forms of thought. To distinguish in such *indefinite terms* between the theories of the quantum physicist and the developing totemic beliefs of an aboriginal child is, inevitably, to come face-to-face with conceptual and linguistic incommensurabilities. And these could not be resolved by an alternative category of explanation despite the plausibility of the thesis from which that aspiration springs; that we all begin life with essentially the same pre-printed neuronal circuits.

On the other hand, the prospect of an infinity of self-authenticating belief systems cannot be sustainable if we are ever to be justified in claiming that some, at least, are internally inconsistent. As Gellner points out, we would be deprived of any theoretical leverage on an important motive for social change; recognition by people of inconsistencies and absurdities in their own beliefs. After all, many paradigmatic examples of critical thinking seem to have arisen precisely because people have successfully challenged problematic aspects of their own intellectual heritage. The paradoxes of Zeno of Elea are more than amusing conundrums. His fable of *Achilles and the Tortoise* was one of several which explicitly addressed logical inconsistencies in a pre-Socratic critical debate about the nature of space and time and the doctrine of a plurality of 'indivisible minima' (Kirk and Raven, 1969, pp. 286-297). Galileo portrayed his argument for heliocentricity as a move within a particular tradition, supplementing the idea of scriptural authority with that of 'divine will, written in nature'. But Cardinal Bellarmine and the Church interpreted it as a decisive move beyond traditional beliefs concerning the rational justifiability of ontological assertions; a case which I have cited against the idea of criteria of rationality specific to times or places. Certain reifications of 'language-games' and 'forms of life' which over-identify them with the homeostatic qualities of tribal lore come perilously close to a vicious regress into scepticism about the possibility of resolving any dispute by appealing to reason or of making sense of ways of life in which we are not fully committed participants.

My second quotation, selected from Le Roy Ladurie's commentary on records of the Inquisition in medieval France flags an argument for subsequent chapters as well as the present one. This is that the linguistic and conceptual repertoire of a community is intimately connected with the availability of instruments for the progressive, argumentative extension of ideas and images, and for reflection upon them. For reasons I will advance, widely diffused literacy is a necessary, though not sufficient, condition for the growth of critical thinking traditions. The catalytic influence of accessible scripts in the development of these traditions bespeaks the social dimension of language and thought and the revolutionising potential of mind in conditions of enhanced dialogue. The largely illiterate Cathar heretics of Montaillou had little sense of an historical past. Their awareness of time and space was couched in the familiar terms of their peasant culture (ibid., pp. 238-240). One result of the narrowly circumscribed, ecclesiastical monopoly of medieval literacy was that the most complete record of Cathar religious dissent was that preserved by the inquisitors who extirpated it. Another irony symbolises the fragility of critical, scientific thought in periods of restricted literacy and dialogue. This is that the New World was discovered by people ignorant of the true circumference of the Earth; a calculation which had been made simply and accurately by Eratosthenes of Alexandria in the pre-Christian era. As Popper has observed, the critical traditions flowered briefly in pagan Greece and then they disappeared, to be revived only a millennium and a half later in the Renaissance. Critical thinking takes place as much between people and between generations as it does between the ears of individuals. It has crucial, intersubjective dimensions.

Vygotsky's biographer, Alex Kozulin, refers to a paradox in the description of historical cultures as logically self-authenticating yet susceptible of change and mutual assimilation, processes which (he suggests) seem to invite extra-logical explanations of *logical* thought. He conjectures that the intellectual and spiritual systems of antiquity, the Middle Ages or the Renaissance should be viewed as, 'self-sufficient cognitive styles that are irreducible to the later, more 'advanced' forms of thinking' - but which are nevertheless intelligible as contributions to an ongoing dialogue which is the defining characteristic of human consciousness (Kozulin, pp. 270-1). In 1904 Franz Boas claimed that, for the Eskimo, the world had always been what it was then - a feature which was distinctive of 'la pensée sauvage' for Lévi-Strauss (Goody and Watt, 1963, pp. 304-345). Totemism and other belief systems may defy classification in terms which satisfy modern, western notions of explanation but they nevertheless seem to be integral to ways of life which have proved sustainable over millennia in challenging environments. But despite its fall from scholarly favour the distinction between 'logical' and 'pre-logical' social mentalities has a certain cogency, as an index of the presence or absence of certain fundamental conditions for reflective, analytical thought.

As I have already pointed out (and will consider further), criteria of rational justification are not exclusive to some privileged modes of cultural experience; they are necessary features of any conceivable language and are thus universal norms of social life. To try to imagine a 'proto-language' which consisted only of simple statements about the observable environment compels recognition of the possibility of error and misunderstanding. Errors may be plausible and there is a need for reasons to be offered in justification of statements if words are to have shared, dependable meanings which distinguish them from the arbitrary expression of affective, individual states. Utterances must be related consistently to one another and to actions. They have to *work* over time in a social context by being shown to have demonstrable applicability in different situations. This is not only the fundamental condition of a language-sharing community but the reason why alien languages can be learned. There is, as Wittgenstein says, 'a common behaviour of mankind' which is 'the system of reference by means of which we interpret and unknown language' (Wittgenstein, 1968, PI, 206). However, it is possible to place different constructions on these commonalties. As I will try to show, Pinker over-accentuates them by conflating universal linguistic and cognitive potentials with particular historical developments of thought. Consequently, he underestimates the significance of cultural assimilation and transmission in precipitating novel and more inclusive categories of explanation in response to recognition of the inconsistencies and shortcomings of traditional understandings.

Critical thinking (in any sense sufficiently different from that universal commitment to the norms of reason and truth which might identify it as a social and educational objective) arose out of awareness of the incommensurabilities between different belief and value systems. Growth of a sense of history and social change, and thus of the relativities of human knowledge, were what stimulated the search for general principles to enable the reasoner to transcend this welter of perceived inconsistency. A sense of history prompts that metacognitive awareness which is an essential ingredient of critical thought. It is trivialised and subverted if it is portrayed as discrete from these historical attempts to achieve a more general grasp of the relationship of language and thought to reality.

The last of my preliminary quotations, from Wittgenstein's *Philosophical Investigations,* draws attention to the many levels at which it is possible to say that one 'understands' another language. In particular, the quotation highlights cases where familiarity with the everyday use of a foreign language fails to dispel a sense of alienation - because there is more to languages than concept-to-concept correspondences between words, sentences and phrases. There are idiomatic configurations of connotation and denotation within a system of language-use which have the effect of charging ostensible meanings with peculiar significance. Words and their referents are related in multiple ways which vary between, and within, cultures and this must defeat any attempt to account systematically for the 'mental representations' of the components of a vocabulary; they 'hang together' in complex and unpredictable ways. The task of individuating meanings is both dialogic and ongoing. Kozulin relates this general characteristic of language, 'activity' rather than 'finished structure', to the early speech of the child:

> Language is not a finished thing, but a creative process; it is not "ergon" but "energeia." Vygotsky's studies of child language also followed this line of reasoning in their attempts to show how linguistic and cognitive structures are engendered by verbal activity, and how the child engages in the creative work of building his or her own language. (Kozulin, 1990, p. 20)

This 'unfinished' internal semanticity in language, thought and behaviour encompasses such familiar cases as discussion between peers and the interpretation by adults of the 'world of the child.' For instance, children's performances on Piagetian problem solving tasks demonstrate an ineradicable ambiguity between researchers' conceptions of those tasks and those of their young experimental subjects. One interpretation is that 'there seems to be no way of determining, with the traditional Piagetian tasks, the *relative contributions* of cognitive or linguistic deficiencies when a child fails to achieve the correct solution' (Siegel and Brainerd, 1978, p. 45, my emphasis). But this explanation evades the central issue by clinging to that same categorical distinction between cognition and language which, it is acknowledged, experimental method fails to sustain. In this situation, the child's thought closely resembles that of Lévy Bruhl's Nuer tribesman; its structure is neither more nor less identifiable than the semantic features of the conversation between researcher and subject. We can certainly explore with them the implications of their words, but we cannot lift the veil of language to see what lies behind it. An important difference, though, is that eventually the child in question would almost certainly inherit a significantly more complex universe of ideas, of linguistic-conceptual possibilities, than that available to her Nuer cousins; one reflection of the potency of exponential cultural traditions in effecting cognitive transformations 'between the ears' of individual people.

Although Wittgenstein's *language games* were intended to direct attention to features of real human activities, they are not bounded phenomena which are therefore amenable to investigation of a purely empirical kind as some linguists have been tempted to argue. They are tokens of the dynamic, unfinished function of word-meaning at the core of human relationships. Awareness of the alien character of other ways of living, thinking and speaking afflicts not only the social scientist or the historian, but is a mundane fact of life. Teenage fashions, repugnant to older generations, may have an involutional appeal to values with which it is difficult or impossible for the non-participant to identify, despite the fact that they share a 'common language'. Nor is it difficult to imagine that individuals with different native tongues from opposite sides of the planet might achieve higher levels of mutual comprehension than two individuals of different social and educational standing in the 'same' small geographical community. 'Forms of life' do not coincide neatly with commonly distinguished modes of social organisation any more than they do with intellectual traditions or formal disciplines.

Indeed, it is this absence of boundary criteria which leads Gellner to complain that despite the apparent empirical implications of the language games concept, there is no 'non-arbitrary way of isolating such self contained games within the flux of our thought' (Gellner, 1968, pp. 166-7). To understand something, he maintains, is usually, 'to see it as a case of something more general' (ibid., page 221). It is this problem, too, which invalidates the construction placed by Oakeshott and McPeck on logically self-authenticating formal disciplines. The key question is whether we are confronted by two clear alternatives; between a relativism in which the meaning and rational status of beliefs are sanctioned by criteria specific to particular world views, and a rationalism upholding the idea of universal criteria which enable us to discriminate consistently between logical and illogical forms of argument, intelligible and meaningless propositions.

I argue, here, against such clear-cut alternatives and against the view that the stances of Wittgenstein and Winch imply the kind of vicious regress into relativism of which Gellner has accused both philosophers. The point of my interpretation is that it concedes the case for internal criteria of intelligibility *without* entailing acceptance that there can never be valid critiques or meaningful and persuasive dialogue between different forms of life and language games. Transactions over criteria of meaning and reason typify the dialogue which takes place in reality; in the evolution and extinction of languages, the mutual assimilation of cultures and, for example, in the adoption by non-literate cultures of the languages, scripts and modes of explanation of literate cultures. What is irreducible is not some imagined internal 'essence' contained within a way of life and its characteristic patterns of linguistic-usage. Language, as Wittgenstein said, is a labyrinth of paths; 'you approach from one side and you know your way about; you approach the same place from another side and no longer know your way about' (Wittgenstein, 1968, PI 203). This is a good approximation to the indeterminacies of exchange between the cultural anthropologist and her subjects, members of different cultural groups, and conversation between adults and children. It is also a description of the endless distinctions and comparisons which are drawn in disciplinary discourse in the interests of clarity, of which philosophical argument is a paradigm. Failure to identify universal, superordinate criteria of rationality does not preclude common anchorages and the adoption of conventions for exploring the implications of these proximal areas of mutual intelligibility. Language games change over time, become extinct and new ones are invented - in a process characterised by *successive dialogical approximations*. No languages are entirely untranslatable, though some may pose severe problems and entail many years of cultural 'acclimatisation'. Nor are the forms of social organisation which they describe impervious to interpretation. But neither are they capable of being rendered mutually explicit in terms of a higher order of commensurable meanings. In a sense, dialogue is a contest of meanings in which there are winners and losers.

Empirical, conceptual and historical dimensions of thought

Winch's philosophical sociology traces the hermeneutic implications of the concept of *forms of life*, directing attention to reciprocities between observer and observed involved in attempts to elucidate the meaning of unfamiliar social practices; the dialogic process of achieving *verstehen*. For Winch, this is fundamentally a philosophical task though it certainly does not follow from what he says that it is so exclusively. Nor, for that matter, does it follow that philosophy falls entirely within the jurisdiction of the professional philosopher. In his polemic against linguistic philosophy, *Words and Things* Gellner attempts to reclaim ground for empirical investigation of the contextual use of language as a key to its semantic import:

> In fact, Linguistic Philosophy calls for sociology. If the meaning of terms is their

> use and context, then those contexts and the activities therein should be investigated seriously - and *without* making the mistaken assumption that we already know enough about the world and about society to identify the actual functioning of our use of words. (Gellner, 1968, page 257)

I believe Gellner is half-right and half-wrong about this. His counter-emphasis on 'seeing what is the case' is a reaction to a misleading stereotype of linguistic philosophy as a homogenous method, and to a hyperbolic interpretation of the maxim, 'meaning is use' which diverts attention away from the important idea of linguistic usage within a nexus of social practices. Toulmin has provided important qualifications on both these counts, claiming that Wittgenstein was *not a linguistic philosopher* (and certainly not of the kind exemplified by the Oxford school) and that his philosophy bears more than a coincidental resemblance to Vygotsky's philosophical psychology, via the mutual influence of research by the Bühlers into linguistics and developmental psychology (Toulmin, 1969, pp. 70-71). One striking resonance between the two thinkers is their reference to *tools* as a pivotal metaphor for describing the diversity of modes of predication, their connection with particular cultural forms and their irreducibility, either to elementary psychological functions or to a uniform, underlying structure of language:

> Thought development is determined by language...by the linguistic tools of thought and by the sociocultural experience of the child. Essentially, the development of inner speech depends on outside factors; the development of logic in the child...is a direct function of his socialised speech. The child's intellectual growth is contingent on his mastering the social means of thought, that is, language. (Vygotsky, 1989, p. 94)

And Wittgenstein, citing such examples as *giving and obeying orders; reporting an event; speculating about an event; forming and testing a hypothesis; play-acting; translating; asking, thanking, cursing, greeting and praying:*

> - It is interesting to compare the multiplicity of the tools in language and of the ways they are used, the multiplicity of kinds of word and sentence, with what logicians have said about the structure of language [Including the author of the *Tractatus Logico-Philosophicus*]. (Wittgenstein, 1968, PI 23)

In other words, as Toulmin puts it, Wittgenstein's concern was about the 'multifarious ways in which "forms of life" create a context for "language games" and how these in turn delimit the scope and boundaries of the sayable' and *not* with the idea of language as the 'self-sufficient subject-matter of philosophy'. But Gellner is correct in his insistence that the investigation of behaviour is an indispensable condition for clarifying the meaning of relationships between forms of language use and forms of life. I will argue, for instance, that critical and scientific thinking cannot be abstracted from the social traditions within which they emerged without distorting our understanding of their character - to the detriment of education. The 'bottom line' is that naturalistic explanation, alone, cannot elucidate behaviour or the use of words, nor is there a system of overarching logical or syntactic principles to provide the necessary criteria - for these are matters for hermeneutic interpretation.

Wittgensteinian idealism and 'essentialism' - a source of misunderstanding

Winch's claims for philosophy do not amount to an argument for an alternative *system* of social analysis, though he occasionally writes as though he believes something like this is the case. The latter tendency is clearest in a passage in which he attacks Popper's conception of *methodological individualism*. Popper describes this as a means of avoiding confusion between abstract or theoretical models and the social behaviour which they purport to describe (for example, Popper, 1969, pp. 89-99). He recommends that these models should be analysed in terms of the attitudes, expectations and relations of individual people; in other words, by preserving the sense that holistic interpretations of social phenomena are heuristic in character. He describes *methodological essentialism* as the false attribution of a monolithic essence to forms of social activity and organisation. But, Winch argues, social institutions are not simply theoretical constructs which we employ to explain human behaviour; concepts like 'war' are constitutive of our understanding of it, and they belong *essentially* to our behaviour (Winch, 1958, p. 128). Any coherent description of the behaviour of individuals is logically parasitic upon the socially mediated concepts which determine the significance of that behaviour for the actors.

Winch concedes that his formulation 'appears to commit the sin' of what Popper calls 'methodological essentialism', though he neither directly confirms nor denies this (ibid., p. 127). However, insistence on the indivisibility of language, thought and social institutions may well be regarded as a form of *sociological holism*; that is, a doctrine which asserts the unity of ideas, beliefs, institutions and practices in any given society, and which proscribes the investigation of any one of these aspects in isolation from the others as inherently distorting. And there are serious logical and practical problems associated with any such attempt to depict social collectives as seamless or monolithic, as Popper and Gellner point out. Quite apart from the implausibility of applying this principle consistently to pluralistic modern societies, except at a hopelessly abstract level of generality, there is the impossibility of distinguishing one social whole from another in terms of non-arbitrary boundary criteria.

This is essentially the same problem as the one which I have identified in the case of attempts by domain-theorists to justify their portrayal of intellectual traditions and disciplines as logically - but internally - homogenous and mutually exclusive. Hamlyn anticipates the danger of a similar essentialist interpretation of Wittgenstein's aphorisms about the foundational nature of *agreement in forms of life* in the context of educational philosophy:

> There has recently been a renewed interest in what Wittgenstein had to say about rule-following and about the extent to which that necessarily implies a social context and even social backing. There are dangers in these emphases. It cannot be right to take Wittgenstein as implying (and it cannot be right in itself anyway) that the individual has to be initiated into the acceptance of those rules which society imposes. (Hamlyn, 1989, p. 221)

Essentialism entails arbitrary judgments about what is to count as a social unit. If only for this reason Gellner's anti-Wittgensteinian thesis is important, though I believe misconceived. He correctly detects the dual implication of the language game metaphor. It offers no consistent principles of discrimination between those empirical features of the world which it appears to designate and the internal rules which determine the semantic meanings those features are alleged to enshrine. In Gellner's colourful words, '...by looking at language *games* we hunt with the empirical-naturalistic hounds; but by accepting their *contents*, we run with the transcendental hares, or any others we care to run with...' (ibid., pp. 166-167). His criticism is consequently two-pronged; while he condemns the alleged arbitrariness involved in the language-game concept, he levels criticisms at Winch's 'radical contextualism', the sociological thrust of language-game analysis which he detects. Moreover, he directly interprets Wittgenstein's notion of forms of life and their internal criteria of intelligibility as an injunction to interpret various kinds of human utterance 'in the light of their function in the culture of which they are a part' (Gellner, 1972, p. 123).

I believe that Gellner's interpretation of this point is distorted. Yet as I have noted already, it leads him to the valid conclusion that the functionalist approach precludes us from making sense of social changes which arise when, 'people sometimes notice the incoherencies of doctrines and concepts and proceed to reform the institutions justified by them.' This is a fundamental blow against the methodology he is attacking because it shifts the criteria of meaningful behaviour away from the internal perspective of participants to another (possibly more general) point of view. But the defence of both Wittgenstein and Winch is quite simply, that *neither philosopher is a functionalist in the sense attacked by Gellner.*

In fact, the distance between Winch and Gellner is not so great as the latter believes, as I shall indicate, below, in my discussion of *institutions* and *models.* Indeed, Gellner finally concedes that despite the possibilities of abuse, 'It is probably impossible...to draw up general rules for delimiting the legitimate and illegitimate uses of (contextual interpretation)' (ibid., p. 147). Winch's solution, contained in the previously quoted summary of his main thesis, is that;

> ...I have linked the assertion that social relations are internal with the assertion that men's mutual interaction 'embodies ideas', by suggesting that social interaction can more profitably be compared to the exchange of ideas in a conversation than to the interaction of forces in a physical system. (Winch, 1958, p. 128)

The imagery of *an exchange of ideas* is crucial here, because Winch's purpose is not to locate the meaning of human thought and behaviour in some unitary social 'essence'. It is rather to suggest, by virtue of the open-endedness and recursiveness of language and thought, that there is no final resting place for interpretations. There are, however, many areas of common understanding within and between cultures, even though they defy classification within a general framework of explanation. This is like saying, apropos of Wittgenstein, that *agreement in form of life* is not a state of affairs which can be defined, once and for all. Like that 'system of reference by means of which we interpret an unknown language', it is a precondition of language and of interpreting its rules meaningfully, in an infinity of possible situations beyond that in which it is originally learned.

Although Wittgenstein was concerned primarily with the philosophy of logic, the kind of relationship between the syntax and semantics of thought and language which he portrayed embraces not only philosophy but the social sciences as well. It might seem paradoxical, therefore, that he admitted the unsystematic nature of his remarks. But it should be noted, too, that this lack of system is one which he attributed, not to the complexity of the subject, but to its nature (Wittgenstein, 1968, PI, vii).

Indeed, if there is a single thrust to the *Philosophical Investigations*, it consists in abandonment of the idea, explored in the same author's earlier *Tractatus*, of a single consistent and underlying logical systematicity in human language and thought, expressed in the form of a soliloquy:

> ...You take the easy way out! You talk about all sorts of language-games but have nowhere said what the essence of a language-game, and hence of language, is: what is common to all these activities, and what makes them into language or parts of a language. So you let yourself off the very part of the investigation that once gave you yourself most headache, the part about the *general form of propositions* and of language...

> ...And this is true. - Instead of producing something common to all that we call language, I am saying that these phenomena have no one thing in common which makes us use the same word for all, - but that they are related to one another in

> many different ways. And it is because of this relationship, or these relationships, that we call them all "language". (Wittgenstein, 1968, PI 65)

And it is in this connection that language games assume their prominence in his thought, with repeated emphasis upon the indeterminacy of relationships and boundaries between them. By the same token, it is not the ontological status of forms of life which is significant in Winch's philosophical sociology, but the epistemological principle that understanding human behaviour is a dialogical process which cannot, without distortion, be reduced to general descriptions of 'how-things-really-are'. Likewise, Gier concludes that Wittgenstein's radical contextualism and pluralism make him virtually unique because although he agrees in some respects with the continental phenomenologists about the correct method for analysing human behaviour, he does not accept that this implies the possibility of a 'general logic of phenomena'.

As I have suggested several times, the value of examples from cultural anthropology is that they help to illustrate the concept of intentionality and its logical force in the explanation of human behaviour. However, this logical force encompasses *all* human thought and behaviour by virtue of the fact that it is specifiable only in relation to its semantic 'inscape' from the point of view of an actor; its *meaning*. The internal rules of thought and behaviour are their characterising features, though this by no means entails the conclusion that they are consistent or complete. Although members of 'the same' or similar communities will share many interpretations of these rules, and it makes perfectly good sense in these cases to treat the language in which they are described as though it is 'transparent', there will always be residual, conceptual questions about the interpretation of such commonalties. There is, however, no absolute standard of comparison against which to make the decision that individuals, groups, communities, social classes, educational elites and ethnic minorities do or do not share *the same* understandings. That is a matter for continuing dialogue.

Different landscapes

Boas, Sapir and Benedict are major figures in an anthropological tradition which stresses the distinctive character of the world views represented by contrasting languages and cultures. Early in the first chapter of her *Patterns of Culture*, Benedict emphasises two implications of her analysis of the differing configurations of pre-literate cultures:

> All over the world, since the beginning of human history, it can be shown that peoples have been able to adopt the culture of peoples of another blood. There is

> nothing in the biological structure of man that makes it even difficult...We must accept all the implications of our human inheritance, one of the most important of which is the small scope of biologically transmitted behaviour, and the enormous role of the cultural process of the transmission of tradition. (Benedict, 1971, pp. 10-11)

Benedict recognises both a common biological inheritance which facilitates cross-cultural communication and the alienage which means that a person cannot 'thoroughly participate in any culture' unless brought up 'to live according to its forms' (ibid., p. 26). Yet she acknowledges the intense controversy between advocates of configurational anthropology, with their emphasis on cultural distinctiveness, on the one hand, and supporters of the view that there is a common naturalistic basis of social phenomena, on the other hand. Her defence is in the form of a challenge to these naturalists to account for 'even a small part of the social phenomena it is necessary to understand' rather than a decisive elenchus (ibid., p. 168-9). I will consider, below, how Pinker has recently launched a direct challenge to the anthropological tradition represented by Benedict on the basis of his concept of psycholinguistic universals. First however, I will briefly examine the genuinely problematic task of comprehending the semantic meanings embedded in alien cultures because it is of a piece with the more abstract, theoretical issues discussed above.

Bruce Chatwin's portrayal of Aboriginal myth and reality suggests how profoundly alien two forms of life may be, and the distortions which are liable to infest descriptions of a culture by strangers to it - because there is *no assured basis of comparison* between the meanings enshrined in differing cultural-linguistic environments. There are, of course, interesting and detailed controversies between anthropologists on just this kind of issue and its methodological implications. Yet Chatwin's account directly conveys a sense of the alien forms of life of aboriginal Australians, without the intervention of models, hypotheses or methodological issues characteristic of western scholarship. His less analytic, poetic and speculative approach conveys a sense of the different conceptual, affective and perceptual world of the Aborigine; a recognition that when the native and the European walk side by side through the Australian bush, their respective experiences and perceptions are profoundly different:

> White men...made the common mistake of assuming that, because Aboriginals were wanderers, they could have no system of land tenure. This was nonsense. Aboriginals, it was true, could not imagine territory as a block of land hemmed in by frontiers: but rather as an interlocking network of "lines" or ways through...all our words for "country", he said, are the same as the words for "line". (Chatwin, 1988, p. 62)

'Trade' involving the exchange of shells, feathers and belts of human hair (for example) once extended over the entire continent and a single item might travel in this way from the Timor Sea to the Australian Bight. 'Trade routes' were the ancient 'songlines,' and the songs themselves conveyed immensely detailed pictures of distant, unvisited landscapes. Moreover, the traded objects were of only secondary importance to the trade in songs, the significance of which was held to be more than their informational content. They were a means of maintaining the order of the original creation. Songs were of such vital importance in sustaining the existence of the world that there had been a time when for a tribesman to sing a verse out of order would have been to incur the death penalty. Chatwin conveys the sense of a vast, interlocking network of ideas, myths and totemic customs whose meaning lay in their semantic interdependence and registered itself in different perceptions of the real world on the part of Aboriginals and Europeans.

Peter Worsley has considered some of the difficulties of accommodating totemic systems to any European explanatory framework. Objects of immensely different categorical significance for Europeans might be included in the same category in an aboriginal classification. The premise of some anthropologists that totemic objects would have a recognisable utility in tribal society founders on the inclusion of mosquitoes, vomit and diarrhoea as totems, as well as the *exclusion* of many objects which have manifest utility in aboriginal life. A similar problem exists with the apparently arbitrary attribution of totemic significance to certain landscape features in preference to others which are equally obtrusive to the alien observer's eye (Worsley, 1972, pp. 204-221). Lévi-Strauss' alternative interpretation, that totemic objects have *utility* as a system of logical classification, has been described as a brilliant demonstration that they are 'the stuff of thinking' in their respective social systems, but his system of binary classification has been criticised on the grounds that it is only a possible and not a necessary method of discrimination, (any information may be analysed in terms of oppositions) and that it fails to account for subtle gradations in the significance of totemic values and prohibitions (Leach, 1972, pp. 183-203). Worsley argues that field research indicates the probability that totems and rituals have been exchanged between tribal groups and that they may be, 'just arbitrary symbols, only connected to the social units that bear them in a purely contingent way - say, through historical accident - which then become "fixed"...' (ibid., p. 208).

Extending his argument against a premature systematisation of totemic beliefs and practices, Worsley invokes a distinction which Vygotsky drew in *Thought and Language*, between *congeries*, *complexes* and *concepts* in the thought of the young child. The first category was distinguished by Vygotsky as consisting of, 'vague syncretic agglomerations' denoted by words, but lacking any discernible principle of association other than the fortuitous, perceived order provided by the social relationships surrounding and including the child. Whatever the merits or otherwise of Vygotsky's distinctions, Worsley uses the analogy to question the tendency to force tribal systems of classification into a mould prescribed by Western schemata, imposing a 'spurious uniformity' on what are more correctly described as *congerie-like* systems of association. To the familiar observer, totemism encompasses not only cognitive ordering but the totality of social life, the order of nature and its perceived relationships to the supernatural - but also significant divergences from prescriptive rules:

> Mechanical analogies, as usual, are of dubious value for the study of human cultural activity, since deviation and manipulation are omnipresent, both because people have differential interests and because they innovate. (ibid. pp. 218-219)

Kluckhohn and Leighton's previously mentioned observations about the incommensurabilities between Navajo and English mark the extent to which cultural isolation over immense periods appears to be associated with modes of language and thought that do not fit easily into the categorical apparatus within which modern Europeans have believed their experience is structured. An empathetic 'leap-in-the-dark' is required to understand how communities can hunt and farm in remote deserts and conduct their secular and religious affairs in languages which appear to differ radically from our own. The pueblo-dwelling Hopi are agriculturists whose tribal territory is surrounded by that of the more nomadic Navajo. Yet striking contrasts between these native American nations are revealed in their languages and social traditions, many aspects of which have been catalogued by Benedict, who asks of the pueblo-dwelling Hopi and Zuni how it came about that:

> ...here in this small region of America a culture gradually differentiated itself from all those that surrounded it and came always more and more drastically to express a consistent and particular attitude towards existence. (Benedict, 1971, p. 42)

An extreme portrayal of the kind of difference in question is offered by Benjamin Lee Whorf; the Hopi tongue contains 'no words, grammatical forms, constructions or expressions' referring to anything like our familiar conceptions of time and space or verbs with our familiar tenses (Whorf, 1959, p. 144 and 263). He places a radical construction on such linguistic contrasts: ...the linguistic order embraces all symbolism, all symbolic processes, all processes of reference and of logic' (ibid., p. 252) and, '...it is possible to have descriptions of the universe, *all equally valid*, that do not contain our familiar contrasts of time and space' (ibid., p. 58, my emphasis).

Whorf thus subscribes to the relativism that Gellner castigates; self-authenticating language-games, forms of life, 'in-the-world' and 'of-the-world' which are immune from effective external appraisal because they are seamlessly self-consistent and comprehensive. Indeed, he might fairly be accused of insisting that sufficient evidence of the meaning and truth of ways of talking and thinking about reality is furnished simply by their persistence. He stresses the homeostatic function of Hopi ritual in countering rivalries with something I will later refer to as *essentialism in action* - the 'combined, intensified and harmonized thought of the whole community' (ibid., p. 151). And he refuses to distinguish the Hopi metaphysics of time and space as more mystical than Western conceptions:

> Hopi postulates equally account for all phenomena and their interrelations, and lend themselves even better to the integration of Hopi culture in all its phases. (ibid., p. 59)

Pinker challenges the scholarship which led Whorf to such an emphatic form of linguistic and cultural relativism and it is certainly true that Whorf's reference to 'all phenomena and their interrelations' is his relativistic Achilles' heel. It provides no rationale for explaining the strained relationships - but relationships nonetheless - between the Hopi and their linguistically and culturally distinct neighbours, the Navajo. It singularly fails to explain how Whorf, an English-speaking American could hope to understand and render intelligible to others so comprehensively alien a way of life. Nor does it shed light on the important question raised by Benedict about the dynamics which might have led to the *gradual differentiation* of the pueblos from other native American cultures. Far from being of peripheral interest, these questions about the commonalties which make cultural assimilation and differentiation possible are central to the relationship between language, thought and culture which the Whorfian thesis addresses. The 'unfinished' character of language is the relevant dynamic; novelty is a universal possibility. Accentuated by the social and technical apparatus of institutionalised dialogue, it also helps to explain how traditions of critical thinking emerged from more monolithic conventions to revolutionise our understanding of the world. And this was possible precisely because common anchorages can be found amongst the very real incommensurabilities between forms of language and life.

Pinker, however, tries to focus on what is common. He dismisses 'anthropological anecdotes' in the tradition to which I have referred as 'bunk' (Pinker, 1995, p. 65) and disposes of 'the assumption of an infinitely variable human nature from anthropology', presenting an array of allegedly universal human traits in more than sixty lines, the full version of which he attributes to Donald E. Brown. Originally inspired by Chomsky's notion of a universal grammar, Brown's list purports to identify 'universal patterns underlying the behaviour of all documented human cultures' (ibid., pp. 413-5). But there are serious problems about the widely varying levels of generality of these 'universals' and, consequently, the leverage they afford to the researcher who, like Pinker, is interested in 'mind design'. Items on this list include 'nonlinguistic vocal communication such as cries and squeals' to 'supernatural beliefs', 'explanations of disease and death' and 'medicine'.

But Pinker does not tell us within what kind of conceptual frame of reference the alleged universality of the practice of medicine is of greater significance than the *difference* between, say, the expulsion of evil spirits by incantation and the bombardment of malignant cells by radioactive isotopes. Even if one accepts that such contrasting practices merit the epithet 'medicine', there can be no doubt that they represent very different configurations of intellectual and practical activity which register significant differences in the way cultural traditions impact on mental organisation. His acceptance of 'supernatural beliefs' as universals begs complex and much-debated questions about the demarcation between science and metaphysics. Yet the gradual differentiation in certain cultures of metaphysics and epistemology from Palaeolithic magic tells us more about universal potentials of mind-design than any taxonomy which is general enough to subsume both under the same heading, as essentially *the same* thing. And this objection stands against Pinker's other, putative universals; 'conjectural thought' which must encompass, amongst many other things, the ancient Greek idea of *indivisible minima* and the *quarks* and *bosons* of modern particle physics. There are connections, no doubt, but in terms of revolutionising traditions of inquiry and their impact on the 'design' of our minds. Arguably, universalising categories such as these represent the kind of thing Wittgenstein had in mind when he referred to the 'common behaviour of mankind' which makes cultural and linguistic exchange possible. But they do not do what Pinker wants them to because they fail to refute the immense variability which one is bound to acknowledge within each of these categories, even if they are acceptable as broad generalisations. And it is this kind of variability which counts, for Pinker's enterprise of describing mind-design as much as it does for the anthropologist he opposes.

It is necessary to indicate the bearing of Pinker's thesis on my own argument. As I have already mentioned, he follows and moves beyond Chomsky on the question of innate universals. However, his stance on this issue seems to owe much to a conviction occasionally voiced parenthetically by Chomsky about the wider significance of linguistic innatism (though of course, not in justification of it). This is his rejection of an Empiricist conception of mind as a *tabula rasa,* equally receptive to dogma and habits of authoritarian submission as to the principles of free, rational conduct, and consequently vulnerable to the caprice of despots (for instance in Piatelli-Palmarini, 1980). Likewise Pinker, who maintains that the Orwellian nightmare of a linguistically and thus intellectually and morally impoverished totalitarian society would inevitably yield to the free psycholinguistic potential of rising generations: '...children...would creolise Newspeak into a natural language, possibly in a single generation' (Pinker, 1995, p. 82).

I believe Pinker's development of the concept of linguistic creativity is wildly over-optimistic and unhistorical, although it highlights the importance of issues concerning the relationship between language and thought. As I noted previously, he claims that 'mental life goes on independently of particular languages' and therefore that, 'concepts of freedom and equality are thinkable even if they are nameless' (ibid.). One obvious objection is that, so long as they remain nameless, these putative libertarian and egalitarian concepts are unlikely to prove socially or politically efficacious; or even detectable features in a cultural repertoire. *That* requires much more than the creolisation of a pidgin tongue into grammatical form; for instance, the fuller and historically rare articulation and dissemination achieved by a Locke, a Paine, a Rousseau or a Mill. Rigidly hierarchical, authoritarian systems have endured over long periods; slavery and related forms of bondage have been nearly ubiquitous in human societies. The fundamental problem confronting Pinker's thesis is that concepts of freedom and equality, defined as innate universals, are consistent enough with their ideological and political antitheses to lack analytical leverage. We are also entitled to ask, by *reductio,* whether all past and possible human concepts are 'thinkable' as Pinker defines it and, if so, whether his particular emphasis on freedom and equality, as distinct from their alternatives, is justified in terms of his theory. The suspicion must be that it is not; that everything that ever has been, or might be thought is 'thinkable' in this tautological sense; that the structural elements of the proverbial block of marble are polymorphous enough to contain not only the form of the angel, but the gargoyle - and so on, *ad infinitum.*

There is, however, another sense in which Chomsky's description of syntactic structures as 'free creation within a system of rules' is of pivotal importance in connecting the universal human language capability with developed conceptions of freedom and equality. For there are institutional implications in the creativity of language and thought which I will consider further in the light of Mill's epistemological justification of individual liberty. As I have previously argued, conceptions of truth and the rational justifiability of assertions are fundamental conditions of any language. If words and sentences are to mean anything, they must be capable, not only of consistent and appropriate usage, but of meeting shared criteria and of conforming to rules governing the kinds of consistency and appropriateness in question. And these rules and criteria are explicable only in terms of cultural traditions and the semantic meanings they enshrine. Chomsky's demonstration that language acquisition is vastly underdetermined by the learner's experience of language-use supports his general theory of innatism. His account of the indefinite creativity of syntax is, in itself, consistent with an indefinite development of semantic meaning. But Pinker's illicit inferential leap to a theory of innate concepts omits the very dynamic which accounts for significant differences in their scope and depth; the exponential influence of dialogue and, in particular, the development of explicit traditions of critical inquiry.

Linguistic-conceptual innovation and prediction in social science

Human decision-making is characterised by the existence of alternative courses of action which are implicit in the linguistic and conceptual rules according to which those decisions are made. And it is in the nature of *these* rules to be indicative rather than programmatic, the case argued by Searle when he asserts that money is whatever people choose to regard as money rather than anything that can be identified with various categories of objective correlates. There is no absolute criterion *outside* a particular mode of discourse or social practice of what constitutes an application, or a breach, of the rules. In other words, accurate prediction in human affairs is fortuitous, unless it is from the standpoint of an observer who shares participants' understandings of rules internal to a way of life:

> ...even given a specific set of initial conditions, one will still not be able to predict the outcome to a historical trend because the continuation or breaking off of that trend involves human decisions which are not determined by their antecedent conditions in the context of which the sense of calling them 'decisions' lies...the point is that such trends are in part the *outcome* of intentions and decisions of their participants. (Winch, 1958, p. 93)

Jack Goody and Ian Watt, in a discussion of the implications of literacy for social science, consider the cases of the Tiv people of Nigeria and the Gonja people of northern Ghana and their oral, non-literate, tradition of tribal 'genealogies.' In both cases, the interpretation of literate colonial administrators was in terms of the European tradition of historical-factual accounts of ancestry. Disagreements between the administration and tribesfolk about officially maintained written records of these oral traditions were frequent. In the case of the Gonja two whole divisions of the tribe disappeared over a 60 year period as a result of internal amalgamations and administrative boundary changes with resulting modifications in the number of tribal ancestors included in the oral version. Goody and Watt conclude:

> What neither party realised was that in any society of this kind, changes take place which require a constant readjustment in the genealogies if they are to carry out their function as mnemonics of social relationships. (Goody and Watt, 1963, pp. 304-345)

In this case, the expectations of the colonial administrators were rooted in a literate tradition which took for granted a certain conception of an objective past and a corresponding function of the orally transmitted genealogy as a record of that past. This, of course, would be precisely the kind of thing which Europeans would regard as relevant to territorial claims. By contrast, Goody and Watt propose the idea of a 'structural amnesia' which enables non-literate communities to maintain a sense of traditional order because it does not depart too greatly from present experience. In tribal lore, it was largely the function of 'genealogies' to explicate present social relationships - because within *their* world, the absence of a writing system precluded systematic comparisons between the present and any previous circumstances which greatly exceeded the direct testimony of living members of the group. It is difficult to grasp, from within a literate tradition, how differently non-literate cultures might interpret the connections between past, present and future; interpretations which may have significant implications for their concepts of permanent future commitment, for example.

Searle refers to socially internalised rules which determine the scope and limits of what is to be regarded as 'making a promise', a deed which might seem to imply a perfectly overt, unambiguous commitment to future action. A concrete illustration is provided by the Navajo of the 19th Century. European officials experienced frustration at their persistent failure to honour 'promises' which they had made freely to desist from raiding white settlements. Foster Johnston suggests that the explanation lay not so much in the moral turpitude of the Navajo as in the fundamentally different nature of their society and beliefs. 'Promises' to abandon raiding were obtained from Chiefs and enshrined in diplomatic treaties. What the European representatives did not realise was that a chief's jurisdiction tended to be limited to his own extended family and immediate neighbours, but certainly not to the largely independent raiding parties of young warriors. Nor were these raids expressions of what European's would describe as 'hostile intent'; they simply marked the continuation of longstanding traditions. But perhaps more fundamentally, a promise tended to be a statement of your disposition at one instant in a changing world rather than the European concept of an undertaking which prescribed or proscribed certain behaviour indefinitely, regardless of how you might feel in the future, or how outward circumstances might change! (Foster Johnston, 1966, p. 22). Navajo promises were not the same thing as European promises, and certainly did not encompass the idea of contractual relationships. The difference boils down, not to a problem of translation so much as a contrast in what Wittgenstein called 'forms of life'. Kluckhohn and Leighton insist that an appreciation of these linguistic/cognitive differentials is important for the non-Navajo administrator because:

> He will be less easily moved to harmful or futile anger at "broken promises," for he will realize that, in many cases, his understanding of an agreement or a situation

> diverged in important particulars from that of the Navajos with whom he was dealing. (Kluckhohn and Leighton, 1960, p. 212)

It must be clear, too, that similar considerations apply to an indefinitely large number of concepts which we use to describe human institutions and practices; that war, love, prayer, violations of taboo and so forth exhibit facets of agreement and disagreement between cultures. An act like 'blasphemy' might evoke responses which are out of all proportion to any consequences which would be predicted by an observer who lacked familiarity with the doctrines of a particular religion and the rules governing its interpretation. Moreover, these rules may vary from the explicit and categorical to the broadly indicative, permitting a range of interpretations which are clearly implicated in the broad and shifting spectrum of beliefs and attitudes prevalent in a way of life.

Alien customs cannot be described exhaustively, nor can they be characterised precisely by reference to a template provided by practices in the social scientist's own culture, for these, too, are subject to residual philosophical ambiguities. Yet the problem is not confined to the finer points of cross-cultural interpretation, because what appear to be no more than verbal niceties to one set of individuals may reach to the core of another's sense of self-identity and moral or spiritual value, possibly with dramatic and violent consequences. To adapt another example provided by Gellner (from Evans Pritchard), there may appear to be little to choose between the respective 'logics' of the Nuer's belief that in sacrificing a cucumber he is sacrificing an ox and the once-dominant western Christian tradition of 'transubstantiation' in the celebration of the Eucharist - except, perhaps, that the Nuer's linguistic-cognitive repertoire does not contain the possibility of conceiving of *representation* or *symbolism*. Beliefs which are ostensibly comparable and susceptible of translation from the language of one culture to another may actually occupy very different co-ordinates within the overall configurations of those values. Ernst Cassirer has described this interplay between like and unlike in the interpretation of mythical thought as follows:

> We cannot expect...any one to one correspondence between our logical forms of thought and the forms of mythical thought. But if there were no connection at all, if they were moving on entirely different planes, every attempt to understand myth would be doomed to failure. (Cassirer, 1967, p. 13)

Concepts, models and 'false consciousness'

Gellner objects to functionalist anthropology on the substantial ground that it blinds us, in *a priori* fashion, to the origins of conceptual and social change and also to the possibility of social control by means of 'absurd, ambiguous, inconsistent or unintelligible doctrines' (Gellner, 1972, p. 141). Philosophy, he says, 'is explicitness, generality, orientation and assessment' and in a biting paraphrase of Wittgenstein, he concludes: 'That which one would insinuate, thereof one must speak' (Gellner, 1968, p. .296). But I have already noted that Gellner, himself, is inclined to renounce as unattainable the idea of general rules which could determine the appropriateness or otherwise of contextual interpretation in particular circumstances in favour of a critical attitude towards the phenomena under investigation. This concession is more significant than its brevity suggests. It hints at the kind of dialogical engagement with unfamiliar ideas which Winch describes with his metaphor for sociological research as a matter of tracing the implications of ideas in the course of a conversation. Gellner has conceded Winch's point; that there is no general, systematic method for determining the rational status or meaning of utterances and beliefs.

Chomsky's hostility to the idea of social control by the manipulative use of dogma seems to be reflected in Pinker's unwarranted faith in the inherent creativity of the *language instinct* to cash itself in substantive concepts like liberty and equality. I have argued that the explicitness and generality of his account of these and other putative human universals is spurious; that it does not even engage effectively with the anthropological tradition he dismisses so lightly. And my own contention is that what stands between oppressive, all-embracing dogma or ideology and human freedom and equality are mature traditions of critical thinking; realisations, through the dialectic of argument and debate, of a *potential* contained in the creativity of language. A crucial point is that there is nothing inevitable about these traditions and their sustainability is contingent on institutionalised recognition of the fallibility of human understanding. And many influences always have militated against that recognition, including some explicitly formulated theories about the relationships between language, thought and behaviour.

Psychological and sociological explanations of ideas and practices are often formulated as 'models' of an heuristic or provisional character, which facilitate systematic study of complex human affairs. There may be variations in the levels of explicitness with which these models are articulated, and, indeed, there are cases where the existence of a model may simply not be acknowledged or where it is proposed as a mechanism or dynamic principle inherent in social organisation or psychological processes. An example of the latter is Freud's conception of the *Id, Ego* and *Superego* which appear to have been originally conceived by him as functions specific to locations in the brain but which subsequently assumed the role of principles for explaining the organisation of conscious and unconscious motivation.

However, there might be little to choose between the political analyst's model of parliamentary institutions and the understanding of those institutions in terms of which well-informed people act out aspects of their lives. Indeed, this kind of model might itself become constitutive of many people's understanding of their own institutions, and there are numerous examples of psychological and sociological theories which become the coinage of people's everyday understanding of their own and others' behaviour. Freudian psychoanalysis and Marxist social theory are cases in point; far from being entertained at high levels of theoretical generality by their adherents, such interpretations of the human condition may penetrate the intimate details of everyday life and mould our perceptions of it.

Winch criticises Popper for talking as though social institutions 'are just explanatory models introduced by the social scientist for his own purposes...The ways of thinking embodied in institutions govern the way the members of the societies studied by the social scientist behave' (Winch, 1958, p. 127). Yet social-scientific models may indeed become powerful, motivating concepts within the intentional behaviour of humans. There is no clear-cut general division between the observer's models and the participants' ways of thinking because, in human contexts, the scientist is bound to become engaged in the behavioural phenomena which she studies. (Winch's criticism of Popper's notion of models should also be qualified by recognition of Popper's own belief in the *provisional* nature of scientific theory and the dialectical, inter-subjective context of true scientific inquiry. This is a closer analogy to Winch's contention that the study of society is like a philosophical argument than he appears to recognise.)

This tendency to assimilate 'external' accounts of one's own behaviour may be insidious, though there is no way of distinguishing absolutely between it and normal enculturation. Both involve the internalisation of general categories of description and evaluation. For example, social scientific conceptions of causal determinism in human affairs have been accused of modifying views about individual moral responsibility. Aspiring, 'value-neutral' descriptions of behavioural psychology have inspired strategies for behaviour modification; the adoption of regimes to provide 'positive' and 'negative' reinforcements of aspects of conduct in special hospitals for the mentally abnormal offender, for instance. In such cases there may be evidence that this is an effective technique for inculcating behaviour which is acceptable within a limited institutional setting. Of course, the method is vulnerable to the criticism that behaviour is only 'good' if it arises from an internalised sense of rightness and wrongness. And such an awareness should be capable of being distributed across the range of an individual's actual and potential behaviour because it consists not only of specific, prescriptive rules but a matrix of valuations about relationships between self and others. To manipulate people into acceptable behaviour is to degrade and dehumanise them; to equate their 'good behaviour' with the obedience of a trained animal.

Methods of this kind are extrapolations from the normal human practice of occasionally rewarding and punishing behaviour of different kinds. In extreme forms what they miss is that such rewards and punishments are merely the punctuation marks in a longstanding dialogue which makes explicit a network of relationships and moral and aesthetic attitudes towards them. And that includes the affective states of parties to the dialogue. The moral awareness of the subject of 'behaviour modification' is closely analogous to the intellect of the 'rote' learner; in important respects, neither really *understands* her own words and actions and, consequently, neither is able to perform the conceptual feat of relating what she learns beyond the immediate context of learning. Her 'skills' do not transfer because they are not integrated within the matrix of consciousness from which the notion of 'skill' has been abstracted.

Human intentionality provides the only basis for an understanding of the social and political processes which capitalise on creativity and foster critical thought. The messages of thinkers as diverse as Nietzsche, Mill and Popper concern a human tendency to sacrifice freedom by adopting the 'false consciousness' embodied in the abstractions of dogma and social theory. All three thinkers portray an alienation which can become the dominant feature of social life and of the means of educating people into a superficial and passive understanding of their society. For Nietzsche the characteristic of this mode of life is 'the herd mentality'; for Mill it is the dogma which can express itself in the 'tyranny of majorities', and for Popper it is the urge for stability expressed in an essentialist philosophy underpinning the 'closed society'.

The significance of 'rule-governed' behaviour

Intentionalistic interpretation is sometimes articulated as a contrast between *rule-governed* and causally determined behaviour, and a salient feature of this contrast is that it is possible to make *mistakes* in applying rules. But there is something enigmatic about the kind of 'rules' according to which people conduct their lives, well illustrated by Searle's examples of the open-endedness of interpretations of what constitutes 'money' or 'marriage' and also in Winch's treatment of 'rule governed behaviour.' For, Winch claims, no formula can infallibly govern the application of rules; 'we must always come to a point at which we have to give an account of the application of the formula' (Winch, 1958, p. 29). And it is no solution to this enigma to postulate secondary rules governing the application of primary rules - and so on, for there is no escape from the necessity of determining what constitutes a correct application of each set of rules. In each case, the question arises as to what we regard as the *sameness* of particular applications, and that cannot come simply from a forceful reiteration of the rules. What is in question is their appropriateness in successively novel contexts. This may be controversial in particular cases, but *controversy* is possible only because there are already established uses; to apply rules of language correctly or incorrectly implies agreement about appropriate use *as a norm.* Rush Rhees emphasises the extensive nature of these rules of interpersonal communication. The various expressions of a language have their meaning within a multiplicity of shared uses in which the criteria of 'sameness' and 'difference' are immanent:

> What we call following a rule in language is not just following orders. That is why we talk about 'taking part in' a language - the language is not any one man's doing more than another's and the rules, if they are rules of language, are not one man's rules. This is essential for understanding. (Rhees, 1970, p. 63)

To some extent descriptions of human situations and behaviour are masked by familiarity; we have a concept of how they 'fit' into the pattern of our lives. The crucial point, however, is that knowing what a particular activity is (e.g. football, collecting fossils, telling a joke) is not simply a matter of observation, nor is it a matter of stipulating a definition of an observed activity. In the latter case, we have no assurance that our definition corresponds with what is observed, unless we are able to relate it to the internal rules and concepts which place the activity in a wider context. Because we are generally able to accept this background of agreement tacitly, definitions of various aspects of behaviour appear seductively transparent and economical. But definitions owe this economy to what is *not* stated more than to what is made explicit; to regressive rules which govern the sense of each of the terms of a definition. And this is why, despite some common areas of agreement, it is possible to misinterpret the intentions and behaviour of others quite radically; to assume that the friendly assurances of a Navajo Chief have the force of a contractual obligation or that a litany of tribal ancestors is a dependable genealogy.

My argument is that identical considerations apply when, for example, attempts are made to explain the intellectual processes which occur when a child, an adult, or perhaps a mentally handicapped adult, attempts to solve a problem which has been set because it appears to researchers, on *a priori* grounds, that the particular test or experiment makes explicit the rules governing intellectual processes. It might bear analogies to other familiar activities. But to *stipulate* definitions of cognitive processes may be to foreclose on the dialogue by means of which a learner assimilates the tacit background of rules which relate the activity meaningfully to other areas of her understanding. And to apply conclusions formulated in the course of such research directly to educational policy can be to preempt the creativity and freedom of human thought by disregarding her own need to make those connections as explicit as possible. I will consider this question of the criterion of identity between a model of particular cognitive processes and the 'inscape' or perspective of a subject in experimental settings further in Chapter 6.

The crucial questions are about the *semantic* features of the situation; the rules of meaningful language-use which are ultimately the only environment within which the differing interpretations of the parties will reach accommodation. By virtue of haggling over properties and meanings, successive dimensions are added to the original formulation of a concept or theory. The relevant methodology is one which involves the mutual exploration of concepts; a form of discourse which is characteristically philosophical and discursive.

6 Between Our Ears?

> The idea of a process in the head, in a completely enclosed space, makes thinking something occult. "Thinking takes place in the head" really means only "the head is connected with thinking." Of course one says also "I think with my pen" and this localisation is at least as good. (Wittgenstein, 1974 p. 106)

> Without the development of an exosomatic descriptive language - a language which, like a tool, develops outside the body - there can be *no object* for our critical discussion. But with the development of a descriptive language (and further, of a written language), a linguistic third world can emerge; and it is only in this way, and only in this third world, that the problems and standards of rational criticism can develop...I suggest that one day we will have to revolutionize psychology by looking at the human mind as an organ for interacting with the objects of the third world... (Popper, 1972, p. 120 and p. 156)

Cognition as a cultural phenomenon

The concepts and categories which structure our views of reality and our situation within it are products of cultural evolution; of social and political history. To concede a universal naturalistic basis for them is not necessarily inconsistent with that claim but neither is it to say as much as many theorists have wished. Basic obstacles frustrate attempts to extrapolate an unambiguous order from the computational matrix so widely believed to underpin the variety of human ideas and cultural expressions. As a result, descriptions of thinking as processes within individual minds are destined to be incoherent, or at least so problematical that they are a seriously inadequate resource for educational theory and for a theory of critical thinking. Nor is my foregoing reference to political history casual; the critical component of thought is implicated in ideas about the nature of authority. Social relationships are reciprocally indebted to ideas about the authenticity of moral, legal and religious values as well as to criteria of reason and truth embodied, but also often in conflict, in science, philosophy and the arts. Essential features of thought are thus obscured by a preoccupation with the operations of individual minds in a cultural vacuum, for social interactions do not simply provide a context for modes of thought; in crucial respects they must be regarded as constitutive of them.

Chomsky and Pinker attribute political significance to their concept of innate linguistic and mental universals as a bulwark against the manipulation of personality and belief. Pinker's optimism about the indestructibility of concepts of freedom and equality does not fit comfortably with historical evidence of the sustainability of repressive authoritarian cultures but I mention it again, here, to stress how readily interpretations of the respective roles of *nature* and *nurture* in the development of language and thought express themselves as theories of society and politics. This anticipates my later discussion of Mill, whose emphasis on the indefinite, universal potential and equality of human abilities does not sacrifice awareness of the different ways in which they can be expressed and *suppressed* within cultures. The issue of critical thinking is pivotal for Mill in realising those potentials; in achieving freedom and equality by liberating people's minds from the crippling effects of dogma and prejudice. And for Popper, the cultural dimension is also definitive; the traditions of critical thinking emerged briefly in Greece before being submerged by alternative social conventions for more than a millennium until the Galilean revolution (Popper, 1963, p. 151).

A great deal depends, then, on how much we can say about the natural organisation of the individual human mind, and how confidently we can ascribe the substantives of language and thought to it. In the present chapter, I examine problems confronting that enterprise, maintaining that the characterising features of language and thought are semantic and dialogic. If the individual mind is bracketed-off from this cultural nexus of meaningful exchange, its content evaporates.

Frank Smith comments sceptically on a current educational preoccupation with connections between words describing aspects of everyday thinking like 'remembering', 'deducing' or 'expecting' and specific brain functions, as well as a related tendency to conflate the latter with *skills* which are learned and improved by instruction (Smith, 1992, p. 6). Norris, for instance, has countered McPeck's *a priori* argument for the domain specificity of thought by calling for scientific investigation of mental structures and processes, which he once compared directly with physical processes, as a necessary step towards understanding familiar abilities like arithmetical calculation (McPeck, 1990, pp. 68-9). Although I will not canvass the difficulties posed by views of this kind as objections to one way of investigating individual cognition, they do place severe constraints on what we should expect it to achieve, particularly in educational settings where research inspired by the idea of determinate cognitive processes has been influential. Teaching critical thinking is not a matter of adopting operational definitions; it requires the elucidation and critical appraisal of certain cultural traditions. And that is not a finite task but one which should constantly infuse the world of education.

Critical thinking *at any level* involves creative interpretation of accepted rules of sound reasoning and inquisitiveness about their epistemological status and wider implications. These implications are infinite, a result of the constant exfoliation of linguistic meaning in social relationships to produce a matrix of interrelated ideas. That is why critical thought can effect cognitive transformations leading to the revision of what may once have been regarded as part of the 'categorical apparatus' of a mode of inquiry (Popper, 1969, p. 220). But such unpredictability must qualify any conception of determinate, underlying processes and structures of thought which translate so readily into programmatic teaching methods. I wish to canvass an alternative; widespread extension of the characteristically open ended discipline of philosophical dialogue throughout education and the progressive dismantling of institutional constraints on conceptual inquiry to liberate the potential of children, in particular, for critical thinking.

A major theoretical constraint on such a learner-centred educational approach is the common belief that language and thought must be understood, fundamentally, as operations of individual minds; that the appropriate way of investigating thought is through analysis of the formal characteristics of these operations and that research of this kind will indicate appropriate pedagogic strategies. Yet there is no settled way of deciding at what point the study of cognition becomes the study of language, or the study of language the study of social intercourse and history. These things are at least as indispensable to an understanding of thinking as anything contained 'between the ears' of the subjects of empirical research. And the present chapter is concerned with the very widespread belief in the possibility of a 'bottom-up' account of cognition and the fallacious pedagogical conclusions which may be drawn as a result.

The biological basis of cognition and 'psychologism'

This perspective on *mind* is so widely accepted that it has become a tacit presupposition of much teaching and research. Symptomatic of the approach is a belief that studies of artistic creativity may safely disregard aesthetic criteria in the search for 'underlying' psychological abilities (for example, Vernon, 1970, pp. 9-10). Of course, the cognitivist perspective encompasses varying theoretical stances, from the naive to the extremely sophisticated. What they tend to share, however, is a commitment to the idea of determinate psychological processes and to their primal efficacy in the thought and behaviour of individuals and *thence* in social processes.

Evidence of the ideological status of this nuclear concept of mind is contained in literature at the popular end of the thinking skills market. Authors are inclined to preface works with tendentious portrayals of brain physiology (sometimes copiously illustrated) in order to establish the 'scientific' status of their prescriptions (for example, Buzan, 1982, 1988). One recent invitation for the public to join *The Learning Revolution* even contains a section on 'simple tips on brain food' (Dryden and Vos, 1994) and much of the popular literature is awash with references to neurones, dendrites, glial cells and left-right brain functions. The magnetic attraction of this physicalist imagery is implicated in neglect of the social dynamics of language and thought and, consequently, in a lack of sensitivity to institutional rigidities which inhibit the creative participation of the learner in her own education.

Popper rejects both the psychologistic idea of the nuclear individual and the ubiquitous illusion that, 'knowledge is a special kind of belief, or a state of mind' - a prejudice he ascribes to the *subjectivist theory of knowledge* and for which he substitutes the concept of 'epistemology *without* a knowing subject' (for example, Popper, 1972, p. 75 and p. 108, my emphasis). His alternative conception of 'world 3', an autonomous human product of accumulating ideas, concepts, arguments, contradictions and errors has the merit of emphasising the staggering diversity and lack of uniformity in the history of what are so often designated 'cognitive processes' - as well as the social conditions which facilitate or inhibit access to this legacy, a central theme in his contrast between 'open' and 'closed' societies. Popper's refutation of 'subjective epistemology' is of a piece with his denial that there is something primal in the constitution of individual minds which authenticates the investigation of language, thought and social institutions in terms of individual psychology. Instead, he emphasises the historical accumulation of ideas through discourse and argument, comprising, not 'epistemic bedrock' but the living material of the critical traditions and the unanticipated possibilities for the development of thought they contain.

A highly articulated version of the alternative convention is Piaget's educationally influential theory of cognitive stages in individual development, part of what Dennis Phillips describes as an unsuccessful 'attempt to orient the foundations of epistemology towards biology and psychology' (Phillips, 1982, p. 13-29). Piaget's enterprise has also been described as 'a search for structure irrespective of content' (Modgil and Modgil, 1982, p. 2). The quest for abstract structure is a plausible intermediate step towards an understanding of thought as brute, physiological process but I believe it is fraught with paradox and fails the ultimate test of distinguishing between the form, content and social context of utterances at a level sufficiently fundamental to vindicate the theory.

The general conception of mind as brain-function, however qualified, too easily places misleading constructions on some powerful evidence from neuroscience; evidence which should not be disregarded but placed in its proper perspective. A chasm still separates our grasp of brain physiology from our understanding of the most rudimentary psychological or intellectual processes. It is quite conceivable that a revolution in our conceptual repertoire, analogous to quantum or 'chaos' theory, would be necessary to provide coherent bridging principles. Nevertheless, we are right to be impressed, as Pinker is, with the linguistic (not to mention computational, graphic and other) performances of a few people known disrespectfully as *'idiots savants'* who may exhibit what he calls 'good language and bad cognition' (Pinker, 1995, pp. 50-54). A vocabulary and grammatical structure which appear to greatly exceed a speaker's understanding of the significance of her words seems compelling evidence of innate, highly structured physiological mechanisms. So, too, are the reported abilities of others to perform prodigious calculations while apparently unaware of *how*, or of relevant and irrelevant applications of those abilities. Of course we all share an inability to describe *how* we do seemingly simple things (like performing, in an instant, the labyrinthine mathematical calculations apparently necessary to catch a flying ball). But perhaps we should be equally impressed by this absence of a sense of relevant application which seems to distinguish the 'savant' from the more familiar 'prodigy'. For what is not in dispute, here, is the necessity for underlying computational functions of an astronomical order if the simplest proposition or thought is to be conceived in terms of mind-brain connections. What *is* in dispute is the prospect of describing these connections coherently, let alone of developing an educationally valid methodology on the basis of a theory which postulates them.

Preoccupation with the brain-mind connection has tended to preempt the investigation of intellectual abilities by repeatedly studying individual competences on predetermined tasks, evidently because they are regarded as the most suitable kind of base for comparing differential performances, whether these are conceived as age- or ability-related. Methodological emphasis is on 'objective' empirical evidence, as against the uncertainties involved in evaluating performance according to concepts and standards instantiated by traditional disciplines, debatable as these invariably are at some level. The salient point is that this distinction between socio-cultural and individual-cognitivist approaches is not just a matter of needing to take account of *interactions* between individuals in the characterisation of language and thought. Whatever the innate features of the individual mind, its behavioural and linguistic precipitates are modes of cultural expression which are qualitatively different. Vygotsky argues for just such a distinction between elementary psychological functions and the higher functions into which they are transformed by assimilation to a culture. The radicalism of his claim is clear in his insistence, against Piaget, that this is not to say simply that there is an interaction between *external* social processes and *internal* cognitive processes in the individual such that both sets may be conceived as distinct areas of investigation:

> Biological factors appear as primeval, original forces composing the psychological substance of the child's mind. Social factors act as an external, "alien" force

> which...replaces the original biological modes of mental life...Piaget does not see a child as part of the social whole. Social factors are shown as an external force that enters the child's mind and dislodges the forms of thinking inherent in the child's intelligence. (Vygotsky, 1989, pp. 44-45)

> ...the first use of signs demonstrates that there cannot be a single organically predetermined internal system of activity that exists for each psychological function. The use of artificial means, the transition to mediated activity, fundamentally changes all psychological operations... (ibid, p. 55)

Whatever our commitment to the idea, *in principle*, of a physical basis for cognition, it cannot provide a satisfactory foundation for the analysis of language and thought because they are influenced dynamically by socially mediated activities; dialogue, practical collaboration, gesture and symbolism. Yet physicalism helps to sustain a mirage of determinate structures and processes, liable to encourage a narrow, skill-oriented pedagogy which obscures the most crucial feature of thinking; that it cannot be captured in finitely specifiable, symbolic form without distortion. Hyland condemns an accelerating trend towards 'competence models of education and training' though he attributes it to a largely defunct *behaviourist* philosophy which also attempts to dispense with internalised meanings in the attempt to attain a level of 'objective' description. As a result, Hyland claims, knowledge and understanding are consistently downgraded against performance on tasks of a stipulative kind:

> All this poses a serious threat, not just to general education, but to any form of education concerned with rationality in teaching and learning and even remotely concerned with the development of knowledge and understanding. (Hyland, 1993, pp. 57-66)

One fault in current educational trends which Hyland draws attention to is an underestimation of the importance of the incomplete, the ambiguous and the conjectural in human dialogue. It is necessary, of course, to represent the operations involved in mathematical calculation (for example) in symbolic form. Symbolic and algorithmic systems are essential tools. But they embody an *ex post facto logic* which does not fully replicate the processes involved in thinking and discovery, a point emphasised by the physicist, Richard Feynman, which I will return to later in this chapter.

The foregoing considerations notwithstanding, many influential efforts to describe formal, abstract characteristics of language and thought have been predicated on the idea that this is an appropriate route to an understanding of physiological infrastructures. Piaget and Chomsky are two eminent exponents of this approach, though they disagree fundamentally on the nature, scope and origins of the 'structures' in question. This conflict of interpretations is instructive. It exposes deep paradoxes in what is probably the most widely held and practically influential view of thinking and its various manifestations; that it is *in principle* reducible to mental states and ultimately, states of the individual organism, though Chomsky repeatedly emphasises the remoteness of such a prospect.

Constructivism versus *nativism*

The difference between the concepts of physical infrastructure represented by Piagetian *constructivism* and Chomskian *innatism* has been expressed succinctly by Seymour Papert as; '...not whether something has to be there from the beginning, but rather *how much* and what kind of something' (Seymour Papert in Piatelli-Palmarini, 1980, p. 268, original emphasis). Piaget's *constructivism* minimises the genetically determined 'fixed nucleus', attributing complexities of structure to successive accommodations by the individual organism to an external environment - which, of course, includes other individuals. By contrast, Chomsky and his followers regard this 'fixed nucleus' as highly specified; to the extent of claiming, by analogy with his idea of an organically determined human linguistic faculty, that numerous human cognitive functions are likely to be pre-programmed and merely 'triggered' by environmental influences, a position shared by Jerry Fodor (Piatelli-Palmarini, 1980, p. 172).

It should be noted that each of these contrasting positions involves a paradox. If, as Piaget maintains, cognitive development is the result of adjustment to external factors a problem arises about how such learning is conceivable in the absence of 'pre-programmed' cognitive structures of sufficient complexity to make possible (a) the recognition, and (b) the assimilation of new concepts and conceptual schemata, a radical objection to constructivism by Fodor, concerning the irreducibility of logical form and learning theory in general (Piatelli-Palmarini, 1980, p. 143). In a manner reminiscent of the theme of *recollection* in Plato's *Meno,* Chomsky and Fodor maintain that very particular features of human language and understanding must be inborn; a universal, inherited language of thought, described by Fodor and adopted by Pinker as 'mentalese'. Piaget's response is to expose another paradox, apparent in such preformationist stances; that a newborn baby would possess 'virtually everything that Galois, Cantor, Hilbert, Bourbaki or MacLane have since been able to realize'. The nativist line of reasoning, by virtue of its postulate of the irreducibility of logical form, pushes explanations of advanced intellectual performance back to the physical attributes of bacteria and viruses, at least for all those who accept the perspective of biological evolution.

Chomsky's idea of a language acquisition device provides a model of what he suspects to be the universal characteristic of cognitive functions; *'a fixed, genetically determined system of some sort (which) narrowly constrains the forms they can assume.'* The principal evidence for his innatist conclusion is the famous argument that the child's use of language is massively underdetermined by the linguistic experience available in any human environment. This evidence *for* innate mechanisms was deployed effectively by Chomsky against behaviourist descriptions of language acquisition as a system of responses to environmental stimuli. Yet there are serious difficulties about the nature of these mechanisms. They arise partly because of the arbitrariness of the decision to treat syntax as an independently analysable system of abstract, formal relationships, and to ascribe the creativity of language to properties of that system, like recursiveness, which make it theoretically possible to produce an infinity of intelligible sentences from finite syntactic rules. In Chomsky's words:

> ...a grammar, represented somehow in the mind, as a system that specifies the phonetic, syntactic, and semantic properties of an infinite class of potential sentences. (ibid., p. 35)

This formulation strongly suggests an asymmetrical dependence of semantic meaning on syntax although Chomsky seems to equivocate between qualitative and quantitative uses of the idea of creativity. He appears to conceive it both as an endless proliferation of grammatical sentences and, more conventionally, as a way of understanding how those sentences relate meaningfully to the world. But the idea that syntactic and semantic aspects of language are sufficiently distinguishable to establish the priority of the former over the latter as the basic dynamic of linguistic meaning and creativity is very questionable, I will argue. Nevertheless, a system of context-free, abstract, structural relationships *is* one kind of thing which would help the nativist to distinguish particular features of language from socially mediated learning and which, consequently, may be identified as inherent characteristics of the individual organism. This requirement was once articulated by Fodor in a critique of 'ordinary-language philosophy'. The human ability to produce utterances not previously encountered;

> ...must rely upon mechanisms which are recursive, and hence it cannot be reduced to any properties of the (necessarily finite) lexicon of the language. (Fodor and Katz, 1971, p. 270)

If languages contained only a finite resource of 'lexical items' it might be credible that the explanation for the language-user's ability to produce an infinity of meaningful sentences is to be found in the modes of composition described as syntax. But this disjunction between syntactic mechanisms and the meaningful components of language rests on that illicit presupposition that the latter are 'necessarily finite', a contention which I dispute here and in subsequent chapters. Of course, Fodor's distinction does not imply total mutual exclusion. The intelligibility of utterances or sentences is logically prior to the identification of any grammatical structure embedded in them, a consideration which he qualifies by saying that an elucidation of the 'compositional mechanisms' requires *not only* a characterisation of the meaning of words in language but of the functional relationships which tie them into meaningful sentences. Yet the initial requirement of intelligibility is minimised by Fodor's assertion of the finitude of the lexicon because this move seems to indicate *syntactic recursivity* as the source of infinite linguistic creativity. Usually, he argues, 'the meaning of a word or expression varies depending on its grammatical role in context' and, '...the development of a theory of semantics requires the prior elaboration of a theory of syntax'.

Fodor's case implies an unjustifiably restricted, 'atomic' conception of semantic meaning, perhaps the result of a tradition in linguistics of analysing sentences and sentence-parts which Bruner has described as the 'small detail' of speech. Of course, it is true that the meaning of a word varies according to its grammatical role in a sentence; but there are other parameters determining the meaning of utterances which obviate such a neatly articulated relationship between grammatical functions and the meanings of component words. The point can be demonstrated by one example from what must be an indefinitely large number of possible sentences which appear at first sight to be grammatically and semantically unproblematic; for example, *'The sun is hot'*.

In the paper cited above, Fodor argues for 'a unique assignment of semantic properties to lexical items,' adding that a theory of meaning is vacuous if it cannot determine when two lexical items exhibit the same, or different, semantic properties. However, *contexts of discourse* are equally relevant in the assignment of meaning to words in sentences and there is no privileged theoretical standpoint from which we can determine the boundaries of those contexts. Consider the implications of qualifying the sample sentence at the end of the last paragraph as follows:

a) 'The sun is hot.............*(- let's have a cold drink!)'*
b) 'The sun is hot ....*(- about 6,000 degrees Centigrade at its surface.)'*

Example (a) is arguably quite different to (b) in that the quality 'hot' might not necessarily predicated of 'the sun' at all, but possibly concerns the general ambience of a summer afternoon. One might as well say 'It's hot - let's have a cold drink!' On the other hand, (b) involves a very specific reference to both subject and predicate, but in a manner which imports certain elements of the cognitive repertoire of modern science. My point is not just that the immediate context of utterance impacts on the semantic role of words and their grammatical relationships, though this is true, but that in the investigation of the meanings of even such simple utterances as 'the sun is hot' or 'the sea is deep' we are faced with the prospect of an indefinite recession of semantically relevant contexts, including facets of the historical evolution of language and ideas.

Languages are both syntactically and semantically recursive. The impossibility of establishing a criterion of semantic identity between any two uses of a single word is even more apparent in the seminal role played by metaphor in extending word-meaning, a point I will develop in the next chapter. Any given word might have an indefinite range of contextualised meanings and the lexicon of a natural language is not finite for this reason. Recursivity cannot be defined in a sense sufficiently independent of social contexts of discourse to justify the prioritisation of formal, syntactic relationships as determinants of semantic meaning. 'Unique assignment' of the semantic properties of words is not possible. Even if it were held to be possible in *some* cases, or classes of cases, the attempted demonstration would inevitably remain in debt to semantic features within it which remained unanalysed in this way.

The impulse to adopt the approach in question might be largely explained by a later observation of Fodor's; that it is important to be able to isolate the fundamental structural features of language, 'or some other interesting psychological sub-domain', because unless one of these sub-domains could be studied 'in a truly independent way' explanation would become too difficult (Piatelli-Palmarini, 1980, p. 270). I will argue in the following chapter that no such separation is feasible because semantic meaning permeates cognition and is a function of cultural history. But it is in the commitment to the specifiability of abstract structures *at the level of the individual mind* that the problem lies; not in any concrete claims which Piaget or Chomsky make about the intrinsic structure of the organism:

> We can leave open for the future the question of how these abstract structures and processes are realized...in some concrete terms, conceivably in terms that are not within the range of physical processes as presently understood... (Chomsky, 1972, p. 14)

Chomsky's view of the nature of the innate 'fixed nucleus'

Chomsky emphasises the significance of linguistics for psychology, identifying both subjects as 'ultimately part of human biology' (Chomsky, 1990, p. 627). He also suggests that a specifically human language-capacity is one of what may be many specialised cognitive functions, susceptible to rigorous theoretical analysis. This idea of ultimate physical explanations of language and thought, even in the sophisticated Chomskian version, is a powerful cynosure exerting constraints on methodology, directing attention to the structural aspects of language. There is an incentive to frame the conceptual apparatus of inquiry so that secondary manifestations of primary physical processes may be analysed in a manner presumed to be *somehow* commensurate with the dynamics of physical causation. Chomsky's position can be summarised as follows:

a. that the physical basis of language is not only *unknown*, but that it may prove incomprehensible according to present understandings of physical processes, and

b. that the appropriate method of inquiry in linguistics is therefore to try to develop an 'abstract theoretical apparatus' which would reveal, independently, principles according to which language and other aspects of mental activity are organised, and

c. that only at some future stage might the attempt be made to relate these abstract principles to physiological mechanisms.

The crucial difficulty facing such a programme is the absence of any method which it envisages (on present understanding, by Chomsky's own admission) for testing whether the formal analysis of language (or thought) corresponds to any fundamental principles of physiological organisation and functioning. Chomsky's solution, the identification of syntactic forms, or other abstract structures, as independently analysable variables must be arbitrary; a choice determined by general conjectures about the probable nature of this *unknown* physical basis. This does not appear to obviate the major difficulty involved in the tautology (which he recognises as 'an obvious truth' but without accepting it as trivial) that all mental processes are *somehow* expressions of physical processes.

This difficulty is as follows: all human experience, all thought or language, is structured in a multiplicity of ways; the alternative is incomprehensible. The physicalist tautology requires that structure of this kind entails structure of some kind in the 'concrete basis.' Yet to say anything significant at all about this latter conception of physical structure, it would be necessary to discriminate within an indefinitely large body of overt linguistic usages, beliefs, and theories in order to identify a limited range of abstract forms which are most productive and therefore elemental. This is essentially the same exercise as Piaget's - the search for universal, generative forms. Chomsky believes that syntactic rules (such as those which seem to apply in the cases of 'bound anaphora' and the 'specified subject condition') are susceptible to this kind of isolation and that they are evidence of the existence of universal physiological constraints.

An objection to Chomsky's enterprise comes from within his own nativist school of thought - and the principle expressed in his words to elucidate Fodor's refutation of constructivism; 'the resources of all the innumerable systems that ever may be invented...are already fixed' (Piatelli-Palmarini, 1980, p. 157). I think Fodor's rejection of the possibility of moving from elementary logical systems to more complex ones by a learning process entails the conclusion that neither Chomsky's nor Piaget's 'abstract theoretical structures' can ever be more than arbitrary, stipulative characterisations of features of language and thought. They *are* arbitrary and stipulative because there can be no way of demonstrating that one formal structure is more elemental than another; the mode of implication from simple to complex concepts within a uniformly abstract system is simultaneous and co-extensive with that system as a whole. And Fodor's refutation of learning theory exploits this feature of abstract systems.

Fodor's rejection of learning-theory - and its significance

Fodor disputes not only Piaget's account of cognitive development by stages and its origin in sensorimotor intelligence, but *any* developmental account of cognition. He establishes a circularity from which it is impossible to break into the fields of physical determination, on the one hand, and semantics and socio-historical development on the other.

> I'll argue not only that there is no learning theory but that in certain senses there certainly *couldn't* be; the very *idea* of concept learning is, I think, confused. (Piatelli-Palmarini, 1980, p. 143)

The crux of Fodor's argument is that whether any given level of cognitive development is conceived as a result of organic predetermination or organism-environment interaction, it must, as a matter of logical necessity, subsume the forms of all subsequent stages. Attempts to save some notion of the acquisition of increasingly powerful cognitive structures by postulating a 'dynamic Kantian' principle', as Piaget does (ibid., p. 150) are destined to founder because, says Fodor, theories about the conceptual plasticity of the organism fail to obviate a strict requirement. This is that in order for us to begin to conceive of, to hypothesise or formulate more powerful concepts, they must already be inherent in *some* sense. He insists that the possibility of this ontogenetic process requires *at least* the capacity at any given stage to hypothesise (anticipate) the logical form of the succeeding stage. This condition, Fodor argues, remains unaffected by the qualification that development from *Stage 0* to *Stage n* involves 'feedback' or trial and error procedures. Whatever mechanisms are invoked, all entail the conclusion that the more complex logical structures are present in some form at elementary levels; the appropriateness of a hypothetical projection from *Stage O* would be determined by its prior correspondence with more complex conceptual schemata of *Stage n*.

What Piaget depicts as sensorimotor activity leading to the *construction* of complex concepts, Fodor interprets as a 'triggering' function which simply activates them. This notion of 'triggering' which he shares with Chomsky, is the demarcation between constructivism and nativism. Somehow, it was all there from the start. The alternatives are limited, Fodor suggests; 'God does it for you on Tuesdays, or you do it by falling on your head, or it is innate' (ibid., p. 155). Here is a deep paradox in the physicalist conception of the origins of thought which, *in some form*, Chomsky asserts, is the only alternative to mysticism. (ibid., p. 263). If we are committed to the notion of physical correlates or causes of all mental phenomena, we appear to be equally committed to the view that all past and future possibilities of thought are immanent at some level in the structure of our physiology.

Fodor's rejection of learning recalls Hume's scepticism about causality or Zeno's paradoxical conclusion that Achilles cannot overtake the tortoise. Just as concepts of cause and the outcomes of differential speeds over given distances are integral to our descriptions of reality, there is everyday evidence of learners acquiring richer conceptual systems on the basis of simpler ones. This, in ordinary language, is what we mean by 'learning' - as Socrates remarks to Meno in the course of his demonstration of 'recollected' knowledge (Plato, Meno, 81, D). Fodor's scepticism might suggest that here is an example of a category-error which misappropriates the concept of *learning* or, that he uses it as a technicality which is irrelevant to questions of educational method. What Fodor's argument actually shows, I believe, is that to abstract formal schemata from the dynamics of thinking and learning is to court the danger of mistaking a model for the essential elements of cognitive systems. But the abstract schemata of logic or mathematics are not *systems* in the requisite sense because their modes of implication are simultaneous and infinite (if incompletely understood). They are refinements of language; *products* of sequential developments from simple to complex concepts through extensions of linguistic meaning.

Yet for this reason, the arguments articulated by Chomsky and Fodor do undermine Piaget's developmental epistemology, leaving a wealth of empirical observations, the value of which may be largely independent of his attempt to achieve a formal level of description compatible with the idea of physiological process. And despite his occasional warnings about the danger of drawing premature pedagogical conclusions from pure research, Piaget's notion of staged development has exercised a major theoretical and practical influence on both educational research and practice (for example, Boyle, 1982, pp. 291-308 and Tamburrini, 1982, pp. 309-325).

Some empirical studies of 'cognitive stages'

Piagetian theory has become a subject of increasing controversy, in some cases because predictions central to the theory have not been confirmed by subsequent empirical research and in others because ingenious variations on the original Genevan test procedures have cast doubt on the status of key concepts. Many of these studies are well known and are referred to here only because of their bearing on the subject of this chapter; the powerful but misleading cynosure exerted by concepts of underlying form, structure or syntax in thought and language. Two critics, Linda Siegel and Barbara Hodkin refer to *methodological* problems in the study of cognitive development within a Piagetian framework, suggesting that assessments of traditional task-performances have often conflated *variables* like social factors, language and attention with cognitive performance:

> The results of the various studies discussed show that in cognitive development tasks we are studying more than logical ability. Ignoring the effects of social context, language, perception attention and memory is particularly illogical when one wants to infer, as many investigators do, the lack of a cognitive operation from an incorrect response. There are many possible reasons for an incorrect response and unless one considers this interpretation, serious errors of inference will be made. (Siegel and Hodkin, 1982, p. 65)

However, the issues in question are not just methodological; they are conceptual and philosophical; the reference to 'variables' leaves intact a spurious notion of cognition *per se*. Siegel and Hodkin build on this emphasis by suggesting a need for 'control and study of the other relevant factors' - implying the possibility of isolating them by experimental means. I suggest that a more appropriate conclusion from the empirical evidence which these authors review is that other factors are not only involved in the assessment of cognitive performance, they are logically and inextricably implicated in it. Manifestations of cognition can be elicited only through linguistic exchange or some other language-dependant method of communication. And the more communication is restricted to eliminate contamination by such 'non-cognitive variables' the less control the researcher has over perceptions, by the subject, of the experimental parameters; her performance becomes a matter of arbitrary interpretation. This is not to deny that by varying experimental apparatus and verbal communication we might gain greater insight into the way children and other subjects think, as indeed variations on Piaget's procedures demonstrate. But that insight will not be into the 'forms of thinking inherent in the child's intelligence' with which Vygotsky takes issue. Social factors, language, thought and perception are not radically distinguishable, a conclusion from these reappraisals of the Piagetian system which I believe is reasonable but uncongenial to aspirations for a 'bottom-up' account of thought and its characteristics.

Most of the studies cited by Siegel and Hodkin concern the central Piagetian idea of stages of increasing cognitive complexity. Consequently they have a direct bearing on the general question of what is involved in the search for unambiguous descriptions of particular cognitive configurations, including Piaget's characterisations of *egocentric* and *animistic* thought in children. Thus, for example, some studies have suggested that conservation of mass develops earlier than conservation of weight and (last of all) volume. Siegel and Hodkin observe that when a putative operation like conservation develops 'it is presumably available to the child...and should not vary with the situation' because 'these conservations are all characterised by *the same process*' (my italics). Although they conclude that differentials in the performance of tasks do not support the stage-model of cognitive development, they do so on the ground that this is 'a result of perceptual, attention and memory effects.' A similar conclusion is reached about cases in which deliberate training has enabled 'pre-operational' children of three and four years of age to solve conservation and class-inclusion problems; 'assessment of cognitive ability is often confounded by effects from *non-logical sources.*' (ibid., pp. 63-65, my italics).

Terminology of this kind supports a picture of cognitive organisation as a constant obscured by variables which intrude into the experimental procedure. But the evidence Siegel and Hodkin cite might just as well be interpreted to mean that cognitive development is logically indistinguishable from language-use, social relationships, perceptual abilities, memory, attention and affective states. Again, there seems to be an assumption here that a determinate relationship *must* obtain between the formal abstractions of logic and mental activity. Indeed, distinctions drawn in ordinary usage between language, perception and so forth seem to be accepted uncritically as tokens of functions of mind which are ancillary to cognition. And, for reasons I will consider, below, the idea of cognition *per se* cannot be found a secure anchorage in logical operations conceived in such a foundational sense.

Piaget's system of genetic epistemology explicitly underwrites this latter sense; structural 'equilibrations' between organism and environment are *the* mode of conceptual development: 'What happens during the sensori-motor level...will constitute the substructure of the subsequent, fully achieved ideas of permanent objects, space, time, and causality' (Piaget, 1970, p. 357). But I believe that at the postulated level there is no conceivable way of distinguishing abstract logical forms from the conventions of language we use to describe and communicate them.

Variations of standard procedures, such as the use of familiar toys in Piagetian tests of egocentricity, intended to 'simplify logical tasks for children by reducing linguistic requirements' (Siegel and Hodkin, 1982, p. 62) may also be described as removing some gratuitous ambiguities inherent in the language used by adults to present tasks to youthful subjects. This approach has undoubtedly been informative and has highlighted the opacity of questions like one asked to test subjects' grasp of the logic of class-inclusion; 'Are there more red flowers or more flowers?' However, insight is achieved at the expense of ambiguities of a different kind. It has been argued in defence of the conventional forms of presentation that; 'removing the conflict between incompatible cues...also removes the problem' (Voneche and Bovet, 1982, p. 89). The image of a template of uncontaminated logical potential is maintained by Siegel and Hodkin, however, in their rebuttal of a claim by Larsen that such experimental variations on standard Piagetian test procedures amounts to the specification of 'qualitatively different tasks'. They interpret the relevant difference as *different operational definitions* of the same 'structures', adding that 'it seems to us that children must use the logical ability in question to succeed on the alternative tasks' (ibid., p. 62).

Conservation of the idea of invariant logical structure is displayed by another critic of stage-theory, Margaret Donaldson. Although extremely sensitive to the role of linguistic meaning in experimenter-subject interaction on standard Piagetian tasks, Donaldson also tends to be influenced by the cynosure of very particular logical forms as definitive of operations. In Chapter 2, I considered her suggestion that differential performances on the *Wason Card Test* are attributable to a greater 'human sense' embodied in modified test materials which, she considers, nevertheless involve 'the *same* task as regards logical structure' (Donaldson, 1990, p. 81). My suggestion, there, was that the two versions of the test were not isomorphic; that the 'logical structure' of the respective tests is inextricable from the language (and language-related relationships, including gestures and symbols) *necessarily* involved in the specification of the tasks. In proportion to increasing efforts to 'pare the task down' to its elements, the more evident it becomes that linguistic conventions are being proposed and these involve *restrictions* and *extensions* of the meaning of terms used in everyday language. Yet Donaldson's idea of 'human sense', and her associated ideas of 'embedded and disembedded' modes of thought are vague but useful indications of the direction in which an answer might lie. I suggest this vagueness arises because she tends towards a psychological rather than a logical conception of 'human sense'. The fluid, multiform textures of everyday thought and discourse are depicted as though they cloud purer structures related to them in a deep, infrastructural sense. This idea touches on a theme in Wittgenstein's philosophy, for example in passages of the *Philosophical Investigations:*

> We want to say that there can't be any vagueness in logic. The idea now absorbs us, that the ideal *"must"* be found in reality. Meanwhile we do not as yet see *how* it occurs there, nor do we understand the nature of this "must". We think it must

> be in reality for we think we already see it there...The strict and clear rules of the logical structure of propositions appear to us as something in the background - hidden in the medium of the understanding...(Logical structure) is like a pair of glasses on our noses through which we see whatever we look at. It never occurs to us to take them off... We predicate of the thing what lies in the method of representing it... (Wittgenstein, 1968, PI, 101, 102, 103 and 104)

Logical *simplification*, the process of abstraction, in other words, is a function of *increasing* semantic complexity; a development of ordinary language using the devices of metaphor and analogy to make explicit what is most general about the intelligibility of language. Like the abstract relationships of mathematics, logic needs to be learned as an activity in order to be fully intelligible. Even *within* mathematics, the idea of 'multiplication' undergoes a conceptual metamorphosis, a metaphorical extension, when applied to fractions or negative numbers.

As though in confirmation of this point, a seven year old when asked, 'Are there more red ones or more marbles?' described this standard Piagetian class inclusion question as 'dumb' and considered the experimental task 'a trick'. Siegel and Hodkin report that he knew 'the correct answer' but recount the case in terms unflattering to the child as one of 'language problems in comprehension' *(ibid., p. 61)*. But he was absolutely correct to criticise the application of this use of the term 'more' in a *novel* language game, the rules of which had been concealed from him by a kind of trickery!

The notion of 'isomorphism'

In his criticism of Piaget's genetic epistemology, Phillips refers to a passage by Feldman and Toulmin consistent with the last sentence of Wittgenstein's which I quoted. It concerns the fallacy involved in judgments of isomorphism between the properties of abstract, formal systems and cognitive functions :

> Just because the theoretical system in question can plausibly be presented as corresponding to some mental system in the mind of the actual child, we may be led to conclude that the formalism of the theoretical system must be directly represented by an isomorphic formalism in the mind of the child...In this way, ontological reality is assigned to the hypothetical mental structures of the theory simply on the basis of the formal expressions by which they are represented in the theory. (Phillips, 1982, p. 23)

Nor do the difficulties associated with this notion of *isomorphism* stand as objections to Piagetian theory alone. They must defeat any attempt to describe thought and language in terms of abstract, formal structures because there is an ambiguity in this concept of 'sameness of form' which can be resolved only by reference to the intentional states of the observer and the observed and the manner in which they articulate these states in a context of dialogue. Nor can this be a final resolution, capable of being confirmed or refuted by reference to criteria beyond those embedded in the semantics of that dialogue. Strictly speaking, the debate about whether or not standard Piagetian tests and modified versions of them are of the same logical form is nugatory because there *is no single criterion of what 'the same' logical form is* - except *within* the conventions of a formal discipline like logic or mathematics. In such cases there are, of course, demonstrable agreements between the parties about what a formal structure represents within a given convention. Thus, in the case of class-inclusion statements or simultaneous equations, the criterion of *isomorphism* between the concepts of peers, teachers and learners (or experimenters and subjects) is that the parties can operate with the relevant concepts and terminology within the conventions of logic or mathematics. And this, I suggest, says little about the *differences* which may nevertheless obtain between such individuals' apprehension of 'the same' formal concept.

Piaget's case is that the child adjusts, *equilibrates*, to structural features of the environment. We cannot directly judge the correspondence between the child's adjusted cognitive structures and those of the environment because the latter are mediated by our own cognitive structures. Piaget, indeed, refutes the distinction between 'exogenous' and 'endogenous' structures (Piatelli-Palmarini, 1980, p. 369) but, for the reasons already stated, this move undermines his assertion of 'the isomorphism of conscious implication and of organic causality', making it, in effect, no more than a restatement of the physicalist tautology; that there must be biological correlates of cognitive configurations.

A test of the 'adequacy' of a particular cognitive representation cannot involve appeal to external criteria; the judgment that one theoretical structure is isomorphic with another (or that any two cognitive operations are evidence of identical cognitive configurations) can be justified solely in terms of those structures and their extensions into the wider matrices of formal implication characteristic of mathematics and logic. And the intelligibility of a formal, abstract (content-free) expression is its functional role in such a system of reciprocal implication. But implication and inference are not symmetrical of course. We know, for example, that there are natural numbers beyond anything a human mind will entertain. In a previous chapter I mentioned that a child might grasp an addition function without appreciating its relationship to the multiplication function. Indeed, it is quite conceivable that some adults have mastered simple addition and multiplication without entertaining the idea of such relationships. The problem is even more apparent in, say, the conversion of algorithms from decimal to binary or hexadecimal notations where a change of base amounts to a significant conceptual difference in the expression of the same algorithmic form - and so forth, indefinitely. Formal, systemic functions extend indefinitely and simultaneously in a way which the mental operations for which they are invoked as explanations do not. Consequently, any judgment of *isomorphism* between different expressions of such a system marks a human decision about the relevant parameters rather than a discrete feature of that system which could be attributed unambiguously to the content of a human mind at a given moment.

Mathematicians may adopt *ad hoc* rules governing what is to be regarded as a particular formal identity and logicians may express a preference for simplicity of form (H rather than ~ ~ H, for example). But it is an inescapable feature of abstract systems of this kind that *decisions* have to be made in order to individuate particular functions and isolate them (for didactic purposes or otherwise) from what, by its very nature is an infinite matrix of implication. And these very simple examples indicate why any decision to depict the content of an intentional mental state as a finite set of formal relationships necessarily involves the arbitrary stipulation of a *particular* concept of isomorphism. And more complex examples make something like Popper's conception of an autonomous 'world 3' plausible - because there is no non-arbitrary way of delimiting the implications of a particular facet in the totality of a theoretical system. Its ramifications are, as it were, public rather than private property. Although it will be possible to validate or invalidate particular ways of expressing a theory or belief, there is no sense in which they may be said to be identical in form with the content of any one, or of all minds. This point is illustrated at the 'cutting edges' of rational, scientific thought where physicists and mathematicians may reach different conclusions about the representational value of mathematical models of 'the same' phenomena (Popper, 1963, pp. 100-101; Gleick, 1992, pp. 242-243). Dilemmas of this kind cannot be resolved by appeal to an external set of formal criteria because the contradictions, themselves, represent the most highly articulated account of the relation between logico-mathematical schemata and reality.

One might distinguish between addition and multiplication as *distinct* algorithmic functions and teach them as appropriate to presumed stages of childhood competence, a common pedagogic strategy. Alternatively, one might emphasise the relationship of mutual implication between addition and multiplication and represent them in various ways (using blocks, for example) - incidentally building new conventions into the commonplace meanings of words like 'and' and 'of' and 'times' as well as introducing new terminology like 'plus' and 'add' and 'multiply'. But where the former method represents the basic functions of 'addition' and 'multiplication' as discrete, the latter represents a more extended moment in the indefinitely wide field of mathematical implication - and the limits to be set upon this procedure by stipulating particular algorithmic operations are ultimately arbitrary. Richard Feynman's indictment of the emphasis on method rather than solutions in the 'new math' introduced in Californian grade schools in the 1960's accentuates the dangers of confusing the use of algorithmic tools with an understanding of the conceptual task:

> We must remove the rigidity of thought...We must leave freedom for the mind to wander about in trying to solve the problems...The successful user of mathematics is practically an inventor of new ways of obtaining answers in given situations. Even if the ways are well known, it is usually much easier for him to invent his own way - a new way or an old way - than it is to try to find it by looking it up. (Gleik, 1992, p. 401)

My point is that any attempt to define a particular stage of mathematical inference is to resort to a description of one arbitrarily selected moment in the infinite matrix of mathematical relationships. This is reminiscent of Fodor's scepticism concerning the acquisition of more powerful conceptual schemata on the basis of simpler ones. There is an artificiality in stipulating mutually disjunctive features of such 'moments' within continuous formal systems. For it is hard to see how anyone could be said to have grasped the *logical form* of the addition function (2 + 2) without also having grasped the *logical form* of the multiplication function (2 x 2), though it seems equally clear that there are stages in the acquisition of mathematical competence where it would be wrong to say that ability to add is equivalent to ability to multiply. But if this is conceded, what *formal* limits could be set upon the inferential process? The conclusion that 'it was all there from the start' - at least in *some* sense - is probably the best answer which could be obtained by anyone who believes that the development of human thought can be understood through the formal, combinatorial abstractions of mathematics, syntax or logic.

Form and content

Formal, abstract notations are essential tools, but they embody an *ex post facto* logic which cannot replicate the processes involved in thinking and discovery. This is even true where the intention is to devise a precise calculus for the purpose of explanation in a paradigmatically rigorous discipline like sub atomic physics, where concepts may deviate bizarrely from those of 'common sense' or those used to explain more directly observable aspects of physical reality. Feynman described his experience of problem-solving in quantum theory in these terms:

> What I am really trying to do is bring birth to clarity, which is really a half-assedly thought-out pictorial semi-vision thing...It's all visual. It's hard to explain...Ordinarily I try to get the pictures clearer, but in the end the mathematics can take over and be more efficient in communicating the idea of the picture...In

certain particular problems that I have done it was necessary to continue the development of the picture as the method before the mathematics could really be done. (Gleick, 1992, p. 244)

Feynman, whose notes include remarks on 'the great value of a satisfactory philosophy of ignorance' stresses the dynamic nature of transactions between ambiguous mental 'vision' and the conventions of formal representation which are the media of intersubjective communication and criticism. This recalls the distinction between modes of discovery and modes of justification, though there are dangers in attributing too radical a significance to it. As I believe Feynman's words suggest, the relation between these modes is one of continuing reciprocity. There always remains the possibility of detecting inconsistencies and unanticipated implications in the rigorous, formal proof. If my argument is correct, current educational enthusiasm for the decomposition of modes of thought (whether they are concerned with history, physics or maths) into *problem-solving skills* and the components of *knowledge and understanding* is particularly dangerous because it preempts the *critical* element of critical thinking. The notion of determinate mental skills and data-files abolishes vital distinctions between *real* and *rote* learning. It insinuates a conservative epistemology which sanctions only established paradigms. And the relevant consideration will be whether or not those skills, as they are defined, are acquired by individuals and not whether they are exercised or developed in novel ways or perhaps used to question the epistemic status of particular data-selections. 'The world', Mill complained, 'already knows everything and has only to tell it to its children'. And the parody of innovatory, critical thought which this attitude instantiates is that of a 'future discoverer' who must first:

...learn all that has already been known, and then to commence an entirely new series of intellectual operations in order to enlarge the field of human knowledge. (Mill, 1832)

Mill's alternative portrayal of critical thinking anticipates much that has subsequently been argued by authors like Vygotsky, Bruner and Lipman. This is that the rudiments of critical rationality are acquired from the earliest stages by minds constantly stimulated to reach 'beyond the information given' in dialogue with elders and peers and to discover that there are rigorous ways of investigating *what is not known*, even about the commonplace. Anomalous aspects of the familiar may stimulate inquiry which precipitates revolutionary departures from what Kuhn describes as 'scientific paradigms'. This kind of discovery has been celebrated by Popper with the example of Einstein's revolutionary departure from Newton's system which not only subsumed and extended its predictive force but substituted a fundamentally different account (for example, Popper, 1969, pages 20 and 27). Yet such discoveries are inherently unpredictable from *within* established descriptive or explanatory frameworks. The array of alternative models, metaphors and images from which a more comprehensive or satisfactory explanation may be derived is potentially infinite. These alternatives will also be drawn from previous traditions, but the salient feature of paradigm-breaking theories is that their particular combination of the familiar and the novel involves a move *beyond* the theories they replace, subject to accepted procedures for appraisal. It is tempting to ask what kind of determinate cognitive schemata could satisfactorily represent states of partial understanding, hypothetical attitudes or sudden insights.

Although epoch-making intellectual revolutions may be infrequent, as Kuhn maintains, they *typify critical thought* in a vitally important sense. For, in his own terms, they demonstrate that neither the *occasion* nor the *form* of novel developments are predictable from within the constraints of existing paradigms. Thus cognitive transformations reflect the incompleteness of the paradigms they replace, or the problems and inconsistencies inherent in them, but the 'underlying cognitive processes and structures' are *in principle* no more specifiable than the conceptual innovations for which they might be canvassed as explanations. Another implication is that the distinction between mere violations of an existing 'Kuhnian paradigm' and genuinely creative departures from it must be in terms of the characteristics of both the established and novel theories and their applicability to the field in question; that is, to a tradition of thought. Moreover, I suggest that its unpredictability means that the Kuhnian 'paradigm-shift' cannot be distinguished systematically from other forms of innovatory thought and that it applies generally - to the discovery of novelties, affinities and analogies between concepts in the arts and humanities as well as in everyday speech, humour and poetry, for example. No method exists *in principle* for isolating cognitive processes from the intentional content of the forms in which they are expressed. It is insufficient, for example, to demonstrate the existence of universal linguistic automatisms which constrain forms of expression if the constraints are still consistent with an indefinite proliferation of those forms of expression. The idea of organic structure and process subsumes all past, and future possibilities of thought and the infinite matrix of combinations which that entails; physicalism becomes a tautology, providing no leverage on the question of how neural architecture is related to particular ideas or forms of speech.

Vygotsky's refutes the idea of a single, predetermined system of organic functions; the *artificial* devices of a culture fundamentally change the nature of psychological operations. Any description of these operations is parasitic on the analysis of language and symbolic systems as well as modes of discourse and the semantic agreements they embody. And these things, I maintain, are the cumulative results of historical traditions.

7 Language, Tradition and Culture

> If language is as old as consciousness itself...then not only one particular thought but all consciousness is connected with the development of the word. The word is a thing in our consciousness...that is absolutely impossible for one person, but that becomes a reality for two. The word is a direct expression of the historical nature of human consciousness. (Vygotsky, 1989, p. 256)

Tradition and critical thinking

In earlier chapters I disputed certain interpretations of the generalizability of critical thinking, and also the opposed idea that critical thought is internally related to cognitive domains. But what is the significance of this alternative conception of *historical tradition?* What can it tell us about the character of critical thinking that is relevant to present day concerns? What makes a tradition critical, or more critical than others? Is irrationality and error not a possibility within a critical tradition? And what is the kind of connection between traditions of critical thinking and democratic, libertarian social institutions to which I have also referred, given that these traditions had to start somewhere and may persist, even in authoritarian cultures? And what are the implications for education?

These are large questions, of course. Hence it might be wiser to adopt the term 'intimations' as an alternative to 'implications' to avoid the connotations of logical inevitability. For one thing, I have claimed consistently that critical thinking cannot be the subject of unambiguous definition and cannot be artificially compressed into pre-specified learning strategies without sacrificing the vital elements of puzzlement, creativity and sceptical reflection. For another, I maintain that, essential though it is for an adequate characterisation of critical thinking, the historical perspective requires hemeneutic interpretation; the provisional assignment of meanings to words and ideas by reference to their interrelationships and to features of the social contexts in which they have evolved. I will try to clarify this point further in the present chapter, claiming that an interpretative approach is necessary in order to grasp the nature of the questions which critical thinking traditions have tried to answer and that it, alone, is consistent with the creativity of language and thought.

An obvious objection is that this is to ignore the rigour associated with critical thinking. However, I do not believe that is the case, for rigour is better understood as an attribute of the process of evaluating and testing understanding rather than its finite product, as the revolutionising development of science suggests. Another objection might be that such emphasis on the cultural and historical diversity of ideas verges on relativism; the conclusion that there is nothing to choose between mutually incommensurable world views and theories or, what is ultimately the same thing, that they are sanctioned by their place in history, their social acceptability or their utility. I reject such conclusions for reasons which should be clear in this and my final chapter. Nevertheless, I maintain that responses to the evident variability of ideas were the first signs of the transformation of ubiquitous human problem solving abilities into explicit traditions of critical inquiry. And there are intimate, even necessary connections between this development and the evolution of concepts of freedom, equality and democracy.

Criteria of truth and rational justification are normative features of language; conditions for the possibility of meaningful verbal communication. Consequently, I have argued, characterisations in terms of *general* criteria fail to support the distinctive senses intended by the use of the term *critical thinking*, at least in the absence of explicit or tacit reference to a recognised field of discourse. Even then there remains the complex, controversial matter of interpreting the specific meaning and relevance of criteria within such a field. On the other hand, the contention that criteria of sound reasoning are internal to logically autonomous domains fails because there are no non-arbitrary ways of identifying their logical boundaries. Faced with the evolution and cultural variability of modes of thought, exponents of this thesis resort to historical and sociological rather than logical characterisations of domain-specificity or to the idea of principles of rationality sufficient to times and places. As well as invoking the contradictory idea of *general* criteria of sufficiency, the latter move ignores the revolutionising potential of thought; novel beliefs and theories are not necessarily related systematically, and thus predictably, to those they supersede.

Consequently, there is no consistent basis for retrospective judgment about the *rationality* of ideas at different periods and places; that could only sanction dogma. We cannot justify medieval belief in a flat Earth as rational according to contemporary standards, for example. The physical phenomena observed by Eratosthenes and the rudimentary apparatus which he used to measure the globe's circumference with tolerable accuracy were as accessible in later millennia as they were in the pre-Christian era. Nevertheless, heliocentric theory, articulated by Aristarchus in the third century BC was considered heretical by some of his contemporaries. It would probably have encountered greater hostility in pre-Copernican medieval Europe. Our appreciation of past ideas also depends on what could, or could not, have been articulated publicly in the prevailing environment of belief and the probable impact of that on individual capacities for insight and expression.

We can form approximate ideas about the nature, scope and limits of the thought of periods and cultures by investigating some of its constituent elements; conceptions of epistemic and spiritual authority; the roles of wider belief systems in prescribing or proscribing the public form in which novel concepts were expressed; conventions of language and discourse; literacy and access to a heritage of ideas, and the impact of the institutional framework in facilitating or inhibiting that access. Social contexts do not just foster modes of thought, critical or otherwise; they comprise their intelligibility. This is not to dismiss the role of *general* criteria of rationality in the critical traditions. Indeed, I have repeatedly identified a conscious search for principles to validate particular ideas in terms of common standards of rationality as an important hallmark of a critical thinking tradition. But these general principles and criteria are subject to evolutionary change, too, and require hermeneutic interpretation.

A scientifically productive criterion like the *principle of parsimony*, perhaps inherited from Epicurus and enshrined in 'Ockham's Razor', may be subject to very different interpretations in different historical and intellectual contexts; controversies over the relationship between faith and reason in late medieval theology; Buridan's heretical refutation of the concept of a 'prime mover' in fourteenth century cosmology; the anti-intentionalist stance of behavioural psychology - or the rejection of 'folk psychology' as irrelevant to the philosophy of 'eliminative materialism'. The task remains of deciding what constitutes a justifiable application of the kind of criterion encapsulated in Ockham's dictum that *'it is vain to do with more what can be done with fewer'*. Indeed, it becomes questionable whether *the same* general criterion is at issue here and whether it even matters once the substantives of a tradition of discourse are grasped. Precision is achieved, not because statements and definitions have unique meanings but because of the conventional significance they have assumed within a tradition. Concepts like *intentionality, logical atomism* or *functionalism* effectively summarise longstanding and many-faceted philosophical debates. Without some knowledge of that historical negotiation of meanings the concepts cannot be understood properly or deployed effectively. And I suggest that the same principle applies in the physical sciences. A belief that it does not, that science can be taught as an inventory of solutions without reference to an underlying history of problems which comprise its meaning, is likely to be the principle reason for widespread under-achievement in those disciplines and for the spectacular public ignorance of science which research is uncovering.

Traditions of inquiry are the only evidence we have that episodes of critical thinking can be increased in frequency by purposive human action; evolving bodies of ideas, theories and methods within a framework of guiding principles which provide a groundwork for further inquiry. Kuhn stresses the disjunctive logics of competing scientific paradigms, maintaining that choice between them cannot be 'logically or probabilistically compelling' (Kuhn, 1970, p. 93-94). But this sense of discontinuity is over-accentuated, even allowing for his recognition of intervening periods of 'normal science'. It is as though he adopts the formal mode of theory-exposition as an exclusive paradigm for representing states of reality and then responds with scepticism at the prospect of incommensurable representations. Revolutionising theories make sense as innovatory contributions to an understanding of the realities asserted by traditions of inquiry, even if they are incommensurate with the logic of the explanations they supersede. After all, the Einsteinian conception of *space-time* amounts to a radical revision of the Newtonian categories, but it was formulated against the background of theoretical concepts, anomalies and inconsistencies which were not available to the medieval or pre-Socratic cosmologist. Although Einstein maintains that 'all concepts, even those which are closest to experience, are freely chosen conventions...' (Einstein, 1991, p. 482), he was equally emphatic that to create a new theory is not to destroy and old one, but '...to regain our old concepts from a higher level' (Sacks, 1997, p. 166). The exponential effect of traditions of inquiry is to provide us with a body of theories and hypotheses, and their attendant inconsistencies or errors; 'something,' as Popper puts it, 'to be critical about' and which provides the theoretical framework within which observations are made, problems are identified and new hypotheses are formulated.

Rare and vulnerable though they have been, these traditions accentuate and sanction the attitude that all aspects of reality can be questioned fruitfully. It is evident in the writings of, for example, Kepler, Boyle and Galileo that this was not always the case; that these authors felt a prior need to defend critical inquiry as a justifiable interpretation of supernatural authority, incidentally contributing as much to 'the critical disposition' as to knowledge. They helped to establish an individual right of inquiry by redefining the nature of epistemic authority, a seminal influence in the proliferation of disciplined investigation. In my first chapter I employed the metaphor of a *penumbra of critical, scientific thought;* the diffuse influence which it exercises on the attitudes and expectations of communities. A search for unambiguous criteria of demarcation between the critical or the scientific and other modes of thought tends to divert attention from these social matrices of tradition. We reject ideas patently at odds with well established theories which, as individuals, we could neither substantiate nor refute for lack of relevant expertise. Such cases are not, of course, examples of *critical* rejection or acceptance but manifestations of the consensual picture of reality which has emerged as a result of inquiry to embrace even young children. But these attitudes involve more than mere prejudice, though they often involve that, too. One of the cumulative effects of critical traditions is that they encourage the formulation of critical questions and sanction expectations that answers are to be found. This situation applies as much between representatives of different disciplines as between lay people and experts, and has an important bearing on the idea of individual, critical autonomy. For this includes a preparedness to seek reasons for accepting or rejecting authoritative statements, possibly not to find them for lack of evidence or expertise, but to recruit the assistance of others who are better placed in these respects. It also includes a preparedness to tolerate conflicting expert views and an institutional framework for resolving conflicts between alternative paradigms through mutual criticism and testing.

Nevertheless, precisely what is retained or rejected by new paradigms is not predictable from within the conceptual and methodological repertoire of a tradition. Irrespective of their differences, Kuhn and Feyerabend affirm the need to characterise the subject by its erratic historical evolution rather than by a general 'logic of scientific discovery'. Even Popper, whose proposal for a conventional demarcation between empirical science and metaphysical speculation turns on the issue of theory testing, maintains that '...there is no such thing as a logical method of having new ideas, or a logical reconstruction of this process'. Discovery always includes elements of the 'irrational' (Popper, 1977, p. 32). And Lakatos' definition of progress in physics, even if intended to provide a criterion of rationality, has been described as a guide to the historian of science rather than the scientist because its scope, on his own admission, is retrospective (Chalmers, 1992, pp. 104-107).

Another consequence of denying the specificity of scientific method, as I have observed in Kuhn's case, is that the possibility of clear distinctions between science and other forms of knowledge evaporates. Feyerabend explicitly rejects such distinctions, arguing that fruitful comparisons must be a matter of historical exegesis rather than the establishment of principles of demarcation (Feyerabend, 1975, p. 253). Nor do these authors provide any reason for consigning incommensurability to the 'cutting edges' of science with the result that their arguments encompass human thought in general. And the force of the appeal to the history of ideas is that we can expect, at best, to find intimations about the best ways to proceed in future, as much in social and institutional terms as in methodology.

The problem of relativism and some institutional ramifications

The relativist tendency of such arguments is clear, though I believe it is important to distinguish between two broadly different ways in which it can be developed. One is to accept the manifoldness of reality and the graduated nature of our certainties about it - for even radical scepticism is predicated on a knowledge of what is it to be certain in *some* cases. The alternative is to refuse to relinquish a particular paradigm of certainty, held to be unattainable by purposeful inquiry, but to relocate it in an alternative interpretation of relationships between mind and reality. Kuhn, for instance, resorts to a sociological characterisation of science rather than the hermeneutic interpretation which seems more compatible with his historical examination of its 'rather ramshackle structure'. His assertion that nothing higher than '...the assent of the relevant community' (Kuhn, 1970, p. 94) could establish the scientific status of a theory is a regressive standard. For what, apart from scientific credentials comprises the special *relevance* of a particular community and its judgments? Expressed as a sociology of knowledge, or in a Whorfian insistence on the *equal validity* of incommensurable world views, relativism involves the self-contradictory, universalising proposition that there are no universal standards of truth or rationality. As soon as expressed, this kind of argument founders on norms to which we are committed by the nature of language and thought. But the ultimate implication of accepting that commitment, in the absence of universal and *substantive* criteria of reason and truth is, nonetheless, an institutional one. It is a Socratic requirement to follow the logic of argument wherever it leads. In Mill's words, we must keep the lists open because 'The beliefs which we have the most warrant for, have no safeguard to rest on, but a standing invitation to the whole world to prove them unfounded' (Mill, 1965, p. 273). And that, as I argue in my last chapter, summarises both a theory of knowledge and a political programme.

Connections are frequently drawn between critical thinking, personal autonomy, freedom and democracy by contributors to the present 'thinking skills debate' as well as in the more sustained manner of precursors like Mill, Dewey and Popper. However, Stephen Norris envisages the possible outcome of this debate as a choice between extremes; abandonment of the educational ideal of critical thinking or unification of the curriculum under its 'umbrella', citing the view of many contemporary authors that *definition* is a decisive issue (Norris, 1992, p. 4). Others predicate a workable theory of critical thinking on clear distinctions between it and associated terms like *problem-solving, metacognition* and *creativity* (for example, Johnson, 1992, p. 41). But I believe the connections between critical thinking, freedom and democracy are more ancient and intimate than anything that could be secured by agreement on operational definitions. The emergence of philosophical ways of thinking in pre-Socratic Greece is the most palpable evidence of the origins of critical traditions. Insofar as critical thinking has universal characteristics, concern about the epistemic status of various forms of knowledge is the most definitive. It is a state of consciousness intimately connected with certain qualities of language-use and social relationship. These qualities encourage discourse and the sceptical appraisal of received wisdom, by default or otherwise, enhancing capacities for the formulation of conscious imagery and the creation of novel ways of thinking. Ancient Greece provides many lessons.

One is that there was a symmetry between the growth of scientific and philosophical speculation and recurrent challenges to political leadership in some of those diminutive city-states; a developing awareness of the fallibility of all authority and of the relativities of cultural beliefs.

Traditions of critical thought are more than a legacy of methodologies and skills; they represent qualitative transformations in the conscious lives of their participants and are implicated in distinctive ways of life. Contrasts must be drawn between critical thinking and its alternatives in terms of the historical institutionalisation of criticism and a consequent exfoliation of the conscious imagery available for the description of reality. Accommodations are reached between conflicting cultural traditions, but not in the absolute sense that all inconsistencies are removed or that there is a vantage point from which they could be resolved; a principle which applies as much between individuals as between cultures. Because language and thought are creative there is a need for the continuing clarification of particular cultural beliefs and disciplinary understandings, but also of differing individual concepts and beliefs within any community.

I will argue that a crucial threshold in the liberation of human critical potentials was the advent of alphabetic literacy. This flexible and easily learned, 'democratic' script could unleash awareness of historical change and cultural variety because it created unprecedented opportunities for public scrutiny of these legacies and for debate about them. Conversely, oral tradition limits dialogue in at least two significant ways; to predominantly face-to-face communication and to ideas which are defined by very particular, tightly contextualised current usages for which there are few, if any, lasting comparisons. Unlike literate tradition, the oral culture is not conducive to the development of a metacognitive awareness, a second-order capacity for concentrated reflection on the meanings and implications of received ideas. It thus affords little scope for the formulation of general principles which would help discriminate between conflicting explanations - even if alternatives occurred to anyone on more than a rare, episodic basis. The significance of alphabetic literacy lies beyond itself; in the way it reveals the indefinite, revolutionising potential of thought in conditions of enhanced dialogue and sustains the political impulse to institutionalise that dialogue.

Social constructions of reality and the relativities of language

Different cultural modes of linguistic meaning intimate different conceptions of fact, even of the notion of facticity itself, and a different consciousness of the relationships between words and their referents. This principle, articulated notably by Sapir and overstated by Whorf, unites the history of cultures and ideas with the development of individual personality and intellect in the child from the earliest years. In the process of enculturation a language laden with historically accumulated, culturally specific meanings is acquired, albeit differentially, by individual people. An examination of some relativities of culture and cognition will highlight significant contrasts between dynamic traditions of critical thinking and more monolithic, homeostatic modes of thought - and these have a current relevance for the debate about educational ideals and objectives.

Despite the paradoxes and uncertainties afflicting theories about the structural elements of language and thought discussed in the last chapter, over-optimism about the accessibility of such universals to research has led to under-emphasis on the cognitive differentials implied by the diversity of cultural norms and linguistic practices. These are also likely to be relevant within what is normally designated a single culture, and most certainly in the interpretation of the cognitive development of children in the course of their adjustment to linguistic conventions in their social milieux.

Piaget, for example, has depicted animism as a structural element of the young child's thought. Some commentators have disputed not only the universality of this phenomenon but also the concept itself. The 'animism' of children from traditional as well as modernising societies, it has been suggested, is not a simple attribution of life-like properties to inanimate objects but a case of over-generalisation from a limited understanding of language and an awareness that animate and inanimate objects have *some* similar properties. Although a child might talk initially as though an object were alive, she is less likely to agree that it shares some definitive attributes of living things; sensory capacities or an ability to grow, for example (Siegel and Hodkin, 1982, pp. 72-74). In other words, the concept of animism dissolves into alternative possibilities; lack of experience of customary uses of the term *alive*; incomplete grasp of the terminological distinctions adults draw in various practical contexts between object functions and animate behaviour. Word-meaning accumulates and is gradually integrated within the various *social* institutions of language. There is no unique relationship between 'lexical items' and referents - and no possibility that they can therefore be grasped 'once and for all' and interpreted as having the same semantic import for children and adults (Vygotsky, 1989, p 61). A young child's conscious apprehension of the interview situation is as inscrutable as that of the Nuer tribesman who asserts, not that a twin is a like a bird, but that she *is* a bird. There is no consistent basis, other than ongoing dialogue, for discriminating between the child's various ascriptions of ontological status and the adult symbolisms manifest in our tendency to treasure heirlooms, or even to first *play* and then *live* a social role. Language remains the common denominator of intelligibility; even in the microcosm of a single word, it is reciprocal and dynamic. And I maintain that exactly the same principle applies in the case of the kind of incommensurable meanings and symbolic systems which I considered in Chapter 5 and which Kluckhohn, Leighton and Whorf stress in their discussions of aboriginal American languages and cultures.

Conceptions of reality may vary markedly between cultures and epochs. The medium of transmission is the language and *language-mediated symbolism* which marks the 'limits' of those respective worlds. As Edward Sapir has put it:

> Language is not merely a more or less systematic inventory of the various items of experience which seem relevant to the individual, as is so often naively assumed, but is also a self-contained, creative symbolic organisation...[Meanings are] not so much discovered in experience as imposed upon it, because of the tyrannical hold that linguistic form has upon our orientation in the world. (Kluckhohn and Leighton, 1960, pp. 207-208)

Sapir's words clearly raise questions about the relationship of language and thought to the world and difficulties about ways of establishing the status of different modes of language and thought vis a *vis* one another if they are all subject to the same relativistic principle. I suggest that there is an important difference between acknowledging the force of arguments for the cultural and linguistic relativities of thought, on the one hand and, on the other, accepting them as a justification for maintaining, as Whorf does, that differing modes are 'equally valid' accounts of reality. But neither can it be defensible to recruit this variability as a justification for postulating alternatives, like *social utility* or *efficiency*, as valid criteria of the rational or epistemic status of differing forms of language and thought. For these concepts cannot provide a more secure foothold than any others within a relativist framework. Their role in the nexus of language is no more securely founded; they have no absolute status in terms of that thesis.

Some critics of relativism try to account for the way 'words hook up to the world' - a strategy which encourages the idea of unique or paradigmatic word-meanings. In my last chapter, for instance, I discussed Fodor's conception of the relationship between syntactic structures and a finite lexicon. This is essentially *semantic atomism;* the view that the intelligibility of any utterance is determined by the meanings of its component elements and the implications of the formal structures within which they are organised. Although an acceptable enough description of the task of assessing 'everyday' statements in a familiar language, it is a misleading account of linguistic meaning *in general.*

In *Philosophical Investigations,* Wittgenstein disputes the 'picture of the essence of human language' articulated in Augustine's *Confessions,* as the correlation of the meaning of a word by means of ostensive definition with the object it represents :

> ...the individual words in language name objects - sentences are combinations of such names. - In this picture of language we find the roots of the following idea: Every word has a meaning. This meaning is correlated with the word. It is the object for which the word stands. (Wittgenstein, 1968, PI, 1)

Entertaining the idea of a primitive language, consisting entirely of 'words' like 'slab', 'block', 'pillar' and 'beam', Wittgenstein tests the cogency of this *atomistic* view of semantic meaning. His 'builders', who speak this 'language', have no resources on the sole basis of the object-meaning correlation for generalising from *this* 'slab' or 'block' to other instances; of deciding whether '*two* blocks' should be construed as the name of an additional object, or perhaps as a way of naming all objects apart from the first ostensively defined block; whether a particular utterance, 'beam', is to be regarded as a name, a description, a question or an order. Interrogatives and imperatives imply possibilities like answers or compliance; they presuppose other uses of words; other ways of using and reacting to words - and *deeds* (ibid., PI, 1-21).

Wittgenstein's case is that the simple language game depicted by his 'builders' could not be a complete account of language-learning or of the meaning of words. Ostensive definition is plainly a typical component of early learning, but one which is (as it were) chemically combined with a multiplicity of preceding utterances and actions. These are what make it possible to refer to objects of different sizes, colours and functions without having to go through the interminable procedure of demonstrating that they can be the same in certain respects and different in others - 'blocks' and 'boxes' for example; 'sticks' and 'pencils', 'leaves' and 'green'. Even in the simple case of a physical object, understanding the meaning of a noun which designates it requires familiarity with the mode of designation itself. It requires a practical grasp of the general *uses* of the word and varieties of abstraction and metaphor which actually lie behind the mature language-user's sense that there is a uniformity about the meaning of a particular word. Thus, to understand a word is *already* to have a tacit grasp of something quite general about the nature of language and its relationship to actions and social behaviour. Reflection on the multi-dimensional background of reference helps to clarify the claim of Vygotsky's with which this chapter opened: language is essentially intersubjective; it is the means by which our consciousness is ratcheted up to successive levels of awareness; a legacy of previous human interaction.

Metaphor, the 'inward' aspect of word-meaning, and myth

In a sceptical commentary on the possibility of artificial intelligence, John Haugeland refutes the 'Fregian ideal' of semantic atomism as a plausible account of natural languages (Haugeland, 1990, pp. 660-670). The 'disambiguation' of an expression might involve reference to any facet of experience; 'in effect, the whole of common sense is potentially relevant at any point'. He illustrates his claim with two sentences:

(a) *I left my raincoat in the bath because it was wet.*
(b) *Though her blouse draped stylishly, her pants seemed painted on.*

In his first example, (a), there is nothing about either the syntax or the lexical items to indicate whether the coat was placed in the bath because it (the coat) was wet or because it (the bath) was wet. The ambiguity of the sentence (which causes no difficulty to a human listener) cannot be solved by resorting to definitions of the functions of baths and raincoats. The solutions depends on an instantaneous apprehension of the way that action as a whole 'fits into' everyday human behaviour. The words contribute an image and their intelligibility is in the act of visualisation which they provoke. An intelligent machine program, an analogy for the theory of semantic atomism, lacks that retrospective reference which facilitates such immediate connections between disparate images. Searle makes a similar point, arguing that to conceive language in the form of hierarchies of propositions would involve spelling out an infinite regress of statements, each defining the truth-conditions of its predecessors (Searle, 1990, p. 594).

Haugeland's second example of ambiguity, (b), illustrates how grasping meanings is so often a matter of 'visualising' our way into situations rather than deducing them from the combination of lexical items and syntax. What kind of propositional hierarchy could sanction the metaphor of a film of paint as a representation of a close-fitting garment rather than the more 'literal' image of paint applied to a garment? Although he acknowledges that there is a significant problem about *how* this act of visualisation is accomplished, Haugeland helps to undermine an obstinate prejudice; that there is some kind of systematic disjunction between cognitive and affective states, on the one hand, and between these disjoint states and the 'visualisation' of events and situations which words describe, on the other. There is an embarrassing lack of verifiability about appeals to subjective states, coupled with the extreme difficulty of capturing the fleeting character of mental imagery in a precise form of words. Yet I suggest that the difficulty is certainly no greater than that of accounting for semantic meaning in atomistic terms. The transition from naming a unique object of experience - a 'slab' of particular shape, position, location, size, composition and colour, for example - to the universal concept, 'slab' as it applies to numerous instances (in which all these characteristics vary enormously) implies a kind of *visualisation*. Human agreement in common usage cannot be shown to depend on unique bonds between words and referents. But perhaps that is the point and origin of language. It dissects immediate experience and abstracts from it, supplying our consciousness with indefinite possibilities for recombination and communication of the images derived from it. Language is a repository of vicarious experiences and, as Popper says, it *allows our hypotheses to die in our stead.* And, incidentally, that could only happen in some cases if, in others, they could be rationally justified.

The enhancement of critical thinking demands recognition of the role of word-imagery and the contrasting forms which it can take. Not only does all representation involve abstraction, anyway, but those mutually inaccessible 'mental images' are both the product of language and the necessary basis of mutual intelligibility in its use. They constitute the meaningfulness of abstract notations; the 'inspired method of picturing' described by Feynman, in my previous quotation, as prior to his mathematical solutions of problems in physics. Feynman is not a unique example. Freeman Dyson agreed with him that Einstein's scientific creativity declined when 'he stopped thinking in concrete physical images and became a manipulator of equations' (Gleick, 1992, p. 244). And, of course, there is the legendary connection between Einstein's teenage fantasy of riding on a beam of light and his development, as an adult, of the theory of special relativity. In other words, trivial though it might seem by comparison, Haugeland's picture of 'painted-on pants' is one microcosm of the relationship of words, sentences and language to thought. Words do not correspond uniquely and unambiguously to features of an objective world; their sense implies a history of prior discourse. The multiplicity of conventions governing their usage invests consciousness with a vast, ever-changing edifice of images with which we visualise our way into situations, make comparisons and draw distinctions. A developed capacity of this kind provides an infrastructure for critical thinking and the accumulation of a repertoire of imagery with which to do it. It might be possible to clarify this point by referring to the crucial historical role of metaphor as a source of novel linguistic meaning.

Language is permeated with the imagery of earlier forms of explanation, the 'word seeds' which, as Ayto says, which '...have proliferated into widely differentiated families of vocabulary' (Ayto, 1990, Introduction). Our word 'character', which has so many different application to people, landscapes and ideas, derives from a Greek word for a 'pointed stake' via the concept of inscribing distinctive marks on objects. The word 'average' appears to have evolved from an Arabic term for 'mutilated' - applied to damaged goods and subsequently to the practice of merchants who would share losses arising from damaged cargoes (ibid., 1991). In this process of adaptation, old usages are overlaid by new ones which extend their semantic scope without necessarily entirely replacing them. We still 'catch' colds; objects 'fall' to earth; children 'suck' drinks through straws; the moon can be 'new' or 'full' - and so forth. These are legitimate descriptions of states of affairs as far as they go and are used without conscious reference to physical, chemical or biological processes presenting significantly different imagery - of which we are also often aware. It is impossible to imagine effective, everyday communication in the absence of a tacit understanding of the many different (often overlapping) levels of description and their relevance to fields of explanation and contexts of dialogue. 'The full moon rises at 8.30 p.m.' is just one example of a statement which can be true.

The proliferation of metaphorical significance revealed by etymological research is evidence of a fundamental characteristic of thought; that it exploits an isomorphism of conscious imagery in order to ratchet itself to new levels of abstraction. The point which requires emphasis is that the isomorphism in question obtains exclusively between features of the shared mental imagery of parties to discourse. The relationship is at the level of imagination and visualisation. Agreement is about the relevance of features of that imagery in contexts of usage and it makes little sense to ask which one of a number of contexts demonstrates the primitive or paradigmatic use of a word. People, rivers and mountain ranges 'run'; smoke and hair 'curl'; we can 'burn' rubbish, toast, or our own hands and, as I suggested previously, we can *mean* very different things by a simple statement like 'the sun is hot'. Of course, we may distinguish the literal from the metaphorical in the case of leaders who 'fall' from platforms or from power. However, this should not obscure the extent to which the meanings of common words, even precise terminological distinctions, rely on an historical infrastructure of usage rather than finite rules governing appropriate application. One index of the elemental contribution of metaphor in forging new, shared meanings is the spontaneity of its appeal in the very ancient art of poetry. Indeed literature is a seriously neglected source of illumination in the investigation of cognition. The deliberate uses of metaphor in this context are hard to explain unless they are expressions of something primitive in the organisation of thought.

Shakespeare's Macbeth, having murdered his King and incriminated the servants, helps to confirm his guests' suspicions of his own guilt in a lament embroidered with extravagant imagery, including this description of the scene of horror:

> Here lay Duncan, his silver skin, laced with his golden blood,
> And his gashed stabs looked like a breach in nature for ruin's wasteful entrance...
> (Shakespeare, Macbeth, Act 2, Scene 1)

Fine words convey premeditation on Macbeth's part at a moment which should command the kind of direct sincerity evident in the responses of Banquo, legitimate heir to Scotland's throne and the laconic MacDuff who finally avenges the regicide. Yet the metaphor of precious metals is appropriate both to the idealised regality of the murdered Duncan, and to the pallor of his corpse - described in a euphemistic but also *visually realistic* way as 'laced' with his blood.

Interpretations of this kind allude to the dependence of word-meaning on a multitude of uses, exploiting the human ability to switch instantaneously between images and even to entertain contrasting images simultaneously. Of course, the isomorphisms of metaphorical usage are always arguable and this is not just because there may be many different ways of visualising a metaphor, but because its relevance is wholly exhausted in the perception of appropriate use; there is no criterion for deciding whether silver resembles the skin of a corpse or whether blood resembles gold. And the significance of the image is not confined to the passage in question, but to its place in the tragedy as a whole and its role in characterising the protagonists. Grasping the meaning of a few words is likely to invoke aspects of experience quite unpredictably, though that experience is mediated by a particular cultural-linguistic matrix:

> ...thinking also follows a network of tracks laid down in the given language, an organization which may concentrate systematically upon certain phases of reality, certain aspects of intelligence, and may systematically discard others featured by other languages. The individual is utterly unaware of this organization and is constrained completely within its unbreakable bonds. (Whorf, 1959, p. 256)

Popper, who deplores the philosopher's addiction to discussing the meaning of words (Popper, 1972, p. 309) nevertheless devotes attention to linguistic evolution. Explicitly in concert with Whorf, he maintains that language 'always incorporates many theories in the very structure of its usages....it is only against a background like this that a problem can arise' (ibid., p. 165). But as Popper would hardly disagree, Whorf overstates the 'unbreakable' determining force of particular languages, at least as a universal. I will shortly consider how the tool of alphabetic literacy helped to break those bonds, creating new possibilities for the development of language and thought, notably with the advent in pre-Socratic Greece of philosophical and scientific inquiry. The revolutionary difference is not to be found in more literal meanings of scientific and philosophical terminology. Although the critical traditions do deal with the subjects of truth and reality, they do not do so in the sense that their terminology is nailed unambiguously to aspects of the 'real world'. Popper's contention is that these traditions are products of myth-making and of *tests;* that the demarcation between myth and science is the formulation of accounts of reality in a manner which leaves them open to refutation (Popper, 1963, p. 38). He questions the common view that the Greeks were the first people to try to *understand* nature, arguing instead that this was just what their 'primitive, myth-making' predecessors had done. Myths *were* and are the explanations of observable phenomena:

> ...the statement that Poseidon is angry is for me a much simpler and more easily understandable explanation of high waves of the sea than one in terms of frictions between the air and the surface of the water. (Popper, 1963, p. 126)

For Popper the route from the ancient myths identifying the turbulence of a storm with the emotion of fury did not involve a direct appeal to some notion of the *brute facts* behind the myth, but was the substitution of new kinds of imagery, new stories which competed in certain respects with the older ones, inviting a sense of the dissonance between the two accounts and a consequent comparison between them which invited evaluation in terms of the observable phenomena they described.

Words accrue meanings in contexts of usage through metaphor, simile and deliberate analogy, expanding consciousness through the exfoliation of imagery. Vygotsky, as I will show, conceives the development of word-meaning as historically continuous and as characteristic of the developing consciousness of the child. This concept of evolutionary word-meanings also helps to explain the revolutionary cognitive impact of rapid linguistic development. There is in this a potential for undermining confidence in the 'givenness' of the links between words and their traditional patterns of reference, stimulating successive attempts to resolve newly discovered ambiguities. A key element in this development might be described as the growing recognition that to name something is not to explain it or identify its essence - an error implicated in the reification of scholarly jargon and also in the puzzlement of a Russian peasant, reported by Vygotsky, who could understand how clever scientists knew so much about the stars, but not how they found out their names.

Words as tools, mediated learning; a 'zone of proximal development'

Vygotsky's philosophical psychology has popularised the notion of a *psychological tool;* a symbol or device which facilitates an 'artificial development' by raising a given psychological function to a 'higher level', increasing and expanding its activity (Vygotsky 1993, p. 45). The idea is that such tools, while lacking intrinsic meaning, enable individuals to assimilate specific features of their culture to consciousness. He cites a variety of unlike examples, including mnemonic devices; knotted handkerchiefs, notched sticks, signs, words - and language. But despite this apparent vagueness, the tool-analogy has been identified as the key idea in understanding his work (Davydov and Radzikhovski, 1985, pp. 52 -61). The idea of linguistic tools has also been used by Wittgenstein (Wittgenstein, 1968, PI, 23) and Popper, who uses the analogy to describe the process by which human consciousness 'bootstraps' itself through *expressive* and *descriptive* to *discursive* and *argumentative* uses of language (Popper, 1972, p. 239). Vygotsky distinguished his own notion of a psychological tool from those of other near contemporaries, including Dewey, because they failed to convey the kind of specificity of relationship between 'behaviour and its auxiliary means' which he had in mind (Vygotsky, 1978, p. 53). The concept is explicitly anti-reductionist; it directs attention to the catalytic role of features of material culture in the transmission of culturally-specific meanings between individuals and generations. It also underlines the plasticity and uncharted potential of human minds under the influences of interaction and dialogue. If words are tools, the differential uses which are made of them gradually contribute to an edifice of common culture and shared understandings - within which there are nevertheless possibilities of divergence. And these possibilities depend on the extent and qualities of dialogue in the various modalities of learning situations.

As argued earlier in this chapter and elsewhere, demonstrable linguistic asymmetries in adult-child communication reveal the existence of complex and diffuse social *conventions* about the ways in which words mean something in different contexts. The specific manner in which attempts are made to resolve these asymmetries plays a crucial role in determining modes and rates of cognitive development. Wood has noted recent research suggesting that qualities of parent-child dialogue can influence the 'metalinguistic awareness' of young children, influencing their ability to learn, reason and regulate their thought:

> ...social interaction and such experiences as talking to, informing, explaining, being talked to, informed and having things explained, structure not only the child's immediate activities but also help to form the *processes* of reasoning and learning themselves. (Wood, 1992, pp. 134-135)

Such an idea, as Wood points out, is consistent with Vygotsky's emphasis on the role and character of mediation in learning situations and with the dynamics of intellectual growth expressed in another of his key concepts, a *zone of proximal development* - 'the discrepancy between a child's actual mental age and the level he reaches in solving problems with assistance' - problems which he will be able to do alone, tomorrow (Vygotsky, 1989, p. 187). Vygotsky's contribution, however, is not just in the incentive he has supplied for investigating the vital contribution of mediation and discourse to intellectual development, although the very importance and novelty attributed to his thesis by many contemporary authors is another indication of the near-monopoly long enjoyed by the idea of relatively fixed potentials and stages of intellectual growth.

The *zone of proximal development*, with its emphasis on social interaction, relates the developing understanding of children to qualitative aspects of the intellectual culture to which they are introduced. Not only the child, but her more capable peer or adult teacher is implicated in determining the 'width' of this metaphorical zone, as are the language and materials, the 'tools' employed as the medium of exchange. Although Vygotsky substitutes this concept for the prevalent notion of definitive levels of individual mental development, preoccupation with empirical research methodology can minimise the comprehensiveness and radicalism of his thesis. Much depends on the weight one attaches to Vygotsky's general theoretical work and to his research in clinical psychology, respectively (for example, Vygotsky, 1993, p. 256). In the context of his general theory, the 'zone' metaphor has a universal significance in human learning; it 'presupposes a specific social nature and a process by which children grow into the intellectual life of those around them' within which language is 'a paradigm for the entire problem of the relation between learning and development' (Vygotsky, 1978, p. 89). His thesis is as much about the transmission and variability of cultural traditions as about individual cognitive growth. And it might be useful to recall that children have grown into cultures which include not only diverse, rapidly changing modern technologies, but the scattered hunter-gatherer communities which have characterised the greater part of human existence. This offers another perspective on the controversial balance between nature and nurture and the impact of factors external to biological inheritance on cognition.

Isolated from the broad context of his social philosophy, Vygotsky's *zone of proximal development* can be viewed as a very specific diagnostic concept rather than as the universal dynamic of enculturation which he clearly also believes it to be. Such interpretations may lead back from the unlimited horizons afforded by the inherent creativity of language to a narrowly defined technique for measuring something interpreted, in the familiar prejudicial way, as an individual intellectual potential to which teaching should be explicitly directed:

> The assessment of the width of a child's zone of proximal development empirically translates into the assessment of how many prompts she needs to solve problem 1, versus problem 2, versus problem 3, and so on...A child judged to have a wide zone of proximal development is one who reduces the number of prompts needed from trial to trial... (Brown and Ferrara, 1989, p. 284)

Brown and Ferrara's interpretation, with its stress on 'standardised prompts' by a teacher or diagnostician, violates the spirit of Vygotsky's extensive references to semantic meaning as the dynamic principle of cognitive development. Even more worrying, the spatial connotations of the term 'zone' seem to have led directly back to the idea that it is a measurable attribute of an individual child's cognitive potential rather than the variable consequence of particular kinds of personal interaction. The child is turned back into a monad and the shortcomings of her human environment are attributed to her intellect because 'standardised prompts' are the antithesis of meaningful conversation. Language is not simply the medium which conveys the message of a lesson; in vital respects it *is* the message of the lesson. Its imagery may be pregnant with ontological and epistemological implications conveying expansive or restrictive world-views by insinuating different conceptions of intellectual authority, facticity and of the legitimacy of questioning these things.

The importance of Vygotsky's concept of this 'zone', with its accent on the exchange of semantic meanings in the process of mediation, is that it helps to reinstate the epistemic viewpoint of the learner as the vital feature of a pedagogic relationship. Any facet of her semantic repertoire might be relevant, quite unpredictably, to the clarification of an idea and only *she* can decide which facet that is. That is why the imposition of predetermined systems can leave her mouthing the alien words of her teachers, simulating understanding, but unable to deploy it effectively because its interconnections with other areas of her understanding have not been established; she has acquired a non-transferable skill or a disconnected 'fact'. I suggest this underwrites the value of Socrates' revered but oft-neglected advice to follow argument wherever it leads.

Literacy, new dimensions of consciousness, and critical thinking

Recent research has highlighted connections between literacy, in cultures and individuals, and 'the emergence of formal logical thinking' as a result of the abstraction from context involved in interpreting written, as distinct from oral, language and a consequent accentuation of formal, linguistic structure (Wood, 1992, p. 178). Olson maintains that 'critical thinking is essentially synonymous with literacy' (Olson, 1992, p. 184). These conclusions, compatible with my own argument, are grounds for concern about the very high levels of illiteracy in democracies like Britain and the United States. But the main point I wish to make here has less to do with the direct connections between literacy and logical thinking in contemporary settings than with the connection between an accessible script, development of a sense of historical change and the origins of the critical thinking traditions. What is important here is the powerful evidence of the revolutionising tendency of thought in conditions of enhanced dialogue which alphabetic forms of literacy were instrumental in providing. An alphabet is a paradigm of the Vygotskian psychological tool and alphabetic literacy has promoted explosive developments of dialectical inquiry by making written language widely accessible and amenable to what McPeck has called 'reflective scepticism'. Some consequences of such modes of thought are illustrated by differences between a non-literate, twentieth century society and the metatheoretical reflections of Thucydides, Athenian historian of the fifth century BC:

> The Tiv do not recognise any contradiction between what they say now and what they said fifty years ago, since no enduring records exist for them to set beside their present views...they are unaware that various words, proper-names and stories have dropped out, or that others have changed their meaning or been replaced. (Goody and Watt, 1963, p. 304-345)

> ...I have made it a principle not to write down the first story that came my way, and not even to be guided by my own general impressions; either I was present myself at the events which I have described or else I heard of them from eye-witnesses whose reports I have checked with as much thoroughness as possible...It will be enough for me, however, if these words of mine are judged useful by those who want to understand clearly the events which happened in the past and which (human nature being what it is) will...be repeated in the future. My work is not a piece of writing designed to meet the taste of an immediate public, but was done to last for ever. (Thucydides, History of the Peleponnesian War, 1966, p. 24)

That ethos of theoretical and metatheoretical disputatiousness which emerged in certain Greek *poleis* is significant for a theory of critical thinking. As both Mill and Popper emphasise, the achievement of a culture of rational inquiry is no guarantee of its sustainability where the acceptance of widespread discourse and controversiality is supplanted by other social commitments. Critical traditions can come and go; widespread literacy might be their necessary condition, but it is not sufficient. However, I believe those dramatic expressions of the first popular form of literacy demonstrate the explosive potential of human minds when social interaction achieves a critical mass. And that because of the fortuitous advent of a novel system of communication and record-keeping which first alerted people to the ambiguous nature of their past, their traditional values and their physical world. Moreover, Greek experience suggests that there is no clear link between sophisticated technology and scientific thought (Wolpert, 1993, p. 25). The differences between the Tiv and the ancient Athenians are far less about the physical resources available to them than the ability to recognise and articulate intellectual challenges posed by historical and cultural dissonances. The tool of a simple, flexible writing system enabled the Greeks to record, reflect upon and transcend those challenges. The distinctive feature of critical thinking is an explicit metacognitive awareness that there are problems about the relationships between language, thought and reality. The Greeks *invented* the critical traditions; they were not taught how to apply the relevant skills:

> To my knowledge, the critical or rationalist tradition was invented only once. It was lost after two or three centuries, perhaps owing to the rise of the Aristotelian

> doctrine of *episteme,* of certain and demonstrable knowledge...It was rediscovered and consciously revived by the Renaissance, especially by Galileo Galilei. (Popper, 1963, p. 151)

Thucydides' introduction to his account of the war between Athens and Sparta and their respective allies contrasts starkly with the lack of historical sense amongst the peasants of medieval Montaillou, mentioned in Chapter 5, and with the unconscious adjustment of past experience to present reality which Goody and Watt describe as the 'structural amnesia' of pre-literate societies. Thucydides contrasted his method of dispassionate inquiry with the mythological tradition of the Homeric epics which were the mainstay of Greek education (Beck, 1964, p. 55-66). He outlined a procedure for checking the accuracy of individual recollections as evidence of past events; and he displayed a clear sense of the relevance of Greek civilisation to the future of human societies. He presented a history, a theory of history, an historical methodology and the concept of a relatively fixed 'human nature'. Thucydides illustrates the point that the discovery of 'history' presages a transformation in the scope of human thought, a radical departure from the conceptual world of the pre- or proto-literate societies which Goody and Watt characterise as follows:

> ...Literate societies...cannot discard, absorb or transmute the past. Instead, their members are faced with permanently recorded versions of the past and its beliefs; and because the past is thus set apart from the present, historical enquiry becomes possible. This in turn encourages scepticism; and scepticism not only about the legendary past, but about received ideas about the universe as a whole. (Goody and Watt, 1963, p. 332)

These authors also draw clear distinctions between alphabetic and other, usually earlier, forms of literacy in terms of accessibility and flexibility. They emphasise reciprocities between social institutions, ideas and the different media of cultural transmission. The accessibility of pictographic and hieroglyphic scripts is restricted by the abundance of their symbols to homogenous, organised elites, usually charged by the nature of their calling with the preservation of orthodoxy. The twenty-odd symbols of the alphabet provide the basic condition for widespread literacy and enhanced critical awareness from which may spring not only a 'scientific' attitude towards the world, but a democratic challenge to traditional institutions which had developed under conditions of 'oligoliteracy':

> Phonetic systems are...adapted to expressing every nuance of individual thought, to recording personal reactions as well as items of major social importance. Non-phonetic writing...tends rather to record and reify only those items in the cultural repertoire which the literate specialists have selected for written expression; and it

tends to express the collective attitude towards them. (ibid.)

The alphabet had evolved gradually, probably a degenerate development of hieroglyphics, answering mundane commercial needs in the ancient Mediterranean. However, it *was* one fortuitous element in a complex of cross-cultural influences. But the combination revolutionised people's conceptions of themselves and their world. The peculiar significance of the alphabet was its inherent capacity to form a multitude of new connections between individual human intellects within communities - and between those communities and posterity. It demonstrates the revolutionary cognitive potential contained in the free exchange of ideas and the awareness of the fallibility which that provokes.

Monolithic and critical 'world-views'

Whorf provides an example of what might be called *essentialism in action,* in which a collective worldview is reinforced by insistent linguistic repetition. He stresses the homeostatic function of Hopi ritual in inhibiting communal rivalries, ensuring the 'combined, intensified and harmonised thought of the whole community' (ibid., p. 151). Nor does he consider the Hopi metaphysics 'more mystical' than western scientific conceptions, claiming that:

> Hopi postulates equally account for *all phenomena* and their interrelations, and lend themselves even better to the integration of Hopi culture in all its phases. (ibid., p. 59, my emphasis)

A characteristic by-product of the critical traditions, however, has been the proliferation of significant phenomena and evolving ways of investigating relationships between them. Nevertheless, anthropology provides impressive examples of problem solving in technologically primitive societies. History and archaeology demonstrate striking intellectual and cultural achievements in rigidly hierarchical social systems. The Sumerian and Mayan cultures displayed both problem-solving on a massive scale and an inability to find solutions to the resulting environmental degradation which led to their decline (Ponting, 1992, pp. 55-87). This is to suggest only that technological ingenuity, as one aspect of critical thinking, may be compatible with institutional rigidity of a self-destructive order. Yet there may be a useful hint here about the need for distinctions between constituent aspects of critical thinking and the social causes to which they are harnessed - *in terms of the semantic content of languages and their impact on individual consciousness.*

Gleick describes how Feynman used the example of the precise Mayan astronomical calculus to support his case against other physicists who considered the prediction of experimental results as definitive of the adequacy of a theory, and who dismissed philosophical interest in its ontological implications as verbal quibbling:

> The Maya had a theory of astronomy that enabled them to explain their observations and to make predictions long into the future. It was a *theory* in the utilitarian modern spirit: a set of rules, quite mechanical, which when followed produced accurate results. Yet it seemed to lack a kind of understanding...There was no discussion of what the moon was. There was no discussion even of the idea that it went around... (Gleick, 1992, p. 167)

Feynman, who shared Whorf's interest in deciphering Mayan hieroglyphics, speculated on the likely futility of efforts by an imaginary member of that culture to promote discussion about the composition of the moon and the nature of the forces acting upon it; the possibility of an alternative kind of astronomical theory which might also have predictive force. The contrast is between the intelligent construction and utilitarian application of a formal system and an urge to speculate about the nature of the phenomena which it describes. Feynman's point was that such philosophical speculation about ultimate realities would have been alien to the Maya but he used the analogy to illustrate the difference between methodological perspectives in quantum physics; the creative impulse to visualise states of affairs represented by a calculus in contrast to the meticulous but servile exploration of its syntax.

Whorf's thesis, that Mayan language and thought projected the imagery of a different but 'valid' reality takes no account of the consideration raised by Feynman, that Mayan cosmology precluded the curiosity and awareness of alternative possibilities which prompts speculation and argumentative engagement about ultimate causes and characteristics. And the reasons for this are likely to include the limitations of a language and symbolism evolved in conditions of relative cultural isolation and homogeneity; a technology adapted to a uniform physical environment and social institutions maintaining a circumscribed system of ideas - as Whorf says of Hopi language and thought, 'an emphasis on persistence and constant insistent repetition' (ibid., p. 151).

The preceding point indicates an important contrast (though not an absolute disjunction) between what might be called 'problem-solving' and 'critical thinking'. Ennis (1992, p. 22) and Johnson (1992, p. 41) draw attention to a network of concepts, including 'metacognition' and 'problem-solving' which are conceptually related to critical thinking. But Johnson's aspiration for a preliminary 'sorting out' of these concepts seriously underestimates the scale of the task and the kind of historical and existential gulf which can separate problem-solving from what Ennis calls the 'higher order' operations involved in mature critical thought. Critical thinking involves a metacognitive investigation of the nature, meanings and implications of problems. It involves the effort to relate solutions to other aspects of a highly developed social matrix of concepts and images which present innumerable points of comparison and opportunities for recombination according to the unique location of individuals within it.

Zeno's paradoxes exemplify the last point. Directed against a dominant tradition concerning the divisibility of space and time, which may or may not be seen as ancestral to atomic theory (Kirk and Raven, 1969, pp. 286-297), they test assertions about the ultimate constituents of physical reality against everyday experience. But Zeno does this, notably, by moving beyond the frame of reference provided by that debate. His fables of *The Stadium, Achilles and the Tortoise, The Flying Arrow* and *The Moving Rows* recruit relatively simple, common images to demonstrate the incoherence of the arcane ideas he opposed. A similar imaginative leap beyond conventional parameters can be seen in Darwin's solution to the 'recondite problem' posed by the honey bee's remarkable architectural powers. His explanation reduced those skills to simple instinct by redefining the mathematical puzzle about the sophisticated cellular structure of hexagonal prisms in the honeycomb. Darwin simply visualised widely spaced bees building spherical cells by turning repeatedly on their own axes, and speculated about the result of reducing the intervening spaces between the bees until the circumferences of their cells intersected in three dimensions. His next step was to confirm these speculations by experiment, and by correspondence with other naturalists and a mathematician (Darwin, 1962, pp. 259-267).

These, and so many other paradigmatic examples illustrate how critical thinking invokes aspects of an accumulated repertoire of ideas and experiences unpredictably in order to obtain a more general overview of the nature of ideas with which the mind is engaged. Perhaps the most basic legacy of the critical traditions is to demonstrate, not *how*, but *that* this can be done. In other words, *critical thinking* is specific to a certain kind of culture and can only be characterised satisfactorily by reference to the historical complex of ideas and values within which it has evolved. A critical, questioning attitude is one way amongst others of experiencing reality. It is worth recalling that passive receptivity to a world of 'given' facts and states can be much more than the mere absence of curiosity; it may be *sanctioned* by an articulated epistemology. Darwin reflected on both the habitual lack of curiosity of his Andean guides and upon the more hostile view of his geological conjectures taken by those who, '...(like a few in England who are a century behindhand), thought that all such inquiries were useless and impious; and that it was quite sufficient that God had thus made the mountains' (Darwin, 1845, Chapter XV).

Creative tensions liberated by attempts to reconcile incommensurable 'world views' are the origin of a disposition for philosophical and scientific inquiry. But sensitivity to these dissonances entails a basis of comparison; a method of recording them and of ensuring public scrutiny. From their beginnings, the critical traditions have been about the transformations of consciousness which are wrought when social relationships assume some of the characteristics of a 'democratic community of inquiry'.

The relativities of understanding and intolerance of ambiguity

Opposition to relativism can be understandably fierce. I have already referred to parenthetical remarks by Chomsky expressing his dislike of the idea of an infinitely malleable human nature and the consequent possibility that human values and behaviour could be harnessed to the whims of totalitarian leaders. Fodor hates relativism more than anything except, perhaps, fibreglass powerboats because of its implications that '...one's values are comprehensively determined by one's culture' and '...one's metaphysics is comprehensively determined by one's syntax'. Meaningful debate can take place only within such comprehensive frameworks and, Fodor says; 'What you can't do is rationally criticize the framework' (quoted in Pinker, 1995, p. 405).

But in Chapter 5 and subsequently, I pointed out the problems associated with the idea that there are any unambiguous frameworks or identifiable contextual boundaries of this kind. The danger of abandoning hermeneutic interpretation is that of arbitrarily stipulating sociological, historical or other criteria. For if principles of rationality are held to be culturally or historically dependant, there is no uncommitted standpoint from which to make universalising claims about which cultural configurations or historical periods are the relevant ones. Interpretations of the language game metaphor which read into it this kind of systematising intent miss the point. Acceptance of the relativities of understanding faces us with the prospect of fighting our corner as best we can according to our assessment of the criteria of rational argument, here and now. And that requires faith in the universality of human commitments to truth and rational argument and our abilities to find common ground from which to proceed. The emergence of critical traditions from more monolithic ways of life and thought are our grounds for confidence that this can be done, despite conceptual discontinuities which deprive us of an infallible formula.

The evolution of scientific and philosophical thought reflects the changeability of principles of rational criticism which Siegel, another severe critic of relativism, acknowledges when he asks; 'If (principles) evolve and change, how can they be impartial and universal? If impartial and universal, how can they change?' (Siegel, 1988, p. 134). Scheffler, sceptical of the idea of universal, innate mental structures, recommends rational tradition as a guide but warns against abstract interpretations of principle:

> The fundamental point is that rationality cannot be taken simply as an abstract and general ideal. It is embodied in multiple evolv*ing traditions*, in which the basic condition holds that issues are resolved by reference to *reasons*, themselves defined by *principles* purporting to be impartial and universal. These traditions, I believe, provide an important focus for teaching. (Scheffler, 1973, p. 79, original emphasis)

The virtue of this formulation, which Siegel echoes, is its emphasis on the conscious articulation of reasons and principles, a characteristic of the critical traditions which distinguishes them from their more monolithic antecedents. But reasons and principles cannot safely be portrayed as culturally or historically specific or sufficient. Conflict between alternative, contemporaneous modes of reasoning has been typical of the critical traditions and I believe that this is the one feature most nearly definitive of them. Galileo's conflict with the Church turned on the adequacy of empirical evidence and individual reason to sustain the *ontological thesis* of heliocentrism in apparent contravention of scriptural authority. As Cardinal Bellarmine made clear to his fellow cleric, Paolo Foscarini, it was this further development of the Copernican *hypothesis*, the assertion of a newly discovered physical reality, which was 'a very dangerous thing...injuring our holy faith and making the sacred Scripture false...' (Goodman, 1979, p. 108).

As I have indicated, an important feature of the critical traditions is the impulse to trace the implications of ideas beyond their accepted terms of reference in order to test their interrelatedness and consistency with other common ideas. A corresponding element in the critical thinker's repertoire is an ability to identify the absurd consequences or internal inconsistencies of entrenched belief or dominant theory. This technique, exemplified par excellence by Socrates, courts the charge of subversion. A token of this is Aristophanes' harsh caricature of Socrates in his satire, *The Clouds*, which identified him with the ethical relativism and nihilism of some of the more extreme Sophists, not to mention his eventual execution.

Despite the problem posed by the historical evolution of modes of reasoning and the criteria embodied in them, Siegel believes that rationality is self-justifying because even to ask 'why be rational?' is to 'acknowledge the force of reasons' - of rationality itself (Siegel, 1988, p. 132). This is an incontrovertible argument against the radical sceptic who tries to refute the possibility of criteria of rationality in general. But hostility to critical rationality rarely takes the form of a denial of the force of *reasons* in general; it is expressed most typically in certain views about the *authoritative status* of reasons. Authority might be attributed, for example, to the esoteric knowledge of a social elite like Plato's 'Philosopher Kings'; to the divine revelation in scripture and ecclesiastical tradition, or to the historically determined collective 'spirit' of nations (Hegel) or the 'consciousness' of social classes (Marx).

Intolerance of the ambiguous relationships between language, thought and reality evokes a typical response. It is underpinned by the fact that everyone, at all times, knows what it is to say that at least something is true. We are often justified in our judgements of truth and falsity, reality and illusion, *and this is a necessary condition of being able to attach any meaning to the words*, even for the relativist. There seems to be a consequent temptation to 'ring-fence' these justifiable commitments to reason and truth by enshrining them in a transcendent certainty and attributing to certain individuals, social groups or conventions a privileged relationship to it.

McPeck and Kuhn, for example, both acknowledge the debatable epistemic status of forms of knowledge. The former, having insisted on the indefinite variety of self-authenticating forms of understanding, inconsistently introduces the idea that some possess the special status of being *in place at a given time*. This must be the springboard for his inferential leap to the recommendation that, despite all he has said about the uncertain epistemological foundations of disciplinary knowledge, learning in the early, formative years should concentrate on the passive assimilation of facts and memorisation (McPeck, 1990, p. 44). Kuhn goes further, even to the point of acknowledging the irony of his prescription:

> When examining normal science...we shall want finally to describe that research as a strenuous and devoted attempt to force nature into the conceptual boxes supplied by professional education. Simultaneously, we shall wonder whether research could proceed without such boxes, whatever the element of arbitrariness in their historic origins and, occasionally, in their subsequent development. (Kuhn, 1970, p. 5)

Yet these authors' preference for dogmatic teaching is the result of a failure to consider an implication of the historical relativities of thought which is of crucial pedagogic importance. This is that a reification of ideas, theories and beliefs which is in sharp contrast to their evolution through the dialectics of criticism is likely to obstruct their intelligibility rather than assist it. Concepts and theories can only be properly realised in the attempt to understand how the images they contain are responses to a history of problems; to what Bonnett describes as the 'incipient sense of the unknown' which cannot be felt 'by those preoccupied with imposing a system on thinking, or any recipe for the structuring of thinking or determining its direction in advance' (Bonnett, 1995, p. 305).

The ability to learn efficiently and rapidly *entails* critical thinking and there are certain affinities between critical thinking and acute sensitivity to the relativities of understanding. Each involves sceptical questioning of the concept of absolute correspondence between thought and reality; each involves an ability to entertain alternative descriptions, explanations and hypotheses; each requires the interpretation of ideas against the background of problem-situations in which they were formulated. But relativistic theses collapse because they cannot let go the idea of the imminent accessibility of an absolute truth which they dispute. They may locate it in the ineluctability of contemporary educational practice or in a sociological, rather than a scientific, criterion of scientific inquiry.

For the vast majority of societies, critical self-consciousness never was an option because the social and linguistic conditions for its emergence were not fulfilled. Human consciousness of the world, including conceptions of time, space and causation have differed quite radically according to the access to a cultural repertoire afforded by particular social, institutional and linguistic forms. And access of this kind is not automatically guaranteed by nominal membership of a modern, 'rationalist' society because there are constructive and servile ways of relating to the critical traditions.

Confirmation of this was contained in that recent UK survey of the public understanding of science which revealed that fewer that two out of three respondents were able to say that the Earth 'goes round' the sun, rather than vice versa and that only about one in three was able to say that it does so in one year (Durant et al., 1989, 11-14). Despite the popular accessibility, even superabundance, of this information, these responses reveal a manifest absence of the cosmological imagery within which these discrete astronomical 'facts' are united for the tolerably well-educated; the overall configuration of the solar system, the position and 'tilt' of the Earth and its effect on regional climates, seasonality and weather patterns. A fact, in isolation from its background of imagery, the legacy of answers to historical problems, is just a dysfunctional form of words. This principle should not only inform the practice of pedagogy but direct attention to another crucial point about critical thinking; that it is liable to atrophy in an educational culture dominated by the idea of communicating particular information and skills rather than encouraging the student to explore problems and question the status of her solutions. Durant asks, pertinently:

> ...what excuse shall we give (not for the public, but for ourselves as scientists and educators) to account for the fact that most of the public appears not to have caught up with Nicholas Copernicus and Galileo Galilei? (ibid.)

It seems that modern education has failed to make the great critical traditions accessible to large numbers of citizens. I will argue that the enhancement of critical thought must be at least as much about the need for social and institutional reform as about educational method; about conceptions of the role of education in society and the individual in society. There can be no methodological or programmatic short-cuts to genuine critical thought; it presupposes a libertarian social ethos which elevates dialogue, debate and the critical analysis of fundamental concepts at every level of education. This is not to say that members of regimented, secretive and authoritarian societies are incapable of critical and creative thought. It is, however, to argue that to whatever extent these things flourish in 'closed' societies, they depend on the intellectual inheritance of an alternative tradition which is liable to stagnate or, perhaps, to linger because cross-cultural exchange between specialists in clearly defined fields is permitted on supposedly utilitarian grounds.

There is the danger that that claims of this kind will be regarded as all very well, but that those at the 'sharp end' of educational research must concern themselves with the practical pedagogic means of teaching thinking in order to fulfil such social aspirations. But measures of the effectiveness of particular 'thinking skills' methodologies may appear to validate what are really very incomplete models of intellectual competencies because they bear a parasitic resemblance to products of a richer tradition. Frank Smith answers this 'businesslike' concern with talking less about critical thinking and getting on with teaching it:

> And given that there is so little agreement about the nature of critical thinking and how it should be defined, an enormous leap of faith is required for the belief that it can be taught through curriculums, instructional materials and tests. Perhaps a quite different approach might be required, employing example rather than instruction, encouragement rather than materials, and opportunities rather than tests. (Smith, 1992, p. 93)

But critical thinking is also a foundational social and ethical ideal; not simply one to be treated as a matter of technique, method or curriculum design within an education system. It must be recognised as the basis for a critique of education systems and for an assertion of the priority of their role in sustaining the critical traditions above other social objectives. For as I will argue in my final chapter, Mill's philosophy gravitates around the elenchus that if critical thinking cannot be justified as an ultimate ideal, the concept of justification, itself, dissolves.

8 The Sovereignty of Reason

> ...when the mind is no longer compelled...to exercise its vital powers on the questions which its belief presents to it, there is a progressive tendency to forget all of the belief except the formularies, or to give it a dull and torpid assent, as if accepting it on trust dispenses with the necessity of realizing it in consciousness, or testing it by personal experience; until it almost ceases to connect itself at all with the inner life of the human being. (Mill, 1965, p. 290)

> Mill was a proselytizer of genius; the ruthless denigrator of existing positions, the systematic propagator of a new moral posture, a man of sneers and smears and pervading certainty. It is in this light that the present generation should view this major prophet of the half articulated 'truths' which hang flabbily in the atmosphere of modern liberalism. (Cowling, 1969, p. 353)

> When, therefore, Mill's followers demand the elevation of skepticism to the status of a national religion, and the remaking of society in that image, they are not reading into his position something that is not there - for all that Mill himself...preserves a discreet silence on the detailed institutional consequences of his position...Mill's freedom of speech doctrine is not merely derivative from a preliminary assault upon truth itself; it is inseparable from that assault and cannot, I contend, be defended on any other ground. It is incompatible with religious or any other belief. (Kendall, 1966, pp. 32-33)

Critical thinking as an ultimate ideal

Some of Mill's sternest critics do most to identify important aspects of his thought. Cowling and Kendall both draw attention to the pivotal role of a theory of knowledge in his moral and political philosophy and to its profound, even subversive implications. Mill provides an epistemological justification of individual liberty as a prior condition and fulfilment of democratic aspirations; critical thinking is the paramount social, ethical and educational ideal. If we have the audacity to 'define some parameters, so that we know what we are talking about when we talk of the desirability of teaching thinking' (Coles and Robinson, 1989, p. 8), Mill's philosophy provides us with benchmarks which have not been explicitly rejected by educational thinkers but, instead, rather comprehensively ignored. Ironically, Mill is commonly recognised as a philosopher of major significance on most aspects of politics and social life apart from education, as I noted in Chapter 1. But commitment to the educational ideal of critical thinking pervades and explains his philosophy.

This neglect must be a result of his alienation from the emerging educational system of his time and the authoritarian values which imbued it. Despite changes in ethos in educational practice, the monolithic tendency has survived; reflected on the one hand in the development of large scale and relatively uniform institutions serving predetermined social ends, and on the other, in increasing preoccupation by educational world with rather narrowly circumscribed institutional concerns, defined largely by the complex system which now exists. Mill says little about organisational aspects of schooling because his concern is with prior questions about different ways of learning and understanding and their social and political consequences. He observed the embryonic Victorian educational system with foreboding; anticipating a servile, populist form of democracy characterised by 'collective mediocrity', a consequence of failure to realise the creative potential and personal autonomy of citizens. He confronts the problem of cultural and historical variability with consistent stress on the involutional character of critical thinking; a demand for metaphysical and epistemological thoroughness which leads some critics, like Kendall, to accuse him of absolute scepticism. But that is not Mill's position. The theme which unites his ethics and politics is a constant stress on the dialogical nature of human understanding and a consequent prioritisation of freedom of expression in the personal search for meaning and truth, as well as in the quest for social progress.

Mill challenges common assumptions about intellectual development and human potentials by directing attention to the negative psychological influences of authoritarian tradition. In his Autobiography, he indicts pedagogical aversion to the radical appraisal of belief for the way it can 'stunt and dwarf' minds by misrepresenting knowledge as an inventory of unproblematic solutions (Mill, 1965, p. 149). A 'single truth' pervades Mill's thought; social provision for critical appraisal of even the most firmly held beliefs is a condition of political obligation. His philosophy should redirect concern with critical thinking from 'the classroom' to the heart of social life and morality.

Mill's education in context

Mill's precocious intellectual achievements have also been largely ignored in the critical thinking debate though they sometimes receive respectful, parenthetical mention for their very uniqueness which Mill was at pains to remedy. Fisher, for instance, acknowledges Mill as 'one of the great critical thinkers of his age' in his book, *Teaching Children to Think*, referring to the way the young Mill was not told the answers to questions but required to find them himself and to subject his ideas to rigorous analysis (Fisher, 1994, p. 68 and pp. 95-6). Nevertheless, Mill's reflections on the nature and importance of critical thinking do not mesh comfortably with the strategic emphasis of the contemporary debate. I suggest this is simply because he did not conceive education for critical thinking in strategic terms, but as a primary requirement for self-realisation and social transformation, and that is his vital contribution. Now that a highly centralised and hierarchically organised system of schooling seems to have become definitive of popular and professional conceptions of education, it is worth briefly reviewing the embryonic but abortive alternative which Mill's experience represents.

In his *Autobiography*, Mill insists that his education was not one of 'cram' (Mill, 1965, p. 28). His understanding never overlaid by derivative information 'as a substitute for the power to form opinions' of his own. He contrasts this approach with the usual tendency of students to become 'mere parroters of what they have learnt, incapable of using their minds except in the furrows traced for them'. In the early pages of his *Autobiography* he describes his father's uniquely severe but anti-dogmatic pedagogy (which began with Greek when John was three). In addition to having to strive for his own conclusions, he was not required to study subjects without as full a justification as possible by James Mill of their relevance; an introduction, from the outset, to the task of clarifying the epistemic basis of disciplines. Although that pedagogical method is notable for its stringency, it should receive due acknowledgement as one which prioritised the epistemic viewpoint of the learner, expressing the insight that real understanding is a function of the manner in which new concepts and methods are integrated within a unique individual cognitive repertoire. (And, of course, it does not follow that such an approach need be accompanied by eighteenth century Presbyterian severity.) The details of this experience are well known and readily accessible, but it is worth noting the pre-eminent role of classical literature, philosophy and logic in Mill's curriculum. Socratic dialectic argument he describes an 'unsurpassed discipline'; the figure of Socrates became for the young Mill 'a model of ideal excellence' (Mill, 1965, p. 22).

The impact on educational theory and practice of this account has been minimal. More attention seems to have been paid by educational authors to the stringency of James Mill's teaching methods and their alleged contribution to John Mill's subsequent 'mental crisis' than to the extraordinary potential of the infant mind which they were designed to reveal. That Enlightenment educational philosophy probably reached its nadir in 1926 when Catherine Morris Cox cited Mill's early accomplishments as evidence of an IQ in the 190-200 range, placing him ahead of Copernicus and Faraday and 286 other high-achievers in *The Early Mental Traits of Three Hundred Geniuses*. Cox was either ignorant of, or indifferent to, Mill's reason for writing the *Autobiography*.

It was, he says most explicitly, to describe these accomplishments as evidence of what he believed to be a *general*, and specifically *not*, a unique individual potential. A similar tendency to dismiss Mill's central message and to remain locked within a vague but evidently compelling framework of deterministic explanation reveals itself in Max Lerner's bland equivocation in his introduction to the *Autobiography* and other works by Mill:

> (Mill) was probably accurate about the head start he was given, but over-modest about what he started with. The boy clearly had the stuff of genius in him. Yet while the potential was there as seed, the soil and nourishment which it needed for flourishing were furnished by that relation of tension between student and teacher which we call an "education". (Lerner, 1965, p. x)

This uncommitted 'seed-soil' metaphor evades the central issue of Mill's belief in the decisive impact of environmental influences in development and, particularly, on the exponential impact on intellectual growth of early introduction to critical, philosophical modes of thought. Nor is his education sufficiently recognised as the focal point in a tradition in which pedagogy was identified as the basis for radical social change to an extent unmatched by the social and educational philosophies which replaced it. Philosophical radicalism was egalitarian, democratic and feminist, connecting the varied ideas of pioneers like Mary Wollstonecraft, William Godwin, Robert Owen, James Mill and Jeremy Bentham through the central influence of Helvetius. The principal doctrine of this movement was that all the inequalities between individuals 'are social and modifiable, not physiological and immutable' (Halévy, 1952, p. 20). Like all traditions, philosophical radicalism merged with others and exerted diffuse influences; for instance, in the 19th Century process of electoral reform and in the eventual establishment of universal, state-supported education. However, this rationalist, Enlightenment tradition was largely eclipsed by more ancient, authoritarian conventions against which John Mill was to argue consistently throughout his life.

James Mill and Bentham had collaborated in the design of John Stuart's curriculum which was to excite widespread interest in philosophical radical circles as a test of Helvetius' ideas. They also actively promoted a national educational system of 'Chresthomatic' schools based on the same pedagogic principles and practices, identifying sites and raising funds, only for the whole programme to collapse in acrimony and conflict in the face of organised opposition - externally, from the established church, and internally from those of the 'dissenting' persuasion who were alarmed at the agnostic and atheist tendencies of the radicals.

When John Stuart was just six years old, James Mill was actively involved in the Lancastrian movement's drive for universal educational provision. However, some specific ideals which inspired that drive, the elimination of social and gender inequalities and the idea of universal suffrage, were to be very inadequately realised or postponed for a century or more. In direct opposition to the utilitarian and increasingly agnostic implications of 'philosophical radicalism', the British National Society was convened under the auspices of the established church (Burston, 1973, pp. 63-76). For the next six years increasingly bitter competition meant that while 'a majority of the population was receiving no education, the establishment of a Lancastrian school in a locality was likely to produce a second school to serve the same district under the auspices of the church' (ibid., p. 67). In 1812 James Mill published his response, *Schools for All, not Schools for Churchmen Only*, claiming with irony that it was only at the prospect of improved standards of general education that the cry went up: 'The Church is in danger!' (James Mill, 1973). And from 1818 the movement he supported was increasingly embroiled in internal religious controversy. James Mill and Francis Place secured the modification of a West London Lancastrian Association resolution requiring that readings in school be taken *only* from the Bible and also of another requirement that all children should be taken to church on Sundays - a measure of the determination of religious interests to maintain control of the embryonic educational system. But the radical initiative collapsed; its direct legacy was the foundation of University College, London - largely as a result of James Mill's activism, and the Mechanics' Institute, largely due to Place (ibid., Burston).

These are events of which John Stuart says nothing in his *Autobiography*. Yet it is reasonable to infer that the failure of the broader aspirations behind his education played a very significant part in his subsequent ideas about society and politics. The central principle of social progress had been subordinated to a comprehensive religious orthodoxy. He avoided practical educational initiatives, becoming preoccupied with the dangers posed by the growth of democracy in the absence of educational commitments to a critically intelligent citizenry. That omission must have contributed substantially to his premonitions of the degeneration of democratic government into a tyranny of dogmatically-minded majorities, an opinion to be confirmed by his reading of de Tocqueville's analysis of American democracy and its uniformist tendencies (Mill, 1963, pp. 173-267). Where John Mill deals explicitly with the subject of education, it is to assert the 'nearly self-evident axiom' that 'the State should require and compel the education of every human being who is born its citizen' but also that education should not be undertaken by the State:

> A general State education is a mere contrivance for moulding people to be exactly like one another - a despotism over the mind exercised by the predominant power in the Government, whether that is a monarch, a priesthood, an aristocracy, or the majority of the existing generation. (Mill 1965, p. 352)

The deep contradiction between 19th Century *laissez-faire* liberalism and the then prevailing views on education partly explains Mill's paradoxical fame as a philosopher of almost-everything *except education.* The idea of learning as a self-authenticating end with beneficial social consequences was officially subordinated to the idea of it as an instrument of social and ideological cohesion; an aim expressed in instructions to Her Majesty's Inspectors in 1840/41, mentioned in Chapter 1, that:

> No plan of education ought to be encouraged in which intellectual instruction is not subordinated to the regulation of the thoughts and habits of the children by the doctrines and precepts of revealed religion. (Morris, 1972, p. 283)

John Mill became increasingly disillusioned and concerned about the difficulties of reconciling the need for state-guaranteed standards and financial support for education with the avoidance of centralised control and uniform, over-prescriptive policies on the substantives of pedagogic method and curriculum content (for example, Mill, 1965, pp. 351-353). He remained committed to a radical vision of what education might accomplish, but also to the task of warning against its likely consequences. This foreboding is illustrated in his occasional correspondence on the subject of schools, educational policies and initiatives. In 1865, for example, he declined an invitation by Thomas Huxley, despite his credentials as Darwin's champion, to stand for nomination to an educational society for the promotion of science and theology. He would, he said, support such a school if it were not proposed to teach theology, though, he added: 'It might be useless in the present state of the public mind to propose such schools' (Mill, 1910, p. 43). Opposition to religious influence in education became a persistent theme in his correspondence of later years.

But Mill's was not simply the hostility of a confirmed agnostic to organised religion; an inordinate attachment to a single issue. He went so far in 1867 as to agree with a clerical correspondent that it was highly desirable that 'parts of the Old and New Testament should be taught in schools', but with the reservation that nearly all teachers would fail to distinguish between religious education and indoctrination (Mill, 1910, p. 74). Organised religion symbolised for Mill a pervasive human tendency to perpetuate existing social orders through the imposition of ideologies which, implicitly or explicitly, identified philosophical speculation and argument as subversive of legitimate authority. Any other specification of comprehensive social and moral ends incurred his equal disapproval. Indeed, Mill was even more uncompromising in his criticisms of Comte's proposals for a secular, rationalist education precisely because of its dogmatic, all-embracing aspirations.

Some of the aims of the philosophical radicals succeeded in part; others ran into the sand. The 1832 Reform Act, a very limited success, was followed at a snail's pace by legislation which achieved universal suffrage only by 1928. Mill's advocacy of women's rights in *The Subjection of Women*, his support, through his daughter Helen Taylor, for a network of women's suffrage associations and his unsuccessful promotion as a Member of Parliament of a Bill to secure female suffrage in 1867 were part-payment of a debt to eighteenth century ideas which remain largely unrealised in the early twentieth century. Universal education was achieved slowly in England and Wales and became compulsory only in the 1880's, and free in the 1890's. A plausible case can be made for saying that the sense of cohesive religious purpose which Mill opposed so trenchantly has never been entirely lost; that it has undergone a partial metamorphosis to emerge in the vision of formal education as a process addressing all the needs, and catering for all the potentialities, of maturing citizens of a society characterised by relatively homogenous and specifiable purposes. Mill is the principal critic of such an ideology; and it is to this that he attributes the failure of education systems to produce effective, critical thinkers and creative participants in democratic society.

Mill's contemporary relevance

The contemporary significance of Mill's educational philosophy is as undiminished as that of his political philosophy because they are essentially the same thing. This, perhaps, can be brought out by identifying some recurrent themes in his work.

The 'sanctity' of critical thought and individual autonomy: Mill places deep moral emphasis on critical thinking which seems alien from most modern perspectives. In this respect his ideas closely resemble the faith of members of the Dissenting movement in the possibility of spiritual enlightenment through intellectual struggle for truth - the 'Unitarian' tendency, which Mill partially attributes to Coleridge, to make 'man's reason and moral feelings a test of revelation' (Mill, 1963, p. 168). There is a persistent Socratic identification of knowledge, virtue and truth in his work which Kendall misses despite correctly interpreting the subversive potential of the theme. These elements are present in his essay on *Civilization* where he recommends that the end of education should be to maximise intellectual power and 'inspire the intensest *love of truth;* and this without a particle of regard to the results to which the exercise of that power may lead' (Mill, 1963, p. 72, original emphasis). James and John Mill shared an Enlightenment conviction in 'the unlimited possibility of improving the moral and intellectual condition of mankind by education', a creed which John Mill described as the most important of his father's legacies, but one which was in outright contradiction to 'the prevailing tendencies of speculation, both in his time and since' (Mill, 1965, p. 69).

Mill's case for personal autonomy owes little to his stance on the issue of priority in the relationship between individuals and society, which Popper attacks as 'psychologistic' (Popper, 1969, pp. 89-99). Indeed, Mill attacks the individualism articulated by Bentham for failing to give a satisfactory account of individual involvement in the social nexus on terms rather similar to those of Popper's criticism of his own view of that relationship (Mill, 1963, p. 99-103). What he really does advance, I suggest, is a defensible conception of *epistemic individualism* in the evolution of thought. This is, briefly, that culturally distinctive ideas and beliefs, however ostensibly homogenous, are always decomposable *in principle* to the variety of forms in which they are received, entertained and expressed by individuals. Cultural evolution, the history of ideas, is ultimately intelligible as the result of individual contributions to, and modifications of, traditional beliefs. In a strict sense, there are no *collective* meanings because they are internalised as a function of dialogue; and they are individuated within the unique matrix of each individual's experience, linguistic competence and relationships with others. This is *the* source of ideational change and creativity, determining its extent and pace. According to Popper, the alternative is to subscribe to 'essentialism'; the idea of an unidentified, mysterious substratum of collective thought. And this is to do more than refer to very extensive bonds of tacit meaning in language and social relations; it is to import the notion of something 'beyond' these reciprocities. Indeed, Popper endorses what he calls Mill's 'methodological individualism' - the explanation of social behaviour as 'the behaviour and...actions of human individuals'.

Mill is acutely aware of the extent to which different cultures restrict or extend the scope of individual contributions to the matrix of ideas and beliefs. His argument is symmetrical with Popper's own about the 'argumentative' and 'discursive' uses of language, displayed so prominently amongst the disputatious Greeks, who contributed disproportionately to the fund of human ideas and to diversification of the thought of individuals.

The *involutional character of critical thought:* Critical thinking is more than the application of techniques and methodologies for the efficient assimilation of traditional knowledge. Writing before the development of the misleadingly clear-cut division between the psychology and philosophy, Mill's account of critical thinking is a fusion of what has come to be known as *metacognition*; reflection on the strategies and routines we deploy in the course of thinking and learning, and more ancient problems of *epistemology*; fundamental conceptual inquiry about the nature of knowledge and the possibility of certainty and truth. Thus when he says in the letter *On Genius* that 'the most important phenomena of human nature cannot even be conceived, except by a mind which has actively studied itself' he is asserting, at the same time, a psychological and philosophical principle; that efficient learning involves simultaneous investigation of the methods by which we attempt to learn about a subject and reflection upon the epistemic status of that subject and our methodology. Mill opens up the prospect of a regressive examination of our firmest convictions, for which 'no routine or rule of thumb can possibly make provision'. This procedure is for Mill, nevertheless, a practical, philosophically justifiable and generalizable learning strategy. His conviction clearly rests on his own extraordinary educational experience and on the spontaneous emergence of Greek rationality for which, he emphasises, there *had* been no previous guidelines. He attaches supreme educational value to 'logic and the philosophy of mind', though with the warning that 'the former will not be taught as a mere system of technical rules, nor the latter as a set of concatenated abstract propositions', because:

> The tendency, so strong everywhere, is strongest of all here, to receive opinions into the mind without any real understanding of them, merely because they seem to follow from certain admitted premises, and to let them lie there as forms of words, lifeless and devoid of meaning...the pupil must be led to interrogate his own consciousness. (Mill, 1963, p. 74)

Mill might be said to have anticipated the kind of institutional pressures which would lead to the photocopyable checklist of fallacies, or problems and strategies for their solution, and to have rejected them in favour of a radical reappraisal of the pedagogical relationship - and of the concept of learning. He would not have been surprised about the problem of 'transfer' in the teaching of 'general thinking skills'.

Critical thinking has an involutional tendency which it is vital to acknowledge. Although justifications have to end somewhere, *in practice,* they should not be considered to do so, *in principle.* The verdict must remain open for continuing reappraisal because it is not possible to predict what undetected inconsistency or novel insight might lead to the wholesale revision of pragmatically 'established' truths (as Newton's were by Einstein, for example). If there are general, transferable thinking skills, Mill seems to say, there are serious dangers in trying to specify them in advance rather than to introduce them as regulative principles in the conduct of dialogical inquiry; and this, I suggest, has quite radical implications for educational practice.

Relevant fields of evidence for educational theory and practice: Class, gender and race are irrelevant to the potential for learning; 'I yield to no one in the degree of intelligence of which I believe (the body of the people) to be capable' (Mill, 1963, p. 12). Existing inequalities, particularly stark in his lifetime and displayed so ubiquitously in the subordination and exploitation of women, are not adequate evidence of inherent limitations. Here, again, the influence of Greek accomplishments is apparent in his earliest and latest works, providing an alternative frame of reference to the modern bias for interpreting performance on specified tasks as a measure of *potential.* The prolific achievements of a tiny, ancient civilisation are not to be dismissed as 'an enigma' - as Lipman has pointed out. The explanation is in terms of their cultural characteristics of inquisitiveness and disputatiousness and not of the innate qualities and limitations of individuals. Mill anticipates Vygotsky with an insistence on the interactional features of learning situations and on modes of teaching and learning as overwhelmingly important in determining the course and level of individual educational attainment. What Vygotsky describes as the 'zone of proximal development' is for Mill the vast but indeterminate cognitive territory which could be opened up by a culture of inquiry.

But Mill's analysis also encompasses the ideological characteristics of cultures which 'stunt and dwarf' human potential, and which have the apparent power both to justify and convey a sense of the inevitability of existing differentials. He urges recognition of the stultifying effect of *subordinating* reason to traditional understanding rather than interrogating it critically; of false conceptions of epistemic authority and passive acceptance of a received world-view. 'Critical thinking' is not a discrete educational issue to be addressed independently of other issues like 'under achievement' or 'exceptional ability'; it is the key to understanding them because it is a criterion of the efficacy of modes of cultural transmission. Much of his condemnation is directed consistently against orthodox Christianity and its authoritarian influence in 'encrusting and petrifying' minds and muting critical debate. But his criticism is broader than this. It is an account of the urge to subordinate reason to traditional dogma for fear of the destabilising consequences of relativistic conclusions - a deep and abiding social prejudice against the idea that traditional verities may be questionable.

Despite growing reservations about a democracy defined almost exclusively in terms of an extended franchise, Mill remained an extreme egalitarian, rejecting 'innatist' dogma and its complacent acceptance of existing inequalities. In his essay *Civilisation* he recommends the learning of history as a valid source of evidence for the 'extraordinary pliability' of human nature reflected in cultural change (Mill, 1963, p. 74). Here and elsewhere, Mill enjoins his readers to confront the historical and cultural relativities of thought to challenge the prejudice that human possibilities are to be attributed to innate qualities and deduced from human achievements within a single culture - for these are usually woven from the sparse strands of authoritarian dogma and blind adherence to custom. His own education reveals how much more could be taught in the aimless early years of childhood than is generally believed (Mill, 1965, p. 11).

Although he adds that any boy or girl of average ability could emulate his progress, this single experiment might be judged inconclusive. Indeed, I have referred above to Lerner's bland dismissal of Mill's thesis. But his well known achievements must raise serious doubts about the idea of organically or psychologically determined age-related competences, as do other instances of extraordinary intellectual precocity. James Mill's educational theory, a development of the psychological associationism of Hartley, Priestley and Helvetius, stressed the two radical themes which were the inspiration for John Mill's home-based education. One was that '...by far the greater part (of the distinctions between individuals, sexes and races) are...produced by circumstances' and are not 'innate' or 'indelible' (Mill, 1965, p. 160). The other was a crucial emphasis on the influence of learning in the early stages of life:

> It is probable, that people in general form a very inadequate conception of all the circumstances which act during the first months, perhaps the first moments, of existence, and of the power of those moments in giving permanent qualities to the mind. (James Mill, 1973, p. 70)

Mill encourages rejection of the mode of inductive inference from the restricted fields of evidence constituted by 'normal' educational attainments and performances for a broader historical and conceptual perspective. But the conservative prejudice he opposes is still widespread. For instance, it has entered the 'critical thinking debate' in the form of McPeck's unsupported claim that to absorb information passively is the 'natural and appropriate way' for young children to learn (McPeck, 1990, pp. 44). Where McPeck claims it is 'simply bad pedagogy to teach the exceptions before one understands the rule', Mill considers rules unintelligible unless they are grasped in terms of their exceptions, implications and nuances of meaning. And, contradicting the Oakeshottian idea of learning to speak before one can understand, he derides dogmatic formulations which a child is expected 'to believe before it can attach any meaning to them':

> At school, what is the child taught except to repeat by rote, or at most to apply technical rules, which are lodged, not in his reason, but in his memory? When he leaves school, does not everything which a young person sees and hears conspire to tell him, that it is not expected he shall think, but only that he shall profess no opinion on any subject different from that professed by other people? (Mill, 1832, p. 38)

Mill's inaugural address to the University of St. Andrews in 1867 makes very clear his apprehensions concerning the general acceptance of unjustifiably restrictive parameters in the assessment of human potential:

> ...this strangely limited estimate of what it is possible for human beings to learn, resting on a tacit assumption that they are already as efficiently taught as they ever can be. So narrow a conception not only vitiates our idea of education, but actually, if we receive it, darkens our anticipations as to the future progress of mankind. (Mill, 1984, p. 222)

His argument, however, apart from the evidence of his own educational performance, is an epistemological one; a theory about the nature of knowledge, its historically cumulative and dialogical character. There simply is no role within his theory for the idea that the 'many-sidedness' of truth and the complex, debatable status of knowledge in all its varied, overlapping and sometimes conflicting fields, can be best conveyed to young minds by misrepresenting the world as one of simple certainties. Helen Taylor expressed Mill's intense hostility to the 'authoritative' teaching by parents of 'anything whatever that one does not from the bottom of one's heart and by the clearest light of one's reason believe to be true'. To act otherwise, she continued: '..is little if at all short of a crime against one's children, against one's fellow creatures in general, and against abstract truth in whatever form it appears most sacred to one's eyes' (Mill, 1910, p. 134). Adults cannot be justified in inflicting upon young minds categories of analysis which the adult mind is incapable of sustaining consistently. The groundwork of critical thinking is laid by critical inquiry, and it is the widespread disregard of the need for such a groundwork, in society generally as well as in educational programmes, which makes the 'gifted' child stand out as a somewhat embarrassing and inexplicable saltation.

Word-meaning, dialogue and social relations: A basic feature of Mill's epistemology and social philosophy is the idea that meaning evolves through constant immersion in the multiplicity of usages, the struggle for mutual intelligibility. In the absence of this struggle, dogma can impose on human minds 'the formularies of belief' which are 'barely connected with the inner life of the human being' (Mill, 1965, p. 290). The theme persists throughout Mill's works and he deploys it in repeated attacks on conventional religious belief as a paradigm for the subversion of the critical awareness which gives words and ideas a dynamic life in the mind. For Mill, the 'rote' learner is a microcosm of the servile society where progress is halted because thought and action are embalmed in the medium of superficial agreement, or unresolved contradiction, about forms of words.

Institutional recognition of the role of critical discourse must be an organising principle in human affairs, generally, if people are to be governed by anything more than coercion or manipulation, the theme of his justification of freedom of thought and expression in *On Liberty.* Confrontation between 'antagonistic modes of thought' is a condition of their intelligibility and thus, eventually, of the rational elimination of conflict. For Mill, concepts of social wellbeing are answerable to the court of reason and entail as unlimited a duty of rational justification as other ends. This is the rationale for his contentions that 'All restraint, *qua* restraint, is an evil' and, in respect of moral and other constraints, that '...if the grounds of an opinion are not conclusive to a person's own reason, his reason cannot be strengthened, but is likely to be weakened by his adopting it'. Political liberty is defined in terms of this requirement to justify constraints, though it is important for Mill, I believe, to recognise that ideals and principles need to be reinterpreted constantly within the framework of evolving cultural traditions. That is why, as Kendall complains, Mill says little about the 'detailed institutional consequences of his position', *and*, I believe, why so many scholars have detected ambiguities within and between his libertarianism and his utilitarianism. No notion of abstract right or principle must stand in the way of the critical examination of even the most apparently secure convictions:

> The beliefs which we have most warrant for have no safeguard to rest on, but a standing invitation to the whole world to prove them unfounded...if the lists are kept open, we may hope that, if there be a better truth, it will be found when the human mind is capable of receiving it; and in the meantime we may rely on having attained such approach to truth as is possible in our own day. This is the amount of certainty attainable by a fallible being, and is the sole way of attaining it. (Mill, 1965, p. 273)

The essay *On Liberty* addressed future rather than present generations (Mill, 1965, p. 149), because a general disregard for the dissemination of critical, philosophical modes of thought was likely to herald a servile, uniform society. With the advent of twentieth-century totalitarianism, at a time when sophisticated industrial democracies are still plagued by functional illiteracy on a huge scale and are characterised by mass uniformity in fashions, entertainment and consumer choice, I suggest that Mill's view of the proper role and method of education in society is prescient. In the final paragraphs of On Liberty he anticipates improvements in transport and communications, the centralisation and homogenisation of the education system and an increasing tendency for politicians to pander to popular prejudice. He could not have envisaged a majority of a nation's population watching the same episode of a television 'soap opera' simultaneously, but he might not have been surprised that an even larger majority would still be oblivious to the Renaissance discovery that the Earth orbits the Sun in the period of about one year.

The central issue; truth as a regulative principle

If principles of rationality evolve and change, asks Siegel, how can they be taken to be impartial and universal? (Siegel, 1988, p. 134). I suggest that this, too, is the central concern of Mill's philosophy and his answer, in the form of the theory of critical thinking, is its unifying characteristic. Mill's major works are a sustained attempt to interpret the ideas of truth and rationality as *regulative* principles and to interpolate them constructively into the flux of human affairs; to descend, as it were, from a plane on which the implications of abstract principles are explored without due acknowledgement of the relativities of human understanding and value.

Mill's *Autobiography* includes the account of his struggle to reconcile the abstract, formal modes of philosophical and social analysis of his father and Bentham with a growing awareness of the 'many-sided' and provisional nature of truth and the relativities of knowledge. Where his father had trusted 'too much in the intelligibleness of the abstract, when not embodied in the concrete' (Mill, 1965, p. 23), Bentham had embarked on the enterprise of reconstructing society *de novo*, dismissing traditions of thought as 'vague generalities' without realising that they 'contained the whole unanalysed experience of the human race' (Mill, 1963, p. 92). It is worth noting the similarity between these words and Oakeshott's portrait of the rationalist as one voluntarily divorced from understandings enshrined in traditional knowledge, referred to in Chapter 3. Mill's thought spans that philosophical divide. The growing distance between his philosophy and that of his mentors emerges in the essays *Coleridge, The Spirit of the Age* and *Civilisation* as a rejection of determinate systems and of systematic deduction from abstract premises; a contrast between the eighteenth and nineteenth centuries which, he says, he ceaselessly tried to transcend. Any philosophy of politics or history, Mill argues, presupposes a theory of human progress. The intelligibility of social institutions and human ends depends on a deeper contextual and historical understanding. But:

> If I am asked what system of political philosophy I substituted for that which, as a philosophy, I had abandoned, I answer, no system: only a conviction that the true system was something much more complex and many-sided than I had previously had any idea of... (Mill, 1965, p. 98-99)

This account is illuminating, I believe, because it casts his subsequent work in a substantially different light to that in which it is often seen. His central task becomes that of translating the insight that all assertions of epistemic or moral authority entail rational justification according to standards which are constantly changing and often opposed. But the onus of justification is rigorous and continuous; rigorous because it must be intelligible to each and all who are held to be subject to authority; continuous because rationality is fallible. Hence, for Mill, all restraint *qua* restraint is evil because it violates that universal requirement. There is still the alternative of coercion, the assertion of will, of course. Nietzsche sees a lack of integrity in the human urge to universalise and in the quest for systematic understanding. In *The Birth of Tragedy* he anticipates a time when science is 'pushed to its limits and, faced with those limits, forced to renounce its claim to universal validity'. The nihilistic ethical consequences of his scepticism are clear in his criticisms of English utilitarianism:

> The welfare of the many and the welfare of the few are radically opposite ends. To consider the former *a priori* the higher value may be left to the naïveté of English biologists. (Nietzsche, 1956, p. 188)

The transcendent role Mill attributes to the normative concepts of truth and reason, I believe, accounts for the apparent inconsistency which some critics have detected in his espousal of a *libertarian* and a *utilitarian* ethic. It is important to recognise the prominence he accords his renunciation of any argument from 'abstract right' in *On Liberty*. Personal freedom and autonomy are justified by Mill in terms of utility, general happiness (Mill, 1965, p. 264). However, *utility* is not some finite state, if it is indeed more than the benevolent face of Mill's agnosticism, but one which entails the freedom to experiment, to criticise and justify traditional values according to the best attainable standards of rational argument. There is, thus, a reciprocal interplay between these principles and the evolv*ing* process of rational debate which is every bit as relevant to contemporary discussion about the relationships between education, liberty, democracy and critical thinking, now as it was then.

Skorupski sees Mill and Nietzsche as polar opposites on a naturalistic continuum which 'goes to the anthropological root of ethical and political life' and which therefore 'has the power to disorientate and disturb all but the most dogmatically entrenched on either side' (Skorupski, 1991, p. 37). The question posed by that naturalistic perspective concerns the place of values in a vacuum of transcendental guarantees of certainty and ethical purpose. The two philosophers are in close agreement that one outcome of the struggle for power is the supremacy of the 'herd morality' and Mill is as antipathetic as Nietzsche to the pre-emptive systematising urge, as his caustic review of Comtian rationalism demonstrates (Mill, 1965, pp. 178-181). But his antipathy cashes itself in an attempt to interpolate a dynamic principle into human affairs in place of traditional precepts upheld indiscriminately by a society 'destitute of faith but terrified at scepticism' (ibid., p. 273). He rejects the anxious quest for rules 'to meet all cases, and provide against all possible evasions' in favour of an open ended commitment to the continuing critical assessment of human values and beliefs. Skorupski provides a felicitous description of Mill's response to the 'naturalistic dilemma' posed by the eclipse of transcendental truths and values which has a bearing on the quotations from Kendall and Cowling at the beginning of this Chapter:

> Mill learnt from conservative historicism the importance of allegiance to a tradition and a community. But *mere* conservatism...which appeals to traditional legitimation alone, shrinks from dialogue and critique for the wrong reasons. *There is a dialectic between criticism and allegiance which Mill tried to register*...But readings which present Mill either as an intellectual authoritarian, or as a shallow debunker of precedent and convention do not recognise the difficulty of the dialectic, or the importance it had in Mill's mind. (Skorupski, 1991, pp. 37-38, latter emphasis mine)

As I have pointed out, liberty is justified, specifically not as an abstract right, but in terms of 'utility in the largest sense, grounded on the permanent interests of man as a progressive being' (Mill, 1965, p. 264). But *Utility*, in this largest sense, requires the *freedom* of individuals to develop 'higher capacities' and these are described as intellectual and moral virtues upon which the utilitarian goals of pleasure and happiness are contingent. It is better, says Mill, to be Socrates dissatisfied than a fool satisfied (Mill, 1968, pp. 260-261). And in *On Liberty* he asks a revealing rhetorical question; if certain beliefs are advocated on the grounds of utility, does it make sense to exclude the question of their truth? 'The usefulness of an opinion is itself matter of opinion; as disputable, as open to discussion, and requiring discussion as much, as the opinion itself' (ibid., p. 274). Truth is paramount; a magnetic pole to which all discourse is attracted or opposed. The route to both individual and general well-being is through the exercise of the critical intellect, and from the verdict of that critical intellect - symbolised by Mill as an unidentified tribunal of 'competent judges' - there can be no possible appeal (Mill, 1968, p. 261).

The problem is to take simultaneous account of the ineluctable commonalties of human understanding, feeling and purpose, expressed through shared language and tradition, and the diverse and often contradictory intimations of that legacy. Mill's resolution of the problem places his belief in critical thinking as an educational ideal at the very centre of human affairs; nothing is more fundamental than the critical appraisal by each individual of traditions, including the critical traditions. Skorupski suggests that Mill's case for individual autonomy could have been strengthened by an explicit acknowledgement that it '...is in its own right a categorical human end' (ibid., p. 21) but he underestimates the significance of Mill's renunciation of abstract right in favour of the epistemological justification of his Liberty-principle. Mill's position is that to justify any human end entails an 'open invitation' to rational appraisal and this leads to massive emphasis on the transparent exercise of authority, individual freedom and the education of reason.

Cowling is correct, in a way, about Mill's elitist and anti-democratic predispositions, yet it is these, perhaps, which bring his educational concerns most sharply into focus. In *The Spirit of the Age*, and in *Civilisation* Mill addresses the problems of authority and the justification of social order. But even at this most conservative phase of his thought, where he inclines towards heavy emphasis on the social cohesiveness of respect for tradition and moral leadership, there is a recurrent appeal to a notion of an authority, exemplified by the leaders of the Athenian demos, which 'did not supersede reason, but guided it' - authority vested in 'forcible appeals to the reason of the people' (Mill, 1963, p. 32). Mill is fiercely antagonistic to social elites and intellectual hegemonies. Paradoxically, it is for that reason that he can be read as both an intellectual authoritarian and a subversive. His real intention was not to produce anything resembling a *blueprint* for a tolerant liberal society but to introduce a dynamic which would 'unsettle the minds' (in Lipman's words) of future generations and forestall the degeneration of democracy into:

> ...the only despotism of which, in the modern world, there is real danger - the absolute rule of the head of the executive over a congregation of isolated individuals, all equal, but all slaves. (Mill, 1965, p. 116)

Cowling sees Mill as fearful of democracy, the propagator of an elite order which, by destroying traditional rigidities, 'would make the world safe for 'rational' education, 'rational' thinking, 'rational' sociology and the assured leadership of the 'rational' clerisy' (Cowling, 1969, page 338). Cowling is right about Mill's anxieties concerning democracy and the prospect of its convergent, monolithic tendencies. But Mill's notion of a 'rational' sociology must be considered in the light of the qualified aspirations he expresses in Book VI of the *System of Logic* for a social science which, though 'quite insufficient for prediction may be most valuable for guidance'. And Mill's attitude towards a *rational clerisy*, if not abundantly clear in his consistent repudiations of dogma and self-authenticating elitism, is apparent in his scathing rejection of Comte's idea of a rational 'sacerdotal order' and the unfavourable comparison he draws between that and the Greek addiction to intellectual speculation:

> Anyone who knows Grecian history as it can now be known, will be amazed at M. Comte's travesty of it, in which the vulgarest historical prejudices are accepted and exaggerated, to illustrate the mischiefs of intellectual culture left to its own guidance. (Mill, 1965, page 189)

That phrase, 'intellectual culture left to its own guidance' is of immense significance for the interpretation of Mill's thought, I believe, and for contemporary justifications of critical thinking. Whatever exigencies in the messy affairs of humans dictate suppression of debate, and this may be inevitable from time to time, they can never stand as justifications, nor can they be claimed as legitimate features of a social order, for Mill's case is that justification and legitimacy entail at least openness to criticism and refutation. Principles inevitably come into conflict at some point, but most fundamental is the requirement for continuing provision for the criticism of authority-claims by all who fall within their ambit. And in *On Liberty*, Mill specifically attacks Comte's notion of intellectual and moral hierarchy as an example of the continuing, perverse desire for control over 'every department of human conduct' masquerading under the slogan of rationality (Mill, 1965, p. 267). Elsewhere, he attacked the concept of intellectual authority according to which Comte justified these scientific social hierarchies - in terms which might be justifiably applied to the dogmatic pedagogic precepts of Thomas Kuhn and his case for the educational hegemony of 'normal' scientific paradigms:

> The teacher (of the Positivist faith) should not even represent the proofs to (the pupils) in a complete form, or as proofs. The object of instruction is to make them understand the doctrines themselves, perceive their mutual connection, and form by means of them a consistent and systematized conception of nature. As for the demonstrations, it is rather desirable than otherwise that even theorists should forget them, retaining only the results. Among all the aberrations of scientific men, M. Comte thinks none greater than the pedantic anxiety they show for complete proof, and perfect rationalization of scientific processes...Of course, M. Comte...does not imagine that he actually possesses all knowledge, but only that he is an infallible judge of what knowledge is worth possessing. (Mill, 1965, p. 178 and 181)

Critical thinking as a standard of social order

Mill's educational and political philosophy can be summed upwithout real distortion, in the following thesis: *if there can be any moral justification for particular ways of living and thinking, and for the concepts of authority and obedience they embody, that justification entails the maximisation of the rational autonomy of every subject.* This is an ideal which for practical reasons cannot be fully realised, but it is nevertheless an ineluctable procedural principle, applying as much in education as in all other aspects of human affairs. The very concept of justifiability entails an appeal to public criteria of rationality; it is an appeal for agreement and an invitation to dialogue. Any assertion of supervening values, commercial advantage or social wellbeing, entails the same, recursive appeal to rational justification. Only through the general exercise of critical reason can we hope to identify anything like *absolute* value; everything else is arbitrary imposition, the assertion of will and the exercise of power. Uncomprehending obedience to moral rules or laws cannot be moral because the agent does not grasp the significance or even the nature of her actions. Pragmatically, there can be no doubt that Mill recognises the inevitability of social and moral constraints. Coercion or interference is a necessary evil in human affairs, but it may be justified to the limited extent that it always remains open to question, and thus to subsequent amendment:

> Complete liberty of contradicting and disproving our opinion, is the very condition which justifies us in assuming its truth for the purposes of action; and on no other terms can a being with human faculties have any rational assurance of being right. (Mill, 1965, p. 271)

Kendall is nearly correct in his emphasis on the radical institutional implications of Mill's epistemology. But he is entirely wrong in ascribing this to 'an assault on truth itself' - for if there is one fixed point in Mill's philosophy, it is the conviction that truth, however complex and obscure, is the one thing which can legitimate a social order or provide a standard for evaluating any social or ethical goal. Mill's challenge to posterity, as relevant now as ever, is that it should acknowledge an intractable problem of epistemology as definitive of the human condition. Knowledge and understanding are subsumed within numerous historical, culture-bound traditions of thought which are often mutually contradictory; it is also and only from within these traditions that criteria of intelligibility and reasoned argument are to be derived. Yet conceptions of truth and certainty are the indispensable norms of language use, without which any proposition would be random and meaningless. If there is a point of equilibrium between these horns of a philosophical dilemma, it must lie in the dialogical exploration of the conflict between opposed systems of thought and belief, for it is only through this interplay that the true meaning of ideas can be clarified by parties to a dispute.

Thus the possibility of justifying traditional institutions and moralities rests in the provision which can be made for the individual to acquire abilities, and exercise opportunities, to engage in rational negotiation. In many circumstances, private judgment must defer to expertise, but as the self-confessedly ignorant Socrates demonstrated, authority may be hollow and can be validated only where it is open to constant scrutiny - and this principle is more fundamental than any concept of general utility. Mill should disconcert all those who feel comfortable with the idea of teaching children to think critically, because he relates educational aims directly - and appropriately - to the unresolved problems of epistemology, ethics and politics which are real sources of human conflict. And he points to the historical evidence, notable in the case of the physical sciences, that agreement and consensus do arise out of controversiality (Mill, 1965, pp. 293-294). Development of the critical faculties, to which all people are potentially heirs, is not a means to an end, nor even one of many desirable ends; it is the primary social end.

If educational objectives are conceived in terms of polarities, one extreme is represented by the view that its task is the 'socialisation' of rising generations and the inculcation of certain fundamental values and social skills. The other is an emphasis on the transformational role of education in realising individual creativity and rationality and thereby achieving social transformation - though with a frank acknowledgement of the unpredictable forms it might take and of the importance of relinquishing a desire for control. It might be objected that these aims are not polar opposites, or that all educational thinkers occupy a position on a continuum between them - some, perhaps, an oscillating position. I suggest that there is an important sense in which the two positions are opposed; one has to opt for one as a more fundamental regulative principle than the other.

Democracy, education and critical thinking

Mill's suspicions of democracy are predicated on his belief that it would increasingly subordinate the individual quest for meaning and truth to an illegitimate sense of *collective* purpose. In this respect Mill differs markedly from Dewey, who, I argue, entertains a holistic or essentialist idea of democratic organisation which leads him to equivocate between the ideals of individual rational autonomy and social consensus. For Mill, by contrast, the specification of social ends and means entails claims concerning the authoritative status of judgements about what they should be and how to achieve them. Legitimation is always, in every instance, a reciprocal, argumentative search for rational agreement between those who claim authority and those held to be subject to it. Mill's stance is that this principle must inform all aspects of the pedagogic relationship and most certainly dialogue between parent and child (Mill, 1910, pp. 134-5), for this is where the seeds of rationality are sown.

Although Dewey's educational and social philosophy is almost certainly the more widely regarded as ancestral to the contemporary thinking skills movement, Mill's is the more incisive. It engages directly with the problem implicit in Dewey's tendency to portray democratic society in 'organic' or 'essentialist' terms and school education as the immediate means of achieving a rational convergence of disparate social ends. Different rational considerations will indicate different points of convergence, or they may undermine the authority of the objective of convergence itself. The contrast between Mill and Dewey on educational aims can be summarised as the contrast between their formulations of the role of teachers and schools; Thus Mill insists:

> Though one man cannot *teach* another, one man may *suggest* to another. I may be indebted to my predecessor for setting my own faculties to work; for hinting to me what questions to ask myself; but it is not given to one man to *answer* those questions for another...Knowledge comes only from within; all that comes from without is but *questioning*, or else it is mere *authority*. (Mill, On Genius, 1832, p. 32, original emphasis)

But Dewey articulates his 'pedagogic creed' in clearly contrasting terms:

> Our task is on one hand to select and adjust the studies with reference to the nature of the individual thus discovered; and on the other hand to order and group them so that they shall most definitely and systematically represent the chief lines of social endeavour and social achievement. (Dewey, 1974, page 421)

> ...the teacher is engaged, not simply in the training of individuals, but in the formation of the proper social life. - every teacher should realize the dignity of his

calling; that he is a social servant set apart for the maintenance of proper social order and the securing of the right social growth. (ibid., p. 439)

Dewey's assertion of the educational priority of social cohesion is not an isolated example. His work is permeated with an ideological commitment to the idea of society characterised by 'a common spirit' and 'common aims' which 'demand a growing interchange of thought and growing unity of sympathetic feeling'. These may be laudable as aspirations, but they are dangerous as educational *priorities*. Admittedly, Dewey's criticisms of the usual pedagogic practice of his time accords closely with Mill's condemnation of rote learning. But Dewey's idea of a solution is to orientate the school curriculum towards activities which are meaningful in terms of his conception of a community of homogenous purpose. This impression is reinforced by references to communal crafts in school as an appropriate introduction to scientific modes of thinking. Now ideas of this kind may be (indeed *are*) very interesting and potentially beneficial, especially in the sense that Dewey uses them to question the way in which '...the school has been set apart, so isolated from the ordinary conditions and motives of life, that (it) is the one place in the world where it is most difficult to get experience of life - the mother of all disciplines worth the name'.

The problem with this view, however, is its partiality; the identification of all 'discipline' with the experience of particular communities - in which contexts it might be (occasionally and superficially) plausible to speak of convergent purposes and common ends. And, of course, the greatest temptation to achieve this kind of convergence is likely to occur in the community of children in a classroom. The question is about fundamental theoretical priorities and the dangers of judging reasons by standards of mutual sympathy and tolerance. Mill's insight is that the affective bonds between people will be strongest where they learn to tolerate and welcome argument because it is used, not as a weapon, but in a search for the truth on any question. One clear assumption in the thought of both men is that rational dialogue will unite people rather than divide them and that the source of evil and suffering is submission to dogma. But from his broad perspective, Mill anticipates a time when a pre-emptive imposition on democracy of arbitrary, monolithic purposes will produce a thoroughly servile society. The route is likely to be through a multitude of good intentions, of which the theoretical prioritisation of psychological consensus in the classroom will be a significant microcosm.

And the difference between these contrasting views of democratic life can be traced to different theories of language, thought and social relations. Tiles compares Dewey's analysis of the social role of language with Wittgenstein's refutation of the idea of a 'private language' and references to 'agreement in use' - but he also notes 'the connotations of mutual aid and succour which festoon Dewey's prose whenever he writes of language and its relationship to thought and social interaction' (Tiles, 1990, pp. 94-103). Mill is crucially aware that though certain levels of agreement are conditions of the possibility of discourse, they are nevertheless initial approximations. Semantic agreements at this level invariably conceal inconsistencies and outright contradictions when their implications are explored. The worst kind of agreement is the superficial one which fails to acknowledge this indeterminacy of language and thought - the adoption by rote of forms of words which do not connect with the 'inner life of the human being'. And the dangers are greatest where the illusion of a democratic pursuit of ill-defined collective ends usurps the role of reflective, sceptical inquiry which, as the Greeks once demonstrated, can achieve quite unprecedented heights. This is what underwrites Mill's perennial contribution to the idea of teaching critical thinking. At the centre of his philosophy, embodying all social possibilities, is the unfathomed potential in the mind of the child - and a *trust* in that.

9 Conclusion: 'A Spirit of Adventure'

To describe critical thinking as an ultimate social ideal and a criterion of the effectiveness of education systems is clearly to express a principle at a level of generality which is unlikely to appeal to the overwhelming majority who find it difficult or impossible to imagine effective alternatives to our present system of mass schooling (Adcock, 1994, p. 5). And to advocate a pedagogy which prioritises the epistemic viewpoint of the learner might seem like an invitation to educational anarchy and a counsel of despair to those who anticipate precise methodological alternatives to current teaching methods. A measure of the importance attached by some to eventual solutions of this kind is Norris' assertion that the outcome of the debate about 'generalizability' could result either in unification of the curriculum under the 'single umbrella' of critical thinking or abandonment of critical thinking as an educational ideal (Norris, 1992, p. 4). High expectations have been generated, as Holroyd recognises in his extensive review of problem-solving in secondary education. Describing the subject as lamentably ill-defined, lacking coherent theoretical underpinnings and so broad as to be 'equivalent to advice on teaching people how to live and how to think' he comments apologetically:

> I have great sympathy with anyone who has read this review...thus far and exclaims in impatience, "This is all very well - but what should I be doing about it? Spell out the messages for classroom practice and for curriculum policy." It may be that the only proper "academic" response is: "I can do nothing to help, go and work out your own salvation". (Holroyd, 1989, 7.1.3)

Smith offers even less encouragement to anyone seeking specific, down-to-earth advice about pedagogic techniques for enhancing students' thinking, freely admitting that nothing in his analysis of the subject 'helps a teacher - or an administrator - who believes that thinking can be taught through systematic instruction' (Smith, 1992, p. 126). Nevertheless, conclusions of this kind have not discouraged the official adoption within some key curriculum subjects of a broad distinction between 'knowledge and understanding' and 'problem-solving' as a basis for student assessment. This tacit repudiation of the idea that real understanding comes only through active engagement with scientific, philosophical, historical and other problems seems to reflect a view that theory is one thing and practice is something else.

Impatient responses to technically inconclusive investigations into thinking skills and problem-solving strategies are likely if the research does not 'cash' itself in very particular pedagogic recommendations. But I suggest that such disappointed expectations reflect a dangerously technocratic conception of education which is deeply implicated in the perceived failures of education systems to produce critical thinkers, as well as many other frequently broadcast educational shortcomings. This conception seriously confuses the organisational priorities of a large-scale, mass educational system, and its inherent requirements for systematic teaching and testing, with the intellectual requirements of learners. One effective test of the educational relevance of such a system, I argue below, is whether a substantial and fairly representative body of students, educated outside that organisational framework, can meet or exceed the prevailing standards of assessment within it.

The industrialisation of education and the 'total' school

It is remarkable that given such high levels of public concern about educational standards in the United Kingdom, so little attention has been paid even to the distinctly different models provided by near-neighbouring countries like the Netherlands, where state funding supports a very wide range of educational initiatives sponsored, characteristically, by groups of parents. To some extent this must be attributable to recognition of the complexity of this important sector of public life and the political and social problems of introducing fundamental reforms, even if the idea were to be seriously entertained. But if critical thinking has the importance ascribed to it in the preceding pages, it cannot be regarded as an aim which is separable from other educational objectives such that it can be introduced, unproblematically, as yet another item into an already overcrowded curriculum. Smith poses the problem that if '...schools currently teach in ways that preclude or hamper the development of thinking, how can anyone be sure that deliberate efforts to teach thinking...will not make matters worse?'

This question, alone, is important because it hints at questions all too rarely asked; what is it about our highly sophisticated and complex educational systems which, in the opinion of so many experts and lay people, appears to encourage passive attitudes to learning and classroom regimes characterised by rote rather than critical inquiry? The educational policies of recent governments distinguish less and less between education and vocational skills training. Recent adoption in the England and Wales of the title, 'Department for Education and Employment' and, north of the border, 'Scottish Office Education and Industry Department' (my emphasis) is symptomatic of an accelerating trend towards an instrumentalism typified by what Hyland describes as 'competence models of education':

> Since the establishment of the National Council for Vocational Qualification...in 1986, the influence of the competence-based approach, which underpins National Vocational Qualifications...has spread beyond its original remit and now extends into schools and higher education... (Hyland, 1993, pp 57-68)

Tracing this development back to the early twentieth-century 'social efficiency' theory in the United States, Hyland points out that the false equation between workplace-skills and intellectual skills is the consequence of trying to '...describe, in behaviourist terms, something which is essentially non-behaviouristic, namely the development of knowledge and understanding.' Hyland's main target for criticism is the view that there is 'no justification for assessing knowledge for its own sake, but only for its contribution to competent performance'.

These last words articulate a view which is diametrically opposed to the ideal of education as a process of self-realisation leading to personal autonomy, emphasising instead criteria of attainment wholly external to the student and to whom little or no justification is offered. Recent educational trends have dramatically reversed previous emphasis on 'progressive' or 'child-centred' education, a well established tradition in educational theory which received official endorsement in the UK with the publication of the Plowden Report in 1967:

> Today we again have a government which aims to limit the power of the teaching profession and also to limit the critical study of education. It has already created both the climate and the framework within which every teacher must now think and work: both climate and framework are inimical to the child-centred tradition... (Darling, 1994, p. 110)

Arguably, that uniform, hierarchical framework never was conducive to an education which starts from the *needs of individual children;* this form of words rarely expressed priorities which were realised in practice. But it is difficult to exaggerate the extent to which cultural transmission has now become professionalised and defined as a centralised, official responsibility. On the one hand, UK education is repeatedly stigmatised by contemporary governments for failures to achieve basic standards of literacy and numeracy for large numbers of students; on the other hand, there appears to be limitless official faith in the possibilities of inculcating basic skills, values, standards of behaviour and academic achievement by minutely detailed specification of what is to be taught, at what stages, mainly, but not exclusively, through the medium of a national curriculum.

Such faith in the omnicompetence of schools is in striking contrast to what is actually achieved, and unfavourable comparisons are routinely drawn by the media between UK educational achievements and those of other countries.

Solutions, however, are canvassed increasingly in the form of industrial management techniques, and official publications are replete with the jargon of 'ethos' and 'performance' indicators, measures of 'whole school performance' and 'quality control'. Morris has argued that, nineteenth century liberal *laissez-faire-ism* notwithstanding, the Victorian state displayed great determination to retain control of the embryonic educational system (Morris, 1972, pp. 281-291). Despite the changes which have subsequently occurred, that urge for centralised control was never very effectively challenged and has now reasserted itself decisively.

A Millian emphasis on the epistemic standpoint of the learner is simply incompatible with the centrally-planned and programmatically delivered curriculum. There must be freedom for students to assert their own epistemic priorities; to explore and question; to integrate new ideas within the framework of their existing repertoires of concepts and images. Aspirations like these sound familiar enough and tend to be accommodated effortlessly by official pronouncements about educational aims and methods. But though the language of 'individual student needs' is retained, each newly perceived failure of the system appears to produce more standardised responses, as though 'individual needs' can be accommodated successfully within a general system of classification and dealt with according to predetermined strategies. Feuerstein's biographer, Sharron, has commented about the provision for educationally disadvantaged children in the UK, that 'We have reduced teachers to a pipeline through which we can transport information' (*The Times Educational Supplement*, 2-4-96, p. 3), even in this special educational sector, where continuing mediation by a teacher is an acknowledged priority. The description recalls Smith's ironical comment about trying to 'teach children to think' where the teacher is so manifestly a conduit for vicarious expression of the ideas of absentee managers of the educational 'process'.

It is unlikely that educational innovations *within* such a system which genuinely try to adopt the student's epistemic perspective as a principle of pedagogic orientation could withstand the momentum of the industrial model long enough to prove their value. Though the phrase 'individual student needs' lingers on, the right of parents to have their children educated and taught in conformity with their religious and philosophical convictions, established by the *Convention on Human Rights and Fundamental Freedoms*, is increasingly constrained by the remit of the 'total' school and its spurious claim to omnicompetence. This, alone, must be a reason for jealously guarding existing parental rights under national legislation to educate their children 'otherwise' than in the established school system. For it might be that only in such alternative contexts can the superiority of learner-centred educational methods be demonstrated. But there is another relevant consideration.

Although I have not addressed the general issue of standardised methods of educational assessment directly, the claims I have made about the limitations of empirical procedures for investigating intellectual operations are, nevertheless, relevant to them. These claims are, briefly, that the more closely assessment relies on standardised measures of performance, the less it will convey of the conceptual differences students bring to what is, putatively, the *same* task. Yet assessment of this kind is becoming definitive of both public and official conceptions of educational achievement. However, standardised measures, no matter how epistemologically inadequate, provide opportunities for comparison which can cut in more than one direction. If, as is increasingly the case, the performances of students and schools are to be judged on the results of such testing, those results also measure the adequacy of the burgeoning industrial model of education which delivers them. And there is some powerful *prima facie* evidence which suggests that if we want higher educational standards, at least in the terms defined by that model, we need neither the factories nor their elaborate hierarchies and management techniques.

Radical alternatives

'The classroom' tends to dominate pedagogic theory to such an extent that the idea of an education in other institutional contexts seems implausible or dangerously lacking in the structure necessary for disciplined learning of a high standard. Yet it might be that it is from precisely these different contexts that some of the most illuminating information is to be obtained. Many thousands of families in the United States and Canada, have withdrawn their children from the formal, public education system for varied reasons, probably much more often connected with religious belief than an aversion to rote regimes in public sector schools. However, motivations are beside my present point. *That* is that if very large numbers of home-educated children consistently outperform their school-educated peers across the range of standardised assessment tests used in the public sector, there must be something very wrong with the schools, the tests, or both. And a large body of research from different states of America and from Canada suggests that 'home-schoolers' do achieve substantially higher average test scores, often by factors of twenty or thirty percent. The frequency of results like this seems to have shifted the burden of proof about adult competence from parents to education authorities in a succession of legal challenges by parents to existing state legislation (Ray, 1990). A study of about 800 home-schooling families carried out on behalf of the Home School Legal Defence Association of Canada suggests that, apart from a very marginal, statistically significant relationship between fathers' levels of educational attainment and their children's performances, neither parental teaching qualifications, family income level, nor structured tuition appear to be significant factors in determining the attainment levels of these home-schoolers. That was said to be at, or above, the 76th percentile on standardised Canadian tests, compared with a national average for school students at the 50th percentile - irrespective of grade levels or of the subjects studied. These included reading, listening, language, mathematics, science and social studies.

Brian Ray, the author of this Canadian report, acknowledges that high parental motivation might account for these results, but suggests that, on the other hand, higher achievements might be due to:

> ...the low student-to-teacher ratio, the greater flexibility that is possible in the private setting, close contact between parent and child, and the enhanced opportunity to individualize curriculum and methodology in response to the gifts and limitations of a particular child. (Ray, 1994)

These claims are dramatic and the abundant statistics merit detailed scrutiny. The analysis might provide valuable insights, not about 'how to teach critical thinking' but how to avoid 'rote-regimes' which must be the almost inevitable result of all-encompassing aspirations of the 'total school', an institution which can readily substitute its jurisdiction in this vital area of cultural transmission for that of the other most potent developmental influence on a child; the home. This is not to suggest that schools and classrooms are obsolete, but that the most effective critiques of their organisation and ethos are likely to emerge from an examination of alternative learning situations which, by design or necessity, place a premium on collaborative discussion and inquiry between intellectual peers, and on increased use of the large but neglected reservoir of expertise in the society beyond the school. The eventual choice is unlikely to be between the monolithic system of education we have at present and an indiscriminate flight from that to home-schooling. Instead, we might begin to appreciate the real possibility of more flexible patterns of education offering examples of good practice in which the epistemic needs of children have a secure place.

I have consistently stressed the dialectical nature of understanding and the constitutive role of debate and argument in the formation of critical traditions and 'the critical consciousness'. I have also tried to demonstrate that the main characteristic of disciplined attempts to reach accommodations between different kinds or levels of understanding closely resembles philosophical discourse; the continuous testing of the epistemic status of ideas, evidence and facts; something almost definitive of the origins of the critical scientific traditions in Greece. There are, of course, various initiatives for teaching philosophy in schools, the best known of which is Lipman's 'Philosophy for Schools' programme. Rather equivocally, in view of his preference for receptive early learning, McPeck has argued for the injection of philosophy into mainstream curriculum subjects, claiming (quite correctly,

I believe) that 'philosophies of...' science, history, art, mathematics and social sciences are the 'major prerequisites for being critical thinkers' (McPeck 1990, pp. 16-18). But he also emphasises the logistical problems of introducing such an unfamiliar discipline within the constraints of contemporary education systems, and the idea is thoroughly inconsistent with the dominant skill-orientated, vocational emphasis. But this kind of organisational consideration should not stand in the way of commitment to the ultimacy of critical thinking as the end of education. Nor need it, if the fallacious assumption that everything that is learned has first to be explicitly taught, and that what must be taught must somehow subsume both the essence of disciplinary knowledge and the norms and skills of social life.

It has been tempting to describe philosophical questioning as 'natural' for young children; the means by which they grapple with the language and ideas of the adult world, assigning tentative meanings and ontological significances to successive experiences of that world; an exploration which is too often cut short by adult intolerance of seemingly unanswerable questions. Such anecdotal evidence, however abundant, might be considered no more justifiable than McPeck's bald assertion that rote memorisation is 'natural' for young children (McPeck, 1990, p. 44). However, I have argued that the critical feature of the critical traditions is commitment, purposive or otherwise, to dialogue governed by a search for agreement about principles of sound reasoning which can unite the differing conceptual perspectives of individuals. And if this discursive search for agreement exploits something fundamental in language and thought, as I have also argued, it is at least as relevant for the child as for the adult.

The idea of educating children in an atmosphere of equality and joint inquiry to maximise each individual child's access to the legacy of the critical traditions might appear to be a high-risk strategy; an invitation to classroom disorder. But that view implies a certain kind of classroom. Democracy is also a high-risk strategy, demanding what Pericles of Athens described as 'a spirit of adventure'. Nevertheless, that spirit was intimately associated with the first great demonstration of the transformational power of critical thinking. Critical thought, and the democratic institutions which are its social and political expressions, do not follow predetermined paths or produce guaranteed outcomes. But neither do their alternatives. And the reason for this, in Mill's words, is that:

> Human nature is not a machine to be built after a model, and set to do exactly the work prescribed for it, but a tree, which requires to grow and develop itself on all sides, according to the tendency of the inward forces which make it a living thing. (Mill, On Liberty, Chapter III)

Bibliography

Adcock, John. (1994). *In Place of Schools.* London: New Education Press Limited.

Anderson, John. (1963). *Studies in Empirical Philosophy.* Sydney and London: Angus & Robertson.

Andrews, John N. (1990). General thinking Skills: are there such things? *Journal of Philosophy of Education,* 24 ,1, pp. 71 - 79.

Archambault, Reginald D. (ed.). (1974). *John Dewey on Education.* Chicago and London: University of Chicago Press.

Ayto, John. (1991). *Dictionary of Word Origins.* London: Bloomsbury.

Bagehot, Walter. (1963). *The English Constitution.* London: Fontana.

Becher, Tony. (1987). Disciplinary Discourse. *Studies in Higher Education,* 12, 3, pp. 261 - 274.

Beck, Frederick A.G. (1964). *Greek Education 450 -350 B.C.* London: Methuen.

Benedict, Ruth. (1971). *Patterns of Culture.* London: Routledge & Kegan Paul.

Bernal, Martin. (1991). *Black Athena.* London: Vintage.

Black, Max. (1968). *The Labyrinth of Language.* London: Pall Mall Press.

Bonnett, Michael. (1995). Teaching Thinking, and the Sanctity of Content. *Journal of Philosophy of Education,* 29 , 3, pp. 295 - 309.

Boyle, Derek. (1982). Piaget and Education: A Negative Evaluation in Modgil, -., Modgil, -., (eds.), *Jean Piaget: Consensus and Controversy,* pp. 291 - 308. New York: Praeger.

Bridges, David. (1993). Transferable Skills: A Philosophical Perspective. *Studies in Higher Education,* 18 , 1, pp. 43-51.

Brown, Ann L., Ferrara, Roberta A. (ed. Wertsch). (1989). Diagnosing Zones of Proximal Development in *Culture, Communication and Cognition,* pp. 273 - 305. London: Cambridge University Press.

Bruner, Jerome S. (ed. Anglin). (1974). *Beyond The Information Given.* London: George Allen & Unwin.

Burden, B., Florek, A. (1989). Instrumental Enrichment in Coles, -.M.J., Robinson, W.D., (eds.), *Teaching Thinking,* pp. 71- 80. Bristol: Bristol Press.

Burston, W. H. (ed.). (1969). *James Mill On Education.* London: Cambridge University Press.

Burston, W. H. (1973). *James Mill on Philosophy and Education.* London: The Athlone Press.

Cassirer, Ernst. (1967). *The Myth of the State.* New Haven and London: Yale University Press.

Casson, Lionel. (ed.). (1965) *Classical Age.* New York: Dell.

Chalmers, A.F. (1992). *What is This Thing Called Science?* Milton Keynes: Open University Press.

Chatwin, Bruce. (1988). *The Songlines.* London: Pan Books.

Chomsky, Noam. (1972). *Language and Mind.* New York: Harcourt Brace Jovanovich.

Chomsky, Noam. (1972). *Problems of Knowledge and Freedom.* London: Fontana.

Chomsky, Noam. (1992). On the Nature, Use and Acquisition of Language in Lycan, -., (ed.), *Mind and Cognition,* pp. 627 - 645. Oxford: Blackwell.

Churchland, Paul M. (1992). Current Eliminativism in Lycan, -., (ed.), *Mind and Cognition,* pp. 206 - 223. Oxford: Blackwell.

Cole, Michael. (1989). The Zone of Proximal Development: Where Culture and Cognition Create Each Other in Wertsch, -., (ed.), *Culture, Communication and Cognition,* pp. 146 - 161. London: Cambridge University Press.

Coles, M. J., Robinson, W. D. (1989). in Coles, M.J., Robinson, W.D., (eds.), *Teaching Thinking: A Survey of Programmes In Education.* Bristol: The Bristol Press.

Collingwood, R. G. (1970). *The Principles of Art.* London: Oxford University Press.

Collingwood, R. G. (1946). *The Idea of History.* Oxford: Clarendon.

Cowling, Maurice. (1969). Mill and Liberalism in Schneewind, -., (ed.), *Mill: A Collection of Critical Essays.* pp. 329 - 378. London and Melbourne: MacMillan.

Darling, John. (1993). The End of Primary Ideology? *Curriculum Studies,* 1, 3, pp. 417 - 426.

Darling, John. (1994). *Child-Centred Education.* London: Paul Chapman.

Darwin, Charles. (1962). *The Origin of Species.* New York: Collier Books.

Darwin, Charles. *The Voyage of the 'Beagle'.* Heron Books (publication undated).

Davydov, V. V., Radzikhovskii, L. A. (1989), Vygotsky's Theory and the Activity-Oriented Approach in Psychology in Wertsh, -., (ed.), *Culture, Communication and Cognition,* pp. 35 -65. London: Cambridge University Press.

Dewey, John. (ed. Archambault). (1974). *John Dewey On Education.* Chicago and London: University of Chicago Press.

Dickinson, Lowes G. (1962). *The Greek View of Life.* London: University Paperbacks/ Methuen & Co. Limited.

Donaldson, Margaret. (1990). *Children's Minds.* London: Fontana.

Dryden, G., Vos, J. (1994). *The Learning Revolution.* Aylesbury: Accelerated Learning Systems.

Durant, J. R., Evans, G. A., Thomas, G. P. (1989). The Public Understanding of Science. *Nature* 340.

Einstein, Albert. (1991). Autobiographical Notes in Ferris, T., (ed.), *Physics, Astronomy and Mathematics*, pp. 577 -590. Boston, Toronto and London: Little, Brown & Co.

Elliot, A., Donaldson, M. (1982). Piaget on Language in Modgil, -., Modgil, -., *Jean Piaget: Consensus and Controversy,* pp. 157 - 166. New York: Praeger.

Ennis, Robert H. (1992). The Degree to Which Critical Thinking Is Subject Specific: Clarification and Needed Research in Norris, S. P., (ed.), *The Generalizability of Critical Thinking,* pp. 21 - 37. New York and London: Teachers College Press.

Ennis, Robert H. (1962). A Concept of Critical Thinking. *Harvard Educational Review,* 32, No. 1, pp. 81-111

Erikson, Erik H. (1963). *Childhood and Society.* Middlesex: Penguin Books.

Feyerbend, Paul K. (1975). *Against Method.* New York: Free Press.

Fisher, Robert. (1994). *Teaching Children to Think.* Hemel Hempstead: Simon & Schuster.

Fisher, Alec. (1989). Critical Thinking in Coles, M.J., Robinson, W.D., (eds.), *Teaching Thinking,* pp. 37 - 45. Bristol: Bristol Press.

Fodor, J., Katz, J.J. (1971). What's Wrong with the Philosophy of Language? in Flew, A., (ed.), *Philosophy and Linguistics,* pp. 269 - 283. London and Basingstoke: Macmillan.

Frazer, James. (1993). *The Golden Bough.* Hertfordshire: Wordsworth Reference.

Fromm, Erich. (1960). *The Fear of Freedom.* London: Routledge.

Gellner, Ernest. (1968). *Words and Things.* Middlesex: Penguin Books.

Gellner, Ernest. (1972). Concepts and Society in Emmet, D., MacIntyre, A., (eds.), *Sociological Theory and Philosophical Analysis,* pp. 115 -149. London: Macmillan.

Gier, Nicholas F. (1981). *Wittgenstein and Phenomenology.* Albany: State University of New York Press.

Gleick, James. (1994). *Genius.* London: Abacus.

Goodman, David C. (ed.). (1973). *Science and Religious Belief 1600 - 1900.* Dorchester: John Wright & Sons & Open University.

Goodman, David C. (ed.). (1979). Galileo and the Church in *The Conflict Thesis and Cosmology* AMST 2831-3, pp. 89 - 124. Open University.

Goody, J., Watt, I. (1963). The Consequences of Literacy. *Comparative Studies in Society and History: An International Quarterly,* 5, pp. 304 -345.

Griffiths, Morwenna. (1986). Hirst's Forms of Knowledge and Korner's Categorical Frameworks. *Oxford Review of Education* 12, 1, pp. 17 - 30.

Hagen, Everett E. (1962). *On the Theory of Social Change.* Illinois: The Dorsey Press Inc.

Halévy, Elie. (Trans. Mary Morris). (1952). *The Growth of Philosophical Radicalism.* London: Faber & Faber.

Hamlyn, D. W. (1989). Education and Wittgenstein's Philosophy. *Journal of Philosophy of Education* 23, 2, pp. 213 - 222.

Hanson, John. (1989). The Oxfordshire Thinking Skills Course in Coles, M.J., Robinson, W.D., (eds.), *Teaching Thinking,* pp. 81 - 89. Bristol: Bristol Press.

Harber, C., Meighan, R. (1989). The Democratic School in Harber, C., Meighan, R., (eds.), *Education Now.* Derbyshire: Educational Heretics Press.

Hare, William. (1995). Content and Criticism: the aims of schooling. *Journal of Philosophy of Education* 29, 1, pp. 47 - 60.

Hargreaves, David. (30/5/1997). Guru Predicts Classroom Exodus in *The Times Educational Supplement,* p. 11.

Haugeland, John. (1992). Understanding Natural Language in Lycan, -., (ed.), *Mind and Cognition,* pp. 660 - 670. Oxford: Blackwell.

Heller, Erich. (1959). Men and Ideas Ludwig Wittgenstein - Unphilosophical Notes in *Encounter,* pp. 40 - 48.

Hirst, Paul H. (1974). *Knowledge and the Curriculum.* London: Routledge & Kegan Paul.

Hirst, Paul H. (ed.). (1983). *Educational Theory and its Foundation Disciplines.* London: Routledge & Kegan Paul.

Holroyd, Colin. (1989). *Problem Solving and the Secondary Curriculum - A Review.* Edinburgh: Scottish Council for Research in Education.

Hooykass, R. (1977). *Religion and The Rise of Modern Science.* Edinburgh and London: Scottish Academic Press.

Hume, D. (1902). *Enquiries Concerning the Human Understanding and Concerning the Principles of Morals.* Oxford: Clarendon Press.

Hunt, G. M. K. (1989). Skills, Facts and Artificial Intelligence in Coles, M.J., Robinson, W.D., *Teaching Thinking,* pp. 23 - 29. Bristol: Bristol Press.

Hyland, Terry. (1993). Competence, Knowledge and Education. *Journal of Philosophy of Education* 27, 1, pp. 57 - 68.

Johnson, Ralph H. (1992). The Problem of Defining Critical Thinking in Norris, S.P., (ed.), *The Generalizability of Critical Thinking,* pp. 38 - 53. New York and London: Teachers College Press.

Johnstone, Denis Foster. (1966). *An Analysis of Sources of Information on the Population of the Navaho.* Washington: Bureau of American Ethnology.

Kamii, Constance. Pedagogical Principles Derived from Piaget's Theory: Relevance for Educational Practice in Golby, -., Greenwald, -., (eds.), *Curriculum Design,* pp. 82 - 93. London: Croom Helm.

Kaufmann, Walter. (1968). *Nietzsche: Philosopher, Psychologist, Antichrist.* New York: Vintage.

Kendall, Willmoore. (1969). The "Open Society" and Its Fallacies in Radcliff, P., (ed.), *Limits of Liberty: Studies of Mill's 'On Liberty'*, pp. 19 - 26. California: Wadsworth.

Kenny, Anthony. (1983). *Wittgenstein.* Middlesex: Penguin Books.

Kimberley, K., Meek, M., and Miller, J. (eds.). (1992). *New Readings: Contributions to an Understanding of Literacy.* London: A & C Black.

Kirk, G. S., Raven J. E. (1969). *The Pre Socratic Philosophers.* London: Cambridge.

Kluckhohn, C., Leighton, D. (1960). *The Navaho.* London: Oxford University Press.

Kozulin, Alex. (1990). *Vygotsky's Psychology.* Hemel Hempstead: Harvester Wheatsheaf.

Kuhn, Thomas S. (1970). *The Structure of Scientific Revolutions.* Chicago and London: University of Chicago Press.

Lash, Joseph P. (1980). *Helen and Teacher: The Story of Helen Keller and Anne Sullivan Macy.* Middlesex: Penguin.

Le Roy Ladurie, Emmanuel. (1980). *Montaillou.* Middlesex: Penguin.

Leach, Edmund. (1972). Telstar and the Aborigines or 'la pensee sauvage' in Emmet, D., MacIntyre, A., (eds.), *Sociological Theory and Philosophical Analysis,* pp. 183 - 204. London: Macmillan.

Lerner, Max. (ed.). (1965). *Essential Works of John Stuart Mill.* New York: Bantam Books.

Levi, Albert William. (1969). The Value of Freedom: Mill's Liberty (1859-1959) in Radcliff, P., (ed.), *Limits of Liberty: Studies of Mill's On Liberty,* pp. 6 -18. California: Wadsworth.

Lipman, Matthew. (1991). Squaring Soviet Theory With American Practice in *Educational Leadership*, pp. 72 - 76.

Lyas, Colin. (ed.). (1971). *Philosophy and Linguistics.* London: MacMillan.

Lycan, William G. (ed.). (1992). *Mind and Cognition.* Oxford: Blackwell.

Lyons, John. (1970). *Chomsky.* London: Fontana/Collins.

Mabbott, J. D. (1969). Interpretations of Mill's Utilitarianism in Smith, -., Sosa, -., (eds.), *Mill's Utilitarianism,* pp. 126 - 132. California: Wadsworth.

Magee, Bryan. (1973). *Popper.* London: Fontana/ Collins.

Malcolm, Norman. (1989). *Wittgenstein: Nothing is Hidden.* Oxford: Basil Blackwell.

Martin, Jane Roland. (1992). Critical Thinking for a Humane World in Norrs, S.P., (ed.), *The Generalizability of Critical Thinking,* pp. 163 - 180. New York and London: Teachers College Press.

Mays, Wolfe. (1985). Thinking Skills Programmes : An Analysis. *New Ideas - psychology* 3, 2, pp. 149 - 163.

McDermott, John J.(ed.). (1981). *The Philosophy of John Dewey.* Chicago and London: University of Chicago Press.

McPeck, John E. (1990). Teaching Critical Thinking in Scheffler, I., Howard, V.A., (eds.), *Teaching Critical Thinking.* New York and London: Routledge.

Meighan, Roland. (1995). *Home-based education effectiveness research - and some of its implications.* Nottingham: Education Now

Merton, Robert K. (1979). Puritanism, Pietism and Science in Russell, -., (ed.), *Science and Religious Belief.* Sevenoaks: Hodder & Stoughton/Open University Press.

Meyer, Barbara. (1982). Education and Patterns of Communication in a Situation of Restricted Literacy. *Scottish Educational Review* 14, 1, pp. 23 - 30.

Mill, James. (ed. Burston). (1969). *James Mill on Education.* London: Cambridge University Press.

Mill, John Stuart. (1900). *A System of Logic.* London: Longmans, Green & Co.

Mill, John Stuart (1910). *The Letters of John Stuart Mill.* London: Longmans, Green & Co.

Mill, John Stuart. (1946). Letter to the Monthly Repository known as 'On Genius', in Borchardt, Ruth (ed.), *Four Dialogues of Plato,* pp. 28 - 40. London: Watts.

Mill, John Stuart. (ed. Gertrude Himmelfarb). (1963). *Essays on Politics and Culture.* New York: Anchor.

Mill, John Stuart. (1965). *Auguste Comte and Positivism.* Michigan: Ann Arbor Paperbacks.

Mill, John Stuart. (ed Lerner). (1965). *Essential Works: Autobiography.* New York: Bantam.

Mill, John Stuart. (ed. Lerner). (1965). *Essential Works; On Liberty.* New York: Bantam.

Mill, John Stuart. (ed. Mary Warnock). (1968). *Utilitarianism,* pp. 251 - 321. London: Fontana.

Mill, John Stuart. (1984). Inaugural Address Delivered to the University of St. Andrews in Robson, -., (ed.), *Essays on Equality, Law, and Education* (CW), XXI.

Modgil, -., Modgil, -. (eds.). (1982), in *Jean Piaget: Consensus and Controversy.* New York: Praeger.

Monk, Ray. (1991). *Ludwig Wittgenstein.* London: Vintage.

Moore, G. E. (1968). *Principia Ethica.* London: Cambridge University Press.

Morris, N. (1972). State Paternalism and laissez-faire in the 1860's in Cosin, B.R., (ed.), *Education: Structure and Society,* pp. 281 -291. Middlesex: Penguin.

Nietzsche, Friedrich. (1956). *The Birth of Tragedy and The Genealogy of Morals.* New York: Doubleday Anchor.

Nisbet, J., Shucksmith, J. (1989). The Seventh Sense - Reflections on Learning to Learn. *Scottish Council for Research in Education.* 86.

Nisbet, J. (1990). Teaching Thinking: An Introduction to the Research Literature. *SCRE Spotlights* 26, pp. 1 - 6. Edinburgh.

Nisbet, J. (1993). Improving Thinking - The Thinking Curriculum. *Educational Psychology* 13, 3 and 4, pp. 281 - 290.

Norris, Stephen P. (1990). Thinking About Critical Thinking: Philosophers Can't Go It Alone, in Scheffler, I., Howard, V.A., (eds.), *Teaching Critical Thinking* (John E. McPeck), pp. 67 - 74. New York and London: Routledge.

Norris, Stephen P. (ed.). (1992). *The Generalizability of Critical Thinking.* New York and London: Teachers College Press.

Oakeshott, Michael. (1933). *Experience and its Modes.* London: Cambridge.

Oakeshott, Michael. (1967). *Rationalism in Politics.* London: Methuen.

Olson, D. R. , Babu, N. (1992). Critical Thinking as Critical Discourse in Norris, S.P., (ed.), *The Generalizability of Critical Thinking,* pp. 181 - 197. New York and London: Teachers College Press.

Passmore, John. (1968). *A Hundred Years Of Philosophy.* Middlesex: Penguin.

Paul, Richard. (1990). McPeck's Mistakes in Scheffler, I., Howard, V.A., (eds.), *Teaching Critical Thinking* (John E. McPeck), pp. 102 - 111. New York and London: Routledge.

Pears, David. (1971). *Wittgenstein.* London: Fontana/ Collins.

Phillips, Denis. (1982). Perspectives on Piaget as Philosopher: The Tough, Tender-minded Syndrome in Modgil, -., Modgil, -., (eds.), *Jean Piaget: Consensus and Controversy,* pp. 13- 30. New York: Praeger.

Piaget, J. (1970). The Stages of the Intellectual Development of the Child in Wason, -., Johnson-Laird, -., (eds.), *Thinking and Reasoning,* pp. 355 - 364. Middlesex: Penguin.

Piattelli-Palmarini, Massimo. (ed.). (1980). *Language and Learning - The Debate Between Jean Piaget and Noam Chomsky.* London: Routledge & Kegan Paul.

Pinker, Steven. (1995). *The Language Instinct.* London: Penguin Books.

Plato. (1966). *Protagoras and Meno.* Middlesex: Penguin.

Plato. (1967). *The Republic.* Middlesex: Penguin.

Ponting, Clive. (1992). *A Green History of the World.* Middlesex: Penguin.

Popper, Karl R. (1961) *The Poverty Of Historicism.* London: Routledge.

Popper, Karl R. (1963). *Conjectures and Refutations.* London: Routledge & Kegan Paul.

Popper, Karl R. (1966). *The Open Society and its Enemies Vol. 1.* London: Routledge & Kegan Paul.

Popper, Karl R. (1969). *The Open Society and Its Enemies Vol. 2.* London: Routledge & Kegan Paul.

Popper, Karl R. (1972). *Objective Knowledge.* Oxford: Clarendon Press.

Popper, Karl R. (1977). *The Logic of Scientific Discovery.* London: Hutchinson.

Price-Williams, D. R. (ed.). (1969). *Cross-Cultural Studies.* Middlesex: Penguin.

Priestley, Joseph. (1904). *Memoirs of Dr. Priestley.* London: H. R. Allenson.

Putnam, Hilary. (1995). *Renewing Philosophy.* London and Cambridge, Massachussetts: Harvard University Press.

Rees, J. C. (1969). A Re-Reading of Mill On Liberty in Radcliffe, P., (ed.), *Limits of Liberty: Studies of Mill's 'On Liberty'*, pp. 82 - 86. California: Wadsworth.

Rhees, Rush. (1969). *Without Answers.* London: Routledge & Kegan Paul.

Rhees, Rush. (1970). *Discussions of Wittgenstein.* London: Routledge & Kegan Paul.

Rieber, R. W., Carton, A. S. (ed.). (1987). *The Collected Works of L. S. Vygotsky Vol. 1.* New York: Plenum Press.

Rieber, R. W., Carton, A. S. (ed.). (1993). *The Collected Works of L. S. Vygotsky Volume 2.* New York: Plenum Press.

Rudner, Richard S. (1966). *Philosophy of Social Science.* Englewood Cliffs, N.J. Prentice Hall.

Russell, Bertrand. (1983). *A History of Western Philosophy.* London: George Allen & Unwin.

Russell, C. A. (ed.). (1979). *Science and Religious Belief: A Selection of Recent Historical Studies.* Kent: Hodder & Stoughton.

Ryle, Gilbert. (1970). *The Concept of Mind.* Middlesex: Penguin.

Sacks, Oliver. (1997). Scotoma: Forgetting and Neglect in Science in Silvers, R.B., (ed.), *Hidden Histories of Science.* London: Granta.

Sambursky, S. (1963). *The Physical World of The Greeks.* London: Routledge & Kegan Paul.

Saunders, A. N. W. (ed.). (1970). *Greek Political Oratory.* Middlesex: Penguin.

Scheffler, Israel. (1973). *Reason and Teaching.* London: Routledge & Kegan Paul.

Schneewind, J. B. (ed.). (1969). *Mill: A Collection of Critical Essays.* London and Melbourne: MacMillan.

Scottish Consultative Council on the Curriculum, (1998). *Higher Still.* Edinburgh: Higher Still Development Unit.

Searle, John R. (1984). *Minds, Brains and Science.* Cambridge, MA: Harvard University Press.

Searle, John R, quoted by Ned Block. (1992). Mental Pictures and Cognitive Science in Lycan, -., (ed.), *Mind and Cognition.* pp. 594 -595. Oxford: Blackwell.

Siegel, Harvey. (1988). *Educating reason: Rationality, Critical Thinking and Education.* New York and London: Routledge.

Siegel, Harvey. (1990). McPeck, Informal Logic, and the Nature of Critical Thinking in Scheffler, I., Howard, V.A., (eds.), *Teaching Critical Thinking* (John E. McPeck), pp. 75 - 85. New York and London: Routledge.

Siegel, Harvey. (1991). The Generalizability of Critical Thinking in *Philosophy and Theory* 21, 1, pp. 18-30.

Siegel, Harvey. (1995). 'Radical' Pedagogy Requires 'Conservative' Epistemology. *Journal of Philosophy of Education* 29, 1, pp. 33 - 46.

Siegel, Linda S., Brainerd, Charles J. (1978). The Relationship of Language and Thought in the Preoperational Child: A Reconsideration of Nonverbal Alternatives To Piagetian Tasks in Siegel, Linda S., Brainerd, Charles J., (eds.), *Alternatives to Piaget,* pp. 43 - 49. London: Academic Press.

Siegel, Linda S., Hodkin, Barbara. (1982). The Garden Path to the Understanding of Cognitive Development: Has Piaget Led Us into the Poison Ivy? in Modgil, -., Modgil, -., (eds.), *Jean Piaget: Consensus and Controversy,* pp. 57- 82. New York: Praeger.

Singley, M. K., Anderson, J. R. (1989). *The Transfer of Cognitive Skill.* Cambridge, M A: Harvard University Press.

Skorupski, John. (1991). *John Stuart Mill.* London: Routledge.

Smith, Frank. (1992). *To Think: In Language, Learning and Education.* London: Routledge.

Tamburrini, Joan. (1982). Some Educational Implications of Piaget's Theory in Modgli, -., Modgil, -., *Jean Piaget: Consensus and Controversy,* pp. 309 - 325. New York: Praeger.

Tawney, R. H. (1966). *The Radical Tradition.* Middlesex: Penguin.

Thucydides. (1966). *History of The Peleponnesian War.* Middlesex: Penguin.

Tiles, J. E. (1990). *Dewey.* London: Routledge.

Times Educational Supplement, The:

(12-2-95). p. 14 (Report on 'thinking skills' conference).

(20-1-95). p. 5. Meighan, R. quoted by Deidre Macdonald. 'As Natural as the Fire in the Hearth.'

(16-2-96). p. 3. Nigel Hawkes. 'Intensive pre-school: key to higher IQ.'

(02-4-96). p. 3. Howard Sharron on Feuerstein's 'I.E.'

Toulmin, Stephen. (1969). Men and Ideas: Ludwig Wittgenstein in *Encounter,* pp. 58 - 71.

Urmson, J. O. (1969). The interpretation of the Moral Philosophy of J.S. Mill in Smith, -., Sosa, -., (eds.), *Mill's Utilitarianism,* pp. 117 - 125. California: Wadsworth.

Vernon, P. E. (ed.). (1970). *Creativity.* Middlesex: Penguin.

Voneche, J., Bovet, M. (1982). Training Research and Cognitive Development: What do Piagetians Want to Accomplish? in Modgil, -., Modgil, -., (eds.), *Jean Piaget: Consensus and Controversy,* pp. 83 - 94. New York: Praeger.

Vygotsky, Lev. (1978). *Mind in Society: The Development of Higher Psychological Processes.* Cambridge MA: Harvard University Press.

Vygotsky, Lev. (1989). *Thought and Language.* Cambridge, MA: M I T Press.

Warnock, Mary. (1969). On Moore's Criticism of Mill's "Proof" in Schneewind, -., (ed.), *Mill: A Collection Of Critical Essays,* pp. 199 - 203. London and Melbourne: MacMillan.

Wenestam, Claes-Goran. (1993). A Critique of Research on Cognition and Cognitive Processes. *British Journal of Educational Psychology* 63, 34 - 45, pp. 34 - 45.

Wertsch, James V. (ed.). (1989). *Culture, Communication and Cognition.* Cambridge: Cambridge University Press.

Whorf, Benjamin Lee. (1959). *Language, Thoughtand Reality.* Massachusetts: Massachusetts Institute of Technology.

Wittgenstein, Ludwig. (1968). *Philosophical Investigations.* Oxford: Blackwell.

Wittgenstein, Ludwig. (1969). *Tractatus Logico-Philosophicus.* London: Routledge & Kegan Paul.

Wittgenstein, Ludwig. (1974). *Philosophical Grammar.* Oxford: Blackwell.

Wolpert, Lewis. (1993). *The Unnatural Nature of Science.* London: Faber & Faber.

Wood, David. (1992). *How Children Think and Learn.* Oxford: Blackwell.

Worsley, Peter. (1972). Groote Eylandt Totemism and 'Le Totemisme aujourd'hui' in Emmet, D., MacIntyre, A., (eds.), *Sociological Theory and Philosophical Analysis,* pp. 204-222. London: Macmillan.

Index